OMG
A Youth Ministry Handbook

OMG

A YOUTH MINISTRY HANDBOOK

Edited by Kenda Creasy Dean

with
Roland Martinson
Rodger Nishioka
Don Richter
Dayle Gillespie Rounds
Amy Scott Vaughn
and
Mike Carotta

Youth and Theology Series
Abingdon Press and the
Princeton Theological Seminary
Institute for Youth Ministry

ABINGDON PRESS / Nashville

OMG
A YOUTH MINISTRY HANDBOOK

Copyright © 2010 by Abingdon Press

All rights reserved.

This book is printed on acid-free paper.

Library of Congress Cataloging-in-Publication Data

OMG : a youth ministry handbook / Kenda Creasy Dean, editor; with Roland Martinson ... [et al.].
   p.   cm.—(Youth and theology series)
   Includes bibliographical references.
   ISBN 978-1-4267-0008-8 (pbk. : alk. paper)
1. Church work with youth.   I. Dean, Kenda Creasy. 1959-   II. Martinson, Roland D., 1942-
BV4447.O34 2010
259′.23—dc22

                                                                                                2009052505

10 11 12 13 14 15 16 17 18 19—10 9 8 7 6 5 4 3 2 1

MANUFACTURED IN THE UNITED STATES OF AMERICA

CONTENTS

CONTENTS

CONTENTS

ACKNOWLEDGMENTS

This book launches the Youth and Theology Series, a collaboration between Abingdon Press and the Princeton Theological Seminary Institute for Youth Ministry that we hope will involve you. The Youth and Theology Series offers practical theological reflection on the church's ministries with young people and is intended for pastors and future pastors, college students and seminarians, church leaders and educators, parents and people who hear Christ calling them to ministry with young people.

Because no single book speaks adequately to every situation in ministry, we invite you to check online for supplements that may address your particular pastoral needs and social contexts. And if no supplement exists that you find useful, we invite you to submit one, following the online publication guidelines at www.ptsem.edu/iym. Our hope is that these pages will provide a launching pad, not a docking station, for conversation about the issues facing youth ministry in the early twenty-first century. So think of this book as the beginning of a conversation that your ministry will help continue, and as a place where you can meet potential partners for the journey.

OMG: A Youth Ministry Handbook was designed to be a team effort. In addition to the names listed on the front cover, countless others helped birth this book behind the scenes. We are extremely grateful for the vision and cooperation of John Kutsko and Kathy Armistead at Abingdon, and for the support of President Iain Torrance, Dean Darrell Guder, and the faculty of the Tennent School of Christian Education at Princeton Theological Seminary. Special thanks must go to Mike Carotta, whose lavish encouragement and careful feedback shed light on every chapter, and who helped bring Catholic youth ministers' contributions to the attention of a writing team made up of talkative Protestants. We were fortunate to have many youth ministers and practical theologians serving in auxiliary roles as well: Amanda Drury and Blair Bertrand offered incisive critical feedback and manuscript assistance as associate editors for the earliest drafts of this volume, while Nathan Stucky and Ryan Timpte—two people whose generosity of time was exceeded only by their generosity of spirit—offered pastoral and editorial advice as they cheerfully gave themselves over to copyediting, footnote-finding, and editor-organizing (the last part being the hardest). Finally, we owe enormous thanks to Katherine M. Douglass, who loaned her boundless energy and unparalleled creativity as a teacher to launch *OMG*'s supplementary materials online, creating opportunities for youth leaders to teach each other how to adapt this book for their particular contexts (www.ptsem/iym.org).

For us, this book represents part of the "bucket brigade of faith," a way to hand on the Living Water that Christ poured into us through saints who have encouraged our ministries over the years, and who on occasion have called us out spiritually and vocationally. We are more faithful (and more honest) pastors, youth ministers, professors, and human beings because of them. Of course, you are part of this bucket brigade of faith too, and our prayer is that the Holy Spirit will use something in this book to pour some Living Water into your bucket as you pass it on down the line.

Finally, words cannot express our gratitude for beloved friends and family members whose sacrifices allowed us to slog our way towards manuscript deadlines. To the friends we ignored and the families we took for granted, to the students we didn't see and the children we too hastily kissed goodnight as this book neared completion, please accept our humble thanks for your love and forgiveness: you teach us the meaning of *grace* every day. We thank the Lord for you: *OMG*.

Kenda Creasy Dean
Princeton, NJ
Holy Week 2009

OH MY GOD: AN INTRODUCTION

Most contemporary young people operate far enough from Moses' moral compass that it never occurs to them that "OMG" ("oh my God," in teenspeak) has anything to do with the Ten Commandments, much less that it breaks one of them. After all, the phrase is a nearly ubiquitous adolescent throw-away line; it is a squeal by the sophomore lockers (*"ohmiGOD!"*), a celebrity website (omg.yahoo.com), a Broadway musical number (in *Legally Blonde*), a cellular-savvy abbreviation (6-6-6-6-4), and a moniker for recession-era youth growing up fast in times of economic crisis ("Generation OMG").[1]

Yet Christians should hear the phrase "oh my God" differently. Youth ministers, parents, teachers—anyone who has ever loved an adolescent—know that "OMG" can be a prayer, a plea, a petition, a note of praise, or an unbidden entreaty that escapes our lips as we seek Christ for the young people we love. It is an urgent petition when our children take the steering wheel without us; it is our joyful praise when they return safely home. It frames our contemporary psalmody when we cry out to God in gladness or terror, wonder or trepidation. Every Christian parent, teacher, coach, pastor, youth minister, Sunday school teacher, and volunteer has prayed "OMG" to invoke God's presence for young people, and for ourselves: "Answer me when I call, O God.... Be gracious to me, and hear my prayer" (Psalm 4:1).

People called to work with young people in the church know that this prayer gets more frequent with experience. The more we know about ministry, the more feeble we feel, and the more often we cry out to God as we look for holy openings in what media guru Henry Jenkins calls "participatory culture"—a culture that young people create as well as consume while relationships, aspirations, and identities are shaped by the norms of the digital age. How is Christ formed within us in such a context? How does God transform creative consumers into believers who participate in the life of God? How do they find a role to play in the divine transformation of the world? How does Christian identity take shape in a religiously plural culture, a world of multiple flocks, all beloved by God, in which Christ calls us to serve as shepherds on his behalf, and in which—Jesus was very clear about this—losing even one sheep simply will not do?

Sometimes it surprises us to realize that the church has always asked such questions and that the issues facing the spiritual formation of young people today are mostly variations of those that generations of church leaders have faced as they took their place in the bucket brigade of faith, handing on to newcomers the Living Water of Jesus Christ that was poured into them. Augustine's *Enchiridion*—as he saw it, a "manual" (literally, a "hand-book") of faith, hope, and love—was written at the request of Laurentius, a new disciple who wanted a book about Christian life that would "never leave his hands" (most books of the time were massive manuscripts consigned to public reading rooms). The book you are holding is also written in response to a request for a handbook for people in ministry with young people. We offer it as a text that wrestles with questions surrounding the spiritual formation of adolescents, written by people who are grappling with these questions along with you.

At the same time, this book also unapologetically belongs to a particular moment in history. The early twenty-first-century church has seen youth ministry's first conscious attempts at self-reflection, with all the intellectual gangliness that accompanies the maturation of a field of study. We still find it easy to skimp on theology while casting our lot with sciences like human development or social psychology, sociology or anthropology, neurobiology or education (as we discuss in chapter 1). Yet while adolescent spiritual formation borrows from all of these disciplines, it cannot be reduced to any of them. Youth ministry—or adolescent discipleship formation, if you prefer—is first and foremost an expression of practical theology for and with young people and the church. Its methodologies involve prayerful reflection and an openness to divine transformation that are altogether alien to social science. This book represents an early attempt to "pin down the corners" of adolescent discipleship formation as an emerging discipline by naming key themes in the conversation, and by stating their significance for a church that longs to share Christ with young people who inhabit, and largely embrace, a frankly secular, postmodern culture.

Think of this book, therefore, as a prism, bending the light illuminating our ministry with young people through six different facets:

☆ *Haunting Questions,* in which we take stock of the church's current practices in youth ministry, and some of the questions these practices raise as youth ministry becomes more self-consciously aligned with practical theology;

☆ *Daunting Challenges,* in which we examine the relationship between the church's ministry with adolescents and the mega-storytellers of global, postmodern culture;

☆ *Enduring Themes,* in which we identify themes in youth ministry that pervade every era of Christian ministry, and that nurture youth ministry's connection to the church universal while tending to the particular needs of the present moment;

☆ *Promising Possibilities,* in which we identify emerging trends that seem to be shaping youth ministry in the twenty-first century, and that bear particular promise for churches' engagement with young people in the future;

☆ *Emerging Competencies,* a discussion of some of the particular vocational gifts necessary for effective ministry with young people in the early twenty-first century; and

☆ *A Maturing Discipline,* a meta-reflection on youth ministry as an interdisciplinary field of study within the broader rubric of practical theology and what this means for the preparation of church leaders.

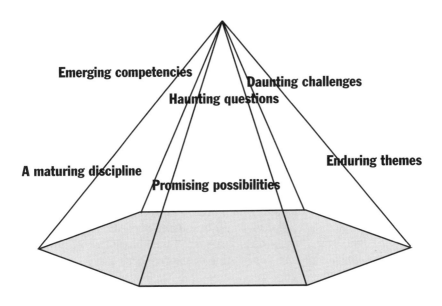

Figure 1.1
Prism for Studying Adolescent Spiritual Formation

This book includes the reflections of six scholars and pastors who have spent their careers contributing to the field of adolescent spiritual formation. Between us we have logged more than 150 years of hands-on ministry with teenagers and emerging adults. That's a lot of lock-ins, Youth Sundays, mission trips, baccalaureate services, and weddings. We have been pastors, youth directors, campus ministers, schoolteachers, camp directors, counselors, denominational youth staff, leaders in youth mission organizations, as well as seminary professors, researchers, administrators, and parents. If you were to ask us, we would all tell you (now that we have day jobs in academia) that we miss the privilege of serving God from the tangled centers of young people's still-emerging lives. Like you, we have more group projects under our belts than we can name, but none of us had ever tried "team" writing before. After imagining the book together, each chapter was drafted by one or two of us, revised by one or two others, edited by yet another, and then given one more editorial tweak. Our hope was to become genuinely collaborative, and we have tried to supply enough connective tissue to make your ride less bumpy as a reader. We decided to let personal examples stand as the author told them. The stories just seemed less contrived that way—which is why it appears that "I" have grown up in six different parts of the country (we have). For whatever patience this requires on your part, we are grateful.

Let me make one final observation. As this is the first book in the Youth and Theology series, we hope this volume fairly represents conversations that are shaping youth ministry in the early twenty-first century, but its contents are not exhaustive.[2] You too are helping to form the future of youth ministry, and the themes of your work—whether or not they are reflected in these pages—decide the church's next steps with young people as well. We have offered anecdotes from our ministries, but you could just as easily offer examples from yours. Online at www.ptsem.edu/iym you will notice an invitation to expand upon these pages for youth ministry in particular settings, so this book can better speak to the churches and young people you know best. (Among other things, you will find guidelines for contributing a study guide, if the one you need does not yet exist.)

This book is unique in the Youth and Theology series in that it offers an aerial view of an emerging field of study, while other books in this series focus more on pastoral issues gleaned from ministry on the ground with young people. But we need this bird's-eye view, for it helps us ascertain what Gregory of Nazianzus (d. 389) called "the scope of our art." Speaking of the teaching office, Gregory offered this eloquent description of the teacher's task:

> The scope of our art is to provide the soul with wings, to rescue it from the world and give it to God, and to watch over that which is in God's image. If it abides, we are to take it by the hand; if it is in danger, to restore it; if it is ruined, to make Christ dwell in the heart by the Spirit.[3]

Gregory's words may poetically describe our vocations as pastors, parents, and youth ministers who tend to the faith of adolescents—but on most days our work seems like anything but poetry. Yet most of us are less focused on giving young people "wings" than on propping them up on very human legs. We want youth to have a faith to stand on, to carry them into the world as people after God's own heart (1 Samuel 13:14). But we also know that we can no longer limit youth ministry to teenagers in the church basement. The "scope of our art," as Gregory puts it, is broader and far more central to the church's identity than most congregations realize, as youth ministry increasingly encompasses those immersed in the first third of life, and as parents serve as the undisputed primary influences on their children's faith. Not only does adolescent spiritual formation require the spiritual formation of adults as well but we can no longer dismiss the experimental spirit common in youth ministry as a passing fancy. On the contrary, the themes and methodologies of the church's ministries with young people offer a glimpse of what the future of the church will look like for young and old alike.

This book, therefore, is written for those who have prayed "oh my God" for the young people whom the Holy Spirit has placed on our paths, in hopes of offering a kind of manual to make us more conversant about young people's spiritual growth, whether we think of "youth ministry" as a specialized field, or merely as ministry with those who happen to be young. We do not propose a particular model or theological outlook apart from the basic biases that reflect our mainstream locations; we are, for example, committed to a Trinitarian understanding of God and to the importance of relationships that reflect and participate in God's relationality. Aside from such basic assumptions, this book offers markers, not fences. It outlines talking points for the twenty-first-century church's reflection on adolescent discipleship formation, aimed at giving young people theological legs to stand on, even as we pray—"oh my God"—for legs of our own.

CHAPTER ONE

HAUNTING QUESTIONS

I thank my God every time I remember you, constantly praying with joy in every one of my prayers for all of you, because of your sharing in the gospel from the first day until now. I am confident of this, that the one who began a good work among you will bring it to completion by the day of Jesus Christ.
—Philippians 1:3-6

If you have a group of twelve kids who don't understand your illustrations and one of them wants to kill you, you have a youth group just like Jesus.
—Mark Yaconelli

It is not just you.

Maybe you haven't put your nervousness into words. But social scientists have, and they are doing it more boldly. Listen to a few who, in recent years, have written about the condition of Christian formation in American young people:

☆ "Most teenagers who have spent years attending church activities [have not integrated their faith] into who they are and how they live" (Barna, 2003).
☆ "Our distinct impression is that very many religious congregations and communities of faith in the United States are failing rather badly in religiously engaging and educating youth" (Smith, 2004).
☆ "Emerging adults' religious beliefs have surprisingly little connection to their religious training in childhood and adolescence" (Arnett, 2004).
☆ "The levels of disengagement among twentysomethings suggest that youth ministry fails too often at discipleship and faith formation" (Kinnaman, 2006).

If you have ever wondered if the hours you spend with children, youth, and emerging adults in the name of Jesus Christ make any difference to them, to the church, or to God, you are clearly in good company.

Barbara is asking these questions too.[1] She wondered why she could not get high school students to attend "The Well," Resurrection Church's Sunday evening Bible study for youth. Teenagers would promise to come, then at the last minute flood her e-mail with excuses about unfinished homework, changed schedules, and last-minute demands from friends or families. Adult leaders posed challenges of their own; of the seven committed adults Barbara had

---

Thanks to Amanda Drury and Ryan Timpte for their research and editorial assistance on this chapter.

trained this year, only three remained after job transfers, pregnancies, and increased work responsibilities took their toll. With fewer volunteers, Barbara worked longer hours herself, and she could feel her resentment grow as the youth program seemed to creep into every crevice of her life.

Furthermore, church leaders seemed disappointed with her performance. Barbara came to them highly recommended, and she began ministry amidst high expectations and excitement. Yet the expectations turned out to be ill-defined and reflected competing goals between Barbara and the church board. Barbara viewed youth and family ministry as taking up life with Jesus Christ and his call to make disciples, evidenced in worship, acts of compassion, and solidarity with the poor. The church board was interested in how many youth attended each event she planned, and whether mission opportunities could "count" for the high school service hours requirement. Barbara sensed the pastor's support, but she knew from staff conversations that he viewed youth ministry as a *potpourri* of programs, events, and strategic relationships. Barbara believed adult education was crucial for equipping parents and grandparents to effectively nurture life and faith in their own children. But parents had little time for such offerings, and like the pastor, most parents seemed to think that Barbara was getting paid to get their teenagers to "enjoy church." Frustration gnawed at Barbara's sense of call. She began to wonder, *Is any of this making any difference? Is this really what ministry is?*

You Are Not Alone

It's not just you. You have plenty of company if you have left a youth gathering wondering if the teenagers heard anything you said; or if you have stared at a stack of budget reports, resource catalogs, or accumulating e-mails from concerned parents and wondered, "Can I really spend the rest of my life doing this?" If the evening news has ever made you wonder whether youth ministry can make a dent in the lives of young people who live in a world swamped by need, the good news is that you are not alone in asking the question. The bad news is that you are right to be concerned.

> If the evening news has ever made you wonder whether youth ministry can make a dent in the lives of young people who live in a world swamped by need, the good news is that you are not alone in asking the question. The bad news is that you are right to be concerned.

If you don't plan to read this book in its entirety, you may want to stop here and go find something with a more comforting opening chapter. Ministry with adolescents inevitably raises questions that deserve the attention of youth ministers, parents, educators, and churches. Spoiler alert: While we open this book with haunting questions, we do not end here. But faithful ministry requires us to be awake to the conditions of people's lives and the contexts surrounding the young people Christ calls us to address. So naming these questions will help us frame the church's work with young people as mission, as a field of study, and as a holy vocation for people who care that young people know and love God. Youth ministry has its lonely moments, but it is neither a solitary nor a trivial pursuit.

So read on. And remember, it is not just you.

Telling the Truth: We Do This for Joy

Let's start by admitting what we already know in our bones: much of what we currently do in the name of youth ministry—much less in the name of Jesus—is not "working," whatever that means. Although most (some estimates say more than four out of five) Christian youth workers are volunteers, with more resources and training opportunities available than ever before, youth ministry has been professionalized to a degree that was unimaginable in the 1970s (a matter we will revisit in chapter 6).[2] Theologically trained youth pastors are more plentiful and longer lasting than a generation ago, and more of them approach youth ministry as their life's calling, rather than as entry-level ministry. Yet study after study suggests that the faith of American teenagers—*even those who attend church*—is extremely tenuous.

Is this what we signed up for? Most of us in youth ministry imagined that our work would produce more visible fruit, more satisfied parents, more vital congregations, more life-changing decisions, and more life-giving practices for young people and for the world they inhabit. That was the ministry we imagined, but much of it has been supplanted by crowded calendars, conflicting expectations, and distracting personal circumstances—in other words, by *life*. We love youth, we really do, but sometimes we think about that job in retail.

> The humbling truth is that none of us do youth ministry because we are good at it. We do it because Christ has called us to it, called us to serve him in this way.

The humbling truth is that none of us do youth ministry because we are good at it. We do it because Christ has called us to it, called us to serve him in this way. God has given us a flock of teenagers and called us to serve Christ in their midst. No sane person, we tell ourselves, would head into such a mission apart from a directive from On High. So why do we stay? What keeps us in youth ministry instead of leaving, say, for a job in accounting (which many Christians do just as faithfully)?

The answer is simple and universal: *Joy*. Most of us cannot imagine another way of life that yields such overwhelming wonder and gratitude. Young people devastate and delight us, but above all they remind us of God's mercy and grace and power. Words do not exist to capture the joy, the awe, the *privilege* of accompanying a young person in his or her journey to Christ, and of

3

knowing that God has somehow used us as vessels of grace along the way. We are often surprised and humbled that youth we barely know consider us significant in this journey. We have learned to hold loosely those teenagers who seem to reject everything we hold dear, knowing that God has not let them go. It is incredible that God trusts us with this work, given our propensity for screwing things up. We share Paul's grateful astonishment when he tells Timothy, "I am grateful to Christ Jesus our Lord, who has strengthened me, because he judged me faithful and appointed me to his service, even though I was formerly a blasphemer, a persecutor, and a man of violence" (1 Timothy 1:12-13).

Still, questions linger.

The Trouble with Research

Fifty years ago, research on youth ministry was almost nonexistent. Churches seldom mined social science as a resource for youth ministry, and social scientists seldom viewed adolescent faith as a topic worth exploring. What little information on adolescent faith formation existed was largely anecdotal, save for the work of developmental psychologists like Erik Erikson (whose theories, even after fifty years of scrutiny, still profoundly influence Christian youth work). Yet as sociologists Christian Smith and Melinda Denton remind us, "Detailed knowledge and understanding of the social world often raises real questions about cultural and institutional practices and commitments that can make real differences in people's lives."[3] Today, thanks to renewed interest in interdisciplinary fields like practical theology and widespread attention from a number of disciplines on the changing nature of adolescence, churches now have several decades of developmental, demographic, sociological, and more recently, neurological and theological research that can inform the way we approach young people, faith, and culture.

Of course, the trouble with research is that, right or wrong, we now have a yardstick by which to assess how youth ministry is doing—and much of this research finds youth ministry lacking. Whether we follow the pioneering findings from the 1970s and 1980s of sociologists like Dean Hoge, Merton Strommen, or educators like Sara Little, Michael Warren, and Sharon Daloz Parks; or glean from the mounds of data harvested annually by Gallup and the Barna Group, the Higher Education Research Institute, or Search Institute; or learn from psychologists and sociologists like Robert Coles, Herschel and Ellen Thornburg, Jeffrey Arnett, Christian Smith, or Robert Wuthnow (the list goes on), much of the research on churches and adolescent faith formation confirms practitioners' suspicions.[4] In fact, a quick scan of these studies reveals that, to a large extent, the questions that bothered us about youth ministry in the 1970s are very much like the questions that bother us today. Again and again, we question the depth of young people's spiritual engagement and wonder about the effectiveness of our ministries with them, the sustainability of youth ministry models, and the faithfulness of youth ministry's mission as a part of the church.

> **Haunting Questions in Youth Ministry**
>
> Does Youth Ministry Matter?
>
> Do Our Practices of Youth Ministry Reflect Christ?
>   Do existing "models and practices" reflect the church's best
>   theological work?
>   Do they accomplish what we imagine?
>   Do they bear any relationship to the church?
>
> Do Our Practices of Youth Ministry Shape Christians?
>
> How Long Can We Keep This Up?
>
> Can we do better?

Does Youth Ministry Matter?

She still had a few minutes before the staff meeting; Maria swerved into the gas station, jumped out of her car, and hit the unleaded button as she shoved the nozzle into her gas tank. As she straightened her back, she caught the eye of a teenage girl standing by the other pump. There was an awkward pause.

"Hey, Maria," the girl said quietly.

"Hi, Carmen," Maria smiled, thankful that the girl's name had suddenly resurfaced. It had been almost a year and a half since Maria had seen Carmen, and she tried not to stare. The shoulder-length black hair Maria remembered was now stained with bright red streaks. Carmen's shoulders were hunched, her clothes were baggy, and her eyes looked dead. A silver stud jabbed into her left eyebrow.

Two summers ago Carmen had accompanied Maria and a dozen other teenagers and adults from their church on a mission trip to Tijuana. On that trip, Carmen seemed to come alive. She jumped at the opportunity to share her experience during mass the Sunday after they returned, and movingly described the way the families they met in Tijuana had helped her see her life differently. Maria remembered that Sunday with pride; she loved seeing spiritual "light bulbs" go on over a teenager's head. Following the trip Carmen had been a regular at church, attending beach volleyball nights and a weekly teen prayer group. Then school started—and then, nothing. Carmen vanished into another world.

Yet here she was. It had only been two years since that summer, but Carmen looked five years older. They shared awkward, superficial chitchat until Maria heard the welcome "pop" of the gas pump indicating the tank was full. Relieved, Maria said goodbye and drove to the church, berating herself. "Why didn't I reach out to her more when I first noticed she stopped coming to mass? Should I have confronted her just now about where she's been?" and—most unsettling: "Was Carmen's experience of Christ on the mission trip real, or was it just some fleeting emotional experience?"

Anyone working in youth ministry knows the joy of new life, the anxiety of stunted growth, and the gut-wrenching disappointment of watching a young person walk away from faith. Sometimes the young people who walk away are the ones we love most; sometimes they are our own sons and daughters. Sometimes they are like Carmen, experiencing dramatic changes in their lives after leaving church. Sometimes they walk away from the congregation but not faith, and sometimes it is the other way around. Sometimes—and this is the most disturbing scenario—young people walk away from faith and the church and experience little discernible difference in their lives at all.

> Does youth ministry make a lasting difference? Do our present practices invite young people to mature and lasting Christian faith?

Does youth ministry make a lasting difference? Do our present practices invite young people to mature and lasting Christian faith? Researchers have been raising questions about the effectiveness of youth ministries within the larger church context for at least the last thirty years. Of course, before we can ask whether youth ministry is effective, we have to define what effectiveness means. Early youth ministry research tended to focus on church attendance as a measure of youth ministry effectiveness. In 1975, sociologist Dean Hoge studied a cohort of twenty-five-year-old Presbyterians who had been baptized as infants and confirmed as teenagers. He found that, somewhere between adolescence and young adulthood, 75 percent of them had quit going to worship regularly (defined as attending at least once a month) and were not engaging in Christian activities.[5] A year earlier, Christian educator Michael Warren had identified a similar pattern emerging in Catholic young people, estimating that "two-thirds of Catholic youth were not being reached in any significant way."[6]

Contemporary studies show similar patterns of participation across the U.S. While teenagers are 10 percent more likely to attend church than their parents, participation declines precipitously throughout adolescence.[7] Younger adults are less involved in churches in the early twenty-first century than they were a generation ago; one survey found that 70 percent of 23- to 30-year-old Protestants who had attended church regularly as youth stopped attending regularly for at least a year between the ages of 18 and 22 (35 percent eventually returned).[8] Catholic teenagers are especially likely to be unengaged in their parishes; according to the National Study of Youth and Religion, two-thirds of Catholic teens who attend churches that sponsor youth groups do not participate in them.[9]

With notable exceptions, the emphasis of most research on adolescent religiosity is less on what young people believe about God or how faith influences their self-understandings than on their level of religious engagement. Youth ministry "works," by these standards, when young people join and remain involved in a community of faith. Today, teenagers are less likely than in previous generations to equate church participation with faith in God; most American young people, even the ones who leave church or have never attended a church, say that religion is a good thing, and that they believe in God and pray regularly (especially when they are in need or crisis).[10] The question that lurks behind the religious formation of these young people is not whether they believe in God (almost all of them do),[11] but whether believing in God *matters*—a question that requires us to go beyond church participation alone to assess youth ministry's effectiveness.

Do Our Practices of Youth Ministry Reflect Christ?

Greg sank deeper and deeper into the pew. For months he had lobbied the Christian education council to cancel Sunday school once a month so teenagers could attend Sunday morning worship. The youth Sunday school class ran concurrently with the Sunday morning worship service—much to the disappointment of the youth leaders. Greg shared their disappointment. As the associate pastor for discipleship, Greg envisioned a worship service with young and old singing side by side, with the sermon addressing younger congregants, and with teenagers leading and participating in worship alongside adults.

The council granted Greg's request, sort of. This was the first Sunday of the month and someone posted a large sign on the door of the youth room: *No Sunday School—Go to Worship*. Greg had seen some of the upperclassmen roll their eyes and slip out a side door, no doubt in search of a pancake house. The rest of the teenagers had trudged their way to the sanctuary and plopped down in the pew next to Greg.

Now, halfway through the worship service, Greg already regretted his request. The singing was listless. The pastor's sermon was painfully dull. No one in leadership seemed to notice that young people existed, much less were in the room. "*This* is where I want youth on a Sunday morning?" he wondered. He began to fear that his efforts to build strong ties between the larger church body and the teenagers would only turn them off more. And, truth be told, he didn't blame them. As the congregation droned through the third hymn, Greg wished he had joined the students looking for pancakes.

This wasn't the first time Greg had raised questions about the relationship between youth ministry and the larger church. He had often wondered how he could cast vision for youth ministry to those who saw youth ministers as glorified babysitters. He wondered how to respond to the adults who seemed uncomfortable around the few students whose faith had caught fire in the past year, and who were walking around with a newfound God-vocabulary. Bottom line, Greg wasn't so sure that the church he knew was the best conduit for spiritual transformation. By the early twenty-first century, questions like Greg's began to haunt people in youth ministry.

> Do existing "models and practices" of youth ministry reflect the church's best theological work? Are we helping young people become part of the larger body of Christ?

Do existing "models and practices" of youth ministry reflect the church's best theological work? Are we helping young people become part of the larger body of Christ or involving them in one more glorified extracurricular activity? Christian identity, by definition, involves immersion in a faith community, but using youth ministry as a defensive measure to stave off church membership losses is practically and theologically problematic. Instrumental approaches to youth ministry—in other words, pastoral relationships that have other, unstated purposes (like getting youth to come to youth group or worship)—represent a distorted view of the Incarnation. Jesus did not call people to come to church; he called them to change and share their lives, to repent, be baptized, take up their crosses and follow him. By the early twenty-first century, the purpose of youth ministry was beginning to be called into question, and with it came questions about youth ministry's status as *ministry*. Does the church's ministry with young people cultivate disciples of Jesus Christ who seek justice, love kindness, and walk humbly with God (Micah 6:8)? Or does it cultivate interpersonal niceness, social acceptability, civic engagement, and—as a primary goal—church membership?

The available data both affirms teenagers' belief in God and challenges that belief's ultimate significance for their lives. Three out of five American teenagers say they regularly attend church (including youth ministry and Christian education programs), but longitudinal research is inconsistent about the influence of adolescent religious training on faith during early adulthood.[12] An Evangelical Lutheran Church in America study found that only about one-third of Lutheran young adults aged 21 to 29 attended worship or engaged in ministry.[13] Sociologist Tim Clydesdale finds this pattern among college freshmen in particular. According to Clydesdale, four out of five college freshmen stow their religious self-understandings in "identity lock-boxes" once they enter college, effectively putting their religious identities under wraps—and on hold—indefinitely.[14] Meanwhile, pollster George Barna sees evidence that people who attend church as teenagers are more likely, as adults, to say that religious faith is very important to them. At the same time, says Barna, "most teenagers who have spent years attending church activities [have not integrated] their faith...into who they are and how they live."[15] Tactfully, sociologist Christian Smith writes that "most teens seem simply to accept religion as taken-for-granted, mostly operating in the background of their lives."[16] Jeffery Arnett is more pointed, observing the faith during the "twenty-something" years bears surprisingly little connection to childhood religious training.[17]

Take a moment for that to sink in.

Decades of research that identifies parents as the primary influences on adolescent faith (not to mention Proverbs 22:6: "Train children in the right way, and when old, they will not stray") call Arnett to closer scrutiny; he seems perplexed by the findings himself.[18] Longitudinal research from the National Study of Youth and Religion also indicates a profound role for religious adults—if not for religious youth programs—in faith that survives emerging adulthood.[19] Yet youth ministers hear in Arnett's observation a faint ring of truth that boils down to this: youth ministry may not be as adept at forming the disciples as we once thought. David Kinnaman, president of the Barna Group, argues for an "overhaul" of American youth ministry that makes faith sustainability the criterion for youth ministry effectiveness, "not because churches fail to attract significant numbers of young people, but because so much of those efforts are not creating a sustainable faith beyond high school."

> There are certainly effective youth ministries across the country, but the levels of disengagement among twentysomethings suggest that youth ministry fails too often at discipleship and faith formation. A new standard for viable youth ministry should be—not the number of "attenders," the sophistication of the events, or the "cool" factor of the youth group—but whether teens have the commitment, passion and resources to pursue Christ intentionally and wholeheartedly after they leave the youth ministry nest.[20]

These are strong words and Kinnaman is not alone in his assessment. Practical theologian Andrew Root tackles the most sacred cow in ministry with young people—relationships between adult youth workers and teenagers—and demands that we examine their motivations and outcomes. Root believes that youth ministry often bends interpersonal relationships with teenagers into vehicles of personal influence with the "unquestioned objective of conversion."[21] Root calls the church to stop using relationships in youth ministry as commodities: "The incarnation is not about influence but accompaniment. It is not about getting us right but bearing what is wrong with us, so that we might find that we are only right in the embrace of a God who loves so much to be with us!"[22]

Do Our Practices of Youth Ministry Shape Christians?

Stephanie described herself as an "A" student and a lifelong Presbyterian who had "come to everything" at her church since she was a baby. Sitting across the table from me at TGI Friday's, she happily chatted about her experience in a congregation not far from where I teach.

I was interviewing Stephanie for a research project, hoping to find out what she believed, how she practiced her faith, how her faith influenced her daily life. Stephanie was in the middle of explaining how much she loved her church youth group, and how close she felt to the youth pastor, who had been a guiding force in her life.

In what way? I asked her.

Oh, in so many ways, she sighed, smiling at the memories. All-night games of sardines in the church. Pranks that involved climbing around on the roof by the church steeple at night, led by the youth pastor. She appreciated the late-night conversations she had with the youth pastor, alone in the church sanctuary, and she admired his decision to ignore drinking at a recent retreat. She loved his ability to "act like a teenager himself" and "have fun" with the kids.

I did a quick mental scan of my students, hoping that Stephanie's youth pastor was not one of them.

"Let's talk about what you believe," I suggested, moving down the interview form. "You said you are a Christian and that you've been involved in this church your whole life. So what would you say makes you a Christian?"

Stephanie looked confused. The chatty Stephanie disappeared and a blank look overtook her.

I pressed: "What do you do, or what do you think about God, that makes you a Christian instead of something else?" Pause. "Does being a Christian make you think about God differently than some of your friends?"

"I guess so."

"Okay, tell me about that. What do you think about God?"

"Um."

"What about Jesus?" I ventured.

"Like, what do you mean?"

"Like, how would you describe Jesus? Does Jesus matter?"

"Not really."

"Okay," I said, trying to think of another way in. "So...what about being a Christian is important to you?"

She brightened up a little. "Well, it makes you nicer. I like being active in church—stuff like that."

And so it went. Is there any difference between the way you live your life and the way your non-Christian friends live their lives? (No, everyone is the same.) So why are you a Christian? (It's how I was raised.) Anything else? (No.) But being a Christian is important to you? (Absolutely.) Why? (My youth pastor is awesome.)

I wondered how a young person like Stephanie, raised and active in a Christian congregation, could have so little to say about being a Christian. I could not shake the sense that church was an important activity in Stephanie's life, but not one that pointed her beyond herself. While her congregation's youth ministry clearly had important social and perhaps developmental benefits for Stephanie, memories of Christian teaching seemed curiously—and disturbingly—absent.[23]

> Recent research has posed yet another set of questions to churches: Do our current practices of youth ministry help young people understand themselves as Christians? Are we passing on adequate understandings of God, the church, and the world?

Recent research has posed yet another set of questions to churches: *Do our current practices of youth ministry help young people understand themselves as Christians? Are we passing on adequate understandings of God, the church, and the world?* After interviewing more than three thousand 13- to 17-year-olds in the U.S., the National Study of Youth and Religion makes a powerful case that the answer to both of these questions is "no." Faith is a low-impact exercise for most American teenagers, even when they are active in their churches. Christian Smith, the study's principal investigator, dubbed the *de facto* religion practiced by contemporary American teenagers as "moralistic therapeutic deism." Smith and his colleagues believe that moralistic therapeutic deism has colonized American churches, supplanting Christianity, and that it now constitutes the dominant religion in the United States.[24] Despite the fact that three out of four teenagers claim to be Christians, the NSYR found that most young people describe their core religious values like this:

Moralistic Therapeutic Deism

1. A God exists who created and orders the world and watches over human life on earth.
2. God wants people to be good, nice, and fair to each other, as taught in the Bible and by most world religions.
3. The central goal of life is to be happy and to feel good about oneself.
4. God does not need to be particularly involved in one's life except when God is needed to resolve a problem.
5. Good people go to heaven when they die.[25]

Like David Kinnaman, Smith and Denton found that most Christian young people do not seem to know much about Christianity, possess little in the way of a theological vocabulary or knowledge of the Bible, and have few tools to help them think about and process life from a Christian viewpoint. By and large they consider religion "a very nice thing," potentially useful but not something they personally need. The National Study of Youth and Religion found little in the way of teen rebellion against religion (on the contrary, young people seemed positive but remarkably complacent about religion, mostly because it mattered very little to them). As Smith and Denton put it, "The problem facing most churches is not teen rebellion, but teenagers' 'benign whatever-ism.'"[26]

Smith and Denton are not the first to suggest that youth, and churches themselves, are in the grips of something like moralistic therapeutic deism.[27] Since the 1980s educators like Michael Warren have focused their research on the ways in which culture, education, and young people interact—a project that has led Warren to unmask consumerism's voracious appetite for converts among young people. As a Catholic educator, Warren's goal is to raise young people's awareness of the processes of consumerism, creating space for critical reflection that helps them recognize how the marketplace vies for their souls. Concerned that churches are not making enough of an effort to resist consumer culture, therefore allowing young people and youth ministry itself to be co-opted by the marketplace, he writes:

If popular culture is in our time an enormous picture window showing people even more fantastic views of what life is all about, then maybe education becomes a kind of tiny peephole not accessible to very many and at which one has to strain to see anything....The magic window is so automatic and easy; the peephole requires more effort.[28]

Warren worries that the power of youth ministry's explicit curriculum pales in comparison to the power of the curriculum of the lived experience of young people.[29] Foreshadowing the "moralistic therapeutic deism" that Smith and Denton would name twenty years later, Warren wrote that—Christian or not—the "real curriculum" in the lives of both youth and their adult leaders makes an idol of "warmth" and interpersonal closeness, and that these core values become the "shaping metaphor" for their lives. He quotes sociologist Richard Sennett:

The reigning belief today is that closeness between persons is a moral good. The reigning aspiration today is to develop individual personality through experiences of closeness and warmth with others. The reigning myth today is that the evils of society can all be understood as the evils of impersonality, alienation, and coldness. The sum of these three is an ideology of intimacy; social relationships of all kinds are real, believable, and authentic the closer they approach the inner psychological concerns of each person. This ideology of intimacy defines the humanitarian spirit of a society without gods; warmth is our god.[30]

Whether the surrogate spirituality is interpersonal warmth or moralistic therapeutic deism, the problem points back to the church's failure to offer the gospel—the story of God as it has been handed down to us in Christian texts and traditions—as a compelling (not to mention transformative) alternative to the creeds of the dominant culture.[31]

How Long Can We Keep This Up?

Adam felt his blood pressure rise as he drove past New Life Community Church, behind the university athletic complex just three blocks from campus.[32] The church had been around for less than five years and already was making an impact on the university community. The praise service on Thursday nights was bursting at the seams, and was already a popular venue for informal preaching and young adult musical talent. New Life's spring break mission trips had more takers than they could handle, and were intentionally linked to university courses that addressed the trips' cultural contexts.

Adam thought about the small group of college students who came to his Bible study at University Church on Sunday mornings. Compared to the hordes in New Life's raked sanctuary, the University Church group looked small and lost in the 1960s multipurpose room where they met.

"I could have big numbers if I ran a circus too," Adam muttered as he pulled into the church parking lot. He was immediately ashamed of his judgmental spirit towards the "rival" college ministry. Anyway, he was too busy to be petty; as University Church's pastor to youth and families, his plate was already full. He had high school leaders to mentor, parents to placate, a Lenten retreat to plan. And now he had a college group to build.

When University Church launched a student outreach program last fall, the chance to reestablish a thriving denominational presence on a state university campus had excited Adam. He adapted to the rhythms of the semester, made himself available during "student hours," organized Bible studies and service opportunities to help students discern God's movement in the world. It was rewarding but wearying work. Next on tap was a discussion group for graduate students at a local pub—though Adam was already dreading the idea of yet another night away from home.

Early on Adam had decided not to sugarcoat the gospel in order to attract students. No Bible-lite. No insulting youth group games involving cotton balls and two-liter bottles of soda. At a state university, he wanted to give students a place to celebrate their theological tradition, though he understood that God was calling him to service, not results. If God chose to bless University Church's college ministry with large numbers, great—but if not, Adam vowed to faithfully tend the flock that showed up. Of course, a larger budget and some committed volunteers would help.

But perhaps he had been naïve. If God was really behind this ministry, more students would be involved, right? "Should I get a wireless connection? A big screen and a gaming system? Maybe a more exotic mission trip?" He wondered if he was selling out.

"What do you want from me, God?" Adam prayed. "Just tell me and I'll do it. I'll gladly do it. I just don't know." One thing Adam did know, however: he couldn't keep up his current pace much longer. "Have you really called me to this, Lord?" he asked. "Because at this rate I don't see how I can devote the next few years to ministry—much less the rest of my life."

Maybe it was time to move on.

> Is our current practice of youth ministry sustainable? Does our understanding of our vocation rest on valid assumptions?

Some questions gnaw at us in youth ministry because deep down we already know the answers. To respond to these questions requires courage more than scholarship—questions like, *Is our current practice of youth ministry sustainable? Does our understanding of our vocation rest on valid assumptions?* In the *Study of Protestant Youth Ministers in America* (2000), Merton Strommen, Karen Jones, and Dave Rahn asked 2,130 full-time youth ministers what they found most encouraging and discouraging in their experience of youth ministry. These pastors identified six experiences that had caused them to seriously consider leaving youth ministry:

1. Feeling a sense of personal inadequacy
2. Experiencing strained family relations
3. Sensing a growing loss of confidence
4. Feeling unqualified for the job
5. Feeling personally disorganized
6. Experiencing burnout.[33]

To address these issues requires more than better self-care. Strommen's team made the unsurprising observation: "Youth ministry is very difficult work, far more difficult than parents and congregational leaders realize. The pressures on a youth minister are enormous, and these pressures are ones for which few have been adequately prepared."[34] Some studies indicate that mastery of a field requires ten years of experience in that field, or 10,000 hours of practice. Pastoral proficiency in youth ministry (i.e., becoming skillful at communicating faith, navigating relationships with youth and parents, working productively within congregational systems, etc.) is no different. Yet youth ministers stay in a church, on average, 3.9 years—which creates an obvious problem: few youth ministers stay in their positions long enough to become effective in them.[35]

By the end of the 1990s, youth ministers themselves sensed the need to change some of their basic assumptions about ministry, even if churches failed to follow suit. Youth ministry literature began to use evocative phrases like "soul-shaping," "contemplative," "Godbearing," "presence-centered," "emerging," and above all, "authentic" to emphasize God's transformative presence in the practice of youth ministry, instead of focusing on programs aimed at making church more fun.[36] Three recurring conversations pushed youth ministry toward a broader sense of purpose, suggesting that youth ministry had as much to offer the church as vice versa. These conversations included:

1. *The "practices" discussion.* A prominent stream of literature encouraged churches to reroute youth ministry (and ministry generally) through Christian "practices"—in other words, to involve young people in the historic actions of the Christian community, such as prayer, biblical interpretation, hospitality, justice-making, and Christian fellowship, to name a few.[37] By borrowing faith practices that have helped centuries of believers encounter God and participate in the self-giving love of Christ, many youth pastors hoped to develop more sustainable, theologically nourishing ways to work with adolescents that would prove life-giving for leaders as well.

2. *Theological dialogue.* Equally important, a new standard for evaluating youth ministry began to challenge unthinking pragmatism: theological intentionality. Reframing youth ministry as a context for divine transformation changed the terms for "effective" youth ministry (this "theological turn" in youth ministry, as Andrew Root calls it, will be explored in chapter 3). Participation was no longer sufficient as a standard for assessing effective faith formation. Youth ministers recognized that some popular approaches to youth

ministry actually undermined the faith that was youth ministry's goal. Theological integrity became an overt standard for ministry with young people, on the assumption that the church's practices, relationships, and methodologies for ministry with teenagers must conform to Christ—even if to do so leads to (hopefully metaphorical) crucifixion and new life.

3. *Dialogue with systems.* Veteran youth pastor and systems consultant Mark DeVries believes that theological integrity and organizational savvy need not serve as opposing poles in sustainable youth ministries. Christ-like patterns of self-giving love can (and must) be translated through congregational systems. When we do so, "sustainable" youth ministry becomes part of a congregation's organizational DNA. DeVries insists that congregations, not gifted youth pastors, are the key to youth ministry effectiveness and sustainability—and in fact, they make theologically intentional ministry possible. As a youth ministry consultant who is deeply indebted to systems analysis, DeVries' work has led him to conclude that most churches struggle in youth ministry for one of two reasons: (1) a congregation invests too little in youth ministry, compromising theological intentionality with a "survival" mentality (e.g., one youth leader for forty kids; a program calendar too full for the number of volunteers who support it; salary levels that implicitly suggest the job of youth director is a short-term position, etc.); or (2) a congregation invests its resources in the wrong things (i.e., new buildings, a "star" youth pastor, the latest program)—things that cannot bequeath life-giving practices of faith, bring teenagers more fully into the Christian community, or engage them in ministries of self-giving love. The solution is for congregations to invest in youth ministry's infrastructure: clarifying the mission and vision of ministry with young people, shoring up volunteers, budgets, and staff relationships, developing sinews between pastors, parents, and volunteers, and so on. Congregations that do this consistently and predictably see "delightful and dramatic" returns on their investments.[38]

> Congregations that wholeheartedly invest in youth ministry's infrastructure consistently and predictably see "delightful and dramatic" returns on their investments.—Mark DeVries[39]

Can We Do Better?

Youth ministers, adult youth workers, and pastors are moving beyond youth ministry "lore" into more theologically intentional and more empirically viable understandings of God, the church, and vocation that profoundly shape young people's lives, not to mention the future of youth ministry itself. The questions that haunt us in youth ministry are more indicative of growing pains than impotence. By now it is utterly clear that youth ministry is more than a defensive strategy to "get young people in church"—or (let's be honest) to keep the few we have from leaving. We know that Christ calls us to be both faithful *and* effective in ministry with young people, which means preparing young people to recognize that Christ has written them into God's story of redemption in which suffering leads to joy. The haunting questions that open this chapter remind us that there is work to be done in leading young people into lifelong commitments, practices, and communities of faith. But the promise of the gospel is that God will be faithful to complete the good work that Christ has already begun in us (Phil. 1:6).

In spite of colossal frustrations, youth ministers are a hopeful breed—a trait noticed even by social scientists. Karen Jones's research reveals that youth ministers are older and staying longer than they did a generation ago; compared to youth ministers of the last century, twenty-first-century youth ministers are more likely to "believe that they are called to youth ministry as a vocation, not a stepping-stone profession."[40] Christian Smith points out, "There is a national discussion now going on across denominations about rethinking the standard model of youth ministry and youth programming. While this beginning conversation doesn't guarantee solutions it is at least a beginning and that is hopeful. Constructive changes seem to be in the works."[41]

> "There is a national discussion now going on across denominations about rethinking the standard model of youth ministry and youth programming. While this beginning conversation doesn't guarantee solutions it is at least a beginning and that is hopeful. Constructive changes seem to be in the works."—Christian Smith

While the moniker "youth ministry" grows increasingly limiting (an issue we will return to later), the scope of the church's work with young people has never been broader. Youth ministers no longer serve congregations primarily by herding teenagers into youth groups for their protection and entertainment; rather, we shape and mobilize overlapping communities—families, peers, congregations, small groups, and so forth—that *all* serve as communities of formation in the service of faith and identity. In the twenty-first-century church, youth ministers must become ecologists more than specialists, orchestra conductors more than the congregation's wind or percussion section, leaders who can deftly weave together multiple constituencies for the benefit of young people and the glory of God.

If the research behind youth ministry's "haunting questions" teaches us anything, it is that adolescent faith grows best in a web of support. Vital Christian faith does not survive long on its own, least of all in teenagers. Although we have assumed that "effective" youth ministry depends on our skill as youth leaders, the truth is that young people's faith never depends on us. Their faith, like our faith, depends upon Christ, and Christ alone. We take our places as gardeners who tend the soil of the adolescent soul until the Word of God takes root there, strengthening them for the daunting challenges that lie ahead.

Further Reading on Themes in This Chapter

Baker, Dori Grinenko, and Joyce Ann Mercer. *Lives to Offer: Accompanying Youth on Their Vocational Quests.* Cleveland: Pilgrim Press, 2007.

Benson, Peter L., ed., et al.. *Spiritual Development: New Directions for Youth Development.* San Francisco: Jossey-Bass, 2008.

Dean, Kenda Creasy. *Almost Christian: What the Faith of Our Teenagers Is Telling the American Church.* New York: Oxford University Press, 2010.

DeVries, Mark. *Sustainable Youth Ministry.* Downers Grove, IL: InterVarsity, 2008.

Fields, Doug. *Purpose Driven Youth Ministry.* Grand Rapids: Zondervan, 1998.

Kinnaman, David, and Gabe Lyons. *UnChristian: What a New Generation Really Thinks about Christianity . . . and Why It Matters.* Grand Rapids: Baker, 2007.

Mahan, Brian, Michael Warren, and David White. *Awakening Youth Discipleship.* Eugene, OR: Wipf and Stock, 2007.

Moore, Mary Elizabeth and Almeda Wright, eds. *Children, Youth and Spirituality in a Troubling World.* St. Louis: Chalice Press, 2008.

Root, Andrew. *Revisiting Relational Youth Ministry.* Downers Grove, IL: InterVarsity, 2007.

Smith, Christian, with Melinda Lundquist Denton. *Soul Searching: The Religious and Spiritual Lives of American Teenagers.* New York: Oxford University Press, 2006.

Yaconelli, Mike. *The Core Realities of Youth Ministry.* Grand Rapids: Zondervan, 2003.

The "Classics" Library

Coles, Robert. *The Spiritual Lives of Children.* Boston: Mariner, 1991.

Erikson, Erik H. *Identity, Youth and Crisis.* New York: W. W. Norton, 1968.

Harris, Maria. *Portrait of Youth Ministry.* New York: Paulist Press, 1981.

Little, Sara. *Youth, World and Church.* Richmond, VA: John Knox Press, 1968.

Martinson, Roland. *Effective Youth Ministry: A Congregational Approach.* Minneapolis: Augsburg Fortress, 1988.

Morrison, John A. *The Educational Philosophy of St. John Bosco.* Los Angeles: Salesian Press, 1979.

Ng, David. *Youth in the Community of Disciples.* Valley Forge, PA: Judson Press, 1984.

Robbins, Duffy. *The Ministry of Nurture.* Grand Rapids: Zondervan, 1990.

Strommen, Merton. *Five Cries of Youth.* New York: Harper & Row, 1979.

Warren, Michael. *Youth, Gospel, Liberation.* San Francisco: Harper and Row, 1987.

CHAPTER TWO

DAUNTING CHALLENGES

At the end of forty days they returned from spying out the land. And they came to
Moses and Aaron and to all the congregation of the Israelites in the wilderness . . . and
they told [them], "We came to the land to which you sent us; it flows with milk and
honey, and this is its fruit. Yet the people who live in the land are strong, and the
towns are fortified and very large." . . . [Caleb] said, "Let us go up at once and occupy
it, for we are well able to overcome it." [But] the men who had gone up with him said,
"We are not able to go up against this people, for they are stronger than we are. . . . All
the people that we saw in it are of great size. . . . To ourselves we seemed
like grasshoppers, and so we seemed to them."
—Numbers 13:25-33

I do live in crazy times.
—Anne Frank

First, don't panic.

That's the advice Sara Savage and her colleagues offer, reporting their research on "Generation Y" in response to 2004's *Mission-Shaped Church* report. The report—an unlikely bestseller in the U.K., penned by a group of Anglican bishops—gained widespread attention for the urgency with which it pointed to the growing cultural gap between the church and the culture of postmodern young people in the United Kingdom.[1]

Savage and her co-writers point out that in each new cultural era, the church "has been faced with a worldview and a way of life that had previously managed perfectly well without the gospel," so has had to learn how to engage with its new cultural setting under the guidance of the Holy Spirit.[2]

> Throughout church history this has been done well and it has been done badly. When done badly it has tended to leave future generations with baggage they could well have done without. But the missionary story also contains many examples of good practice. Some cultures may prove harder for the Church to connect with than others, but none are harder for the Holy Spirit. There is no effective alternative to inculturation, to engaging people with the gospel within and as appropriate to their own culture and worldview.[3]

Savage's conclusions remind us that postmodern Christians are not the first generation to feel overwhelmed and outnumbered. Rewind to Numbers 13, after Joshua and Caleb and team return from scouting out the culture next door. If you have ever tried to familiarize yourself with the cultural icons, artifacts, or rituals of the teenagers in your church, you know what Joshua and Caleb must have felt like on the scouting expedition to Canaan. On the one hand, popular culture seems to be flowing with milk and honey; it is replete with visions of "the good life," brimming with resources and opportunities. Surely the church can occupy this culture, enjoy its beauty, borrow its images, and baptize its traditions for the gospel! After all, haven't we already translated football's high holy days into opportunities to raise money to fight hunger, and haven't we drawn on everything from film to hip hop to translate our prayers into a popular vernacular?[4]

> The most thoroughgoing program of formation in North America is the one molding young people into consumers.

On the other hand, the media juggernaut that propels Western ideologies around the world seems irresistible, even when we make the gospel available through clever translations. It is not clear who "wins" when churches borrow from popular culture; does culture become more attuned to the gospel in these efforts, or does the church become swallowed by the culture? The most thoroughgoing program of formation in North America is the one molding young people into consumers. Relentless, zealous, and insidious, this program of formation "brands" young Americans before they can talk.[5] Like the spies in Canaan, Christians often feel intimated by the magnitude of these cultural forces; we know they are stronger than we are. The global scope, the incessant pace, the consumer narratives that equate adolescent worth with product consumption—these are Goliath-sized challenges for youth ministry. We seem "like grasshoppers" beside them, microscopic citizens of Who-ville who yell from our speck of dust in hopes of being heard by adolescents before we are run over by them.[6]

Of course, in the Dr. Seuss story, it took every last Who down in Whoville to make a racket loud enough to be heard by giant-sized Horton and his friends.[7] But American churches do not clamor very loudly when it comes to young people. Marketers also view us as grasshoppers—which is to say they are not very worried that the church might derail their ambitions to cast teenagers in the role of consumers-in-training. More often, churches cooperate in this training venture, treating faith as a product to be acquired, and consequently reinforcing our own consumer mentalities.

Spying on Canaan

Most youth ministers have a little bit of Caleb in us, or we wouldn't be in the foolhardy business of immersing consumer-minded teenagers in an alternative story about who they are and why they are here—a story that so radically undermines our homage to progress, success, and personal fulfillment that you can understand why teenagers find it hard to swallow. I (Don) am currently a confirmation sponsor for Thomas, an articulate ninth-grader from my congregation. Thomas attends Sunday worship with his parents and his younger sister every week, takes academic courses on the Bible at school, and can tell you more about the kings of Israel and Judah than any adult I know. For the past few years, Thomas has participated in a Thursday morning before-breakfast Bible study, which teenagers take turns leading. "Those guys really know the Bible," Thomas remarks. "They get me. They see who I am."

For all this, Thomas is not sure whether he believes in God. He's even less sure that "joining" the church makes any sense, other than to please his parents. The God he reads about in the Bible troubles him; God sometimes seems capricious and unfair, which for Thomas makes God unworthy of worship and allegiance. And unless Thomas can write a personal statement of faith with integrity, he does not want to be confirmed.

> Two-thirds of American teenagers believe that people do not need to be involved in a religious congregation to be religious and spiritual.

Thomas's attitude toward the church squares with those of the young people interviewed for the National Study of Youth and Religion, mentioned in chapter 1. Two-thirds of American teenagers believe that people do not need to be involved in a religious congregation to be religious and spiritual.[8] Most young people treat faith as an individual choice, like considering a product they might want to buy, rather than as a communal undertaking. Smith and his colleagues observe:

> This individualistic, antiestablishment proclivity lives, ironically, in the heart of much of American institutional religion itself. And it has helped to form an important popular cultural distinction between "an authentic faith"—which is personally chosen, regularly practiced, and spiritually meaningful—and an "empty faith," which is ritualistically rote, spiritually dry, and invested more in organizational associations than "real," personal experience.[9]

Historically, youth ministry has challenged the church by insisting that it reflect its cultural location. Christians may be called "to be in the world but not of the world," but (as a friend of mine says) churches shouldn't be "out of it" either.[10] Yet changes in both the adolescent lifestage and the North American context influence the way we will approach ministry with young people—and perhaps even underscore a new role for youth ministry in the church.

```
┌────────────────────────────────────────────────────────────────┐
│           Daunting Challenges for Youth Ministry                 │
│ The Challenges of a Changing Lifestage                           │
│     Expanding Adolescence?                                       │
│     Ending Adolescence?                                          │
│ The Challenges of a Changing Context                             │
│     A New Sense of Place: The Challenge of Getting Grounded      │
│     A New Sense of Time: The Challenge of Changing Tempo         │
│     A New Sense of Stuff: The Challenge of Living Generously     │
│     A New Sense of Self: The Challenge of Branding               │
│     A New Sense of Story: The Challenge of Telling the Truth     │
│ Challenges Ahead: Serving Christ in a Post-Christendom Church    │
│ Learning to Be Church (Again)                                    │
└────────────────────────────────────────────────────────────────┘
```

The Challenges of a Changing Lifestage

The adolescent lifestage is a modern, Western invention. Until quite recently in human history, you were either a child or an adult; societies invoked rites of passage to announce a young person's readiness to mate, but there was no period of "becoming" that prepared youth for social responsibility unless you were one of the privileged few who could afford the moratorium offered by travel or formal education. What changed in Western society was industrialization. With the technology of the Industrial Revolution, labor demands shifted dramatically, and pressure increased to prevent youth from taking jobs from their elders, and to occupy their free time as a result of their newfound unemployment. In the middle and upper classes, school became the preferred holding tank (although secondary education in the U.S. did not become compulsory, or universally available, until after World War II). This left hundreds of thousands of young people, no longer essential in an agricultural economy, without a prescribed route into adult society—so by the mid-1800s, they were flocking to the cities in search of employment and adventure.

On the heels of the Second Great Awakening, organizations like the YMCA (1844) and YWCA (1855) sprang up to organize urban young people with time on their hands. The expressed desire of the YMCA was to offer young people an "evangelical creed" to help them resist urban temptations.[11] By the late nineteenth century, "child-centeredness" had become a middle-class virtue, and small-town, middle-class Protestants began to look for ways to protect their children's childhood and forestall "precocious" adulthood. In cities, the "child saver" movement, an effort to rescue youth from a draconian court system by keeping them busy with organized youth activities, helped teenagers avoid decisions leading to adult responsibility. Historian Anthony Platt points out,

> Many of the child savers' reforms were aimed at imposing sanctions on conduct unbecoming youth and disqualifying youth from the benefit of adult privileges.

The child savers were more concerned with restriction than liberation, with the protection of youth from moral weaknesses as well as physical dangers.[12]

This was the milieu that sired the "youth group," the peer-intensive model of youth ministry so familiar to us today. In 1904, when G. Stanley Hall penned his tome *Adolescence*, he established, securely if erroneously, young people's newfound cultural status as objects of both fear and fascination. Hall described adolescence as a period of "storm and stress" (a view quickly discredited by subsequent research, but the description has been maddeningly persistent).[13] For Hall, the outcome of the stormy, stressful lifestage was conversion—not the evangelical conversion sought by American revivalism, but a harmonization of drives and instincts that led to sexual and ethical maturity.[14]

In this religious and social context, *youth* suddenly became more than a concept: it became fact. By the twentieth century, the pontoons on which the idea of "adolescence" had been floating were replaced by the steel girders of protection, restriction, and dependence. Churches did their part by establishing "youth ministries" bolstered by early literature in psychology and education.[15] After World War II, universally available secondary education laid the tracks for an age-stratified society, allowing "youth" to coalesce into "peer culture" and Madison Avenue to treat "teenagers" and their newly disposable income as a marketing niche (in 1956, the average American teenager had a weekly income of $10.50—and by 1999, $94 a week).[16] Writing in the 1950s and 1960s, developmental psychologist Erik H. Erikson launched generations of research on "ego-identity formation" as the defining task of adolescence. Erikson's "moratorium," a socially sanctioned "time out" between childhood and adult commitments, became widely accepted as necessary for helping young people successfully prepare for adult roles in a complex modern society. In short, as young people responded to society's response to them, "adolescence" was no longer the exception. It had become psychologically and culturally normative.[17]

> In 1956, the average American teenager had a weekly income of $10.50—and by 1999, $94 a week.

Expanding Adolescence?

Today, adolescence starts sooner and ends later than it did in 1950, with great ambiguity on both ends. The most obvious markers are biological. Normal puberty (the attainment of fertility) takes between 1.5 to 6 years to complete, and in the last century the average age for the onset of menstruation has dropped from age seventeen to twelve, with secondary sex characteristics (e.g., pubic hair and breast buds) appearing before age 8 for a large number of girls. African American and Mexican American girls start menstruation about six months earlier than girls of European descent.[18] Boys also start puberty earlier than in previous generations, though the change is far less dramatic.

Precocious puberty has both social and biological consequences. Early developing girls are more likely to develop breast cancer, become pregnant, perform poorly in school and become victims of physical and sexual violence. Environmental health researcher Sandra Steingraber explains, "Girls get their first periods, on average, a few months earlier than girls 40 years ago, but they get their breasts one to two years earlier."[19] The reasons for these changes remain unclear, and probably can be attributed in part to both improved health care and nutrition and patterns of obesity, though many researchers also cite environmental factors (especially hormone-mimicking chemicals commonly found in plastics, fire retardants, and other household items).

An early start to puberty, however, does not signal an early completion of the adolescent lifestage. On the contrary, adolescence ends *later* than it did a generation ago, and has even provoked some researchers to observe a transitional stage in the lifecycle emerging as the tasks associated with identity formation extend beyond the teenage years. Most contemporary young Americans eschew the title of "adult" until their late twenties or early thirties (one University of Chicago study found that most Americans think adulthood begins at age twenty-six).[20] Developmental theorists generally agree that identity formation is the signature task of adolescence—but the tasks associated with identity formation (negotiating commitments of love, work, and ideology) are increasingly postponed. Psychologist Jeffrey Arnett thinks this postponement signals a new stage in the lifecycle, "emerging adulthood," when these tasks are now accomplished.[21] Significantly, these developmental tasks include coming to terms with questions of faith, whether young people think of themselves as "religious" or not. As Arnett puts it, human beings "invariably address religious questions as part of our lives.... Forming religious beliefs appears to be a universal part of identity development."[22]

> Human beings "invariably address religious questions as part of our lives.... Forming religious beliefs appears to be a universal part of identity development."—Jeffrey Arnett

Ending of Adolescence?

Biological markers signal the beginning of adolescence, but the end of adolescence is far more ambiguous. If fertility is no longer the sign of adulthood, then what is? Some scholars argue that since adolescence no longer functions as a transition into adulthood, it should be abandoned. They believe that middle-class interests have artificially reinforced and prolonged adolescence, infantilizing young people who are sexually, intellectually, and psychologically capable of making adult commitments far sooner than our laws or our morals allow. "Teens have become the last group whose disempowerment is invisible because it is so much taken for granted," argues psychiatrist Philip Graham.[23] These scholars maintain that social forces not only invented adolescence; they have prolonged it long past its due. Psychologist Robert Epstein criticizes religious communities for their uncritical buy-in of a view of adolescence similar to G. Stanley Hall's in 1904, in which teenagers are weak and incompetent and in need of strict adult supervision.[24] Instead of creating structures that reinforce these stereotypes, Epstein believes, social institutions like churches should accord teenagers the same power and privileges they offer adults, enabling youth to live into the roles and responsibilities of adulthood.

Epstein grossly oversimplifies religious communities' attitudes toward young people (and maturation in general); young people are often prophetic leaders in churches, and youth ministry has frequently served as a venue for leadership formation in and beyond the church.[25] But many youth ministers (including the authors of this book) share the intuition that American social institutions expect too little of teenagers, disenfranchising and infantilizing them—and churches are no exception. Practical theologian and youth minister David White writes perceptively that this attitude is no longer tenable in American culture:

> Until recent years, the bargain of adolescence—*dependence and education now, responsibility and independence later*—has worked reasonably well for many, due primarily to its brief span and the certain reward of middle class employment. However, recent cultural developments have made problematic this unwritten treaty with youth. These developments relegate youth to institutions in which they have less than full power for longer than any age cohort in the history of the world, leaving them considerably less free to make their distinctive mark on history, and are quickly shaping them as passive consumers rather than active agents and shapers of history.[26]

American social institutions expect too little of teenagers, disenfranchising and infantilizing them—and churches are no exception.

While scholars like Epstein argue that adolescence should be terminated as an unnecessary step toward adulthood, others argue that adolescence has already ended by virtue of its conflation with adulthood. By the late twentieth century, adolescence had become a lifestyle as well as a lifestage, possible to cultivate and prolong by choice. As a result, many people who were chronologically adults remained socially (and sometimes psychologically) adolescent. Some people have always made the "bargain of adolescence" that White describes—a moratorium way of life marked by dependence, preparation, and postponed responsibilities—somewhat permanent, but for most people the need to pay bills generally made this a short-term arrangement. Today, consumer culture thrives on blurring the borders of adolescence, hawking adult toys to youth (and children) and marketing youth-like lifestyles to adults. Purchasing power, not maturity, is the prerequisite for full participation in consumer culture (and adolescents do a fine job of this without an integrated identity). Whether extended moratoria lead to (or cause) either the "slacker" stereotypes once associated with Generation X, or the "risk averse" mentality said to characterize their younger siblings—or whether social attitudes simply encourage us to stay "young" as long as possible—the upshot is that today's adolescents and adults often look very like one another, making the adolescent lifestage seem increasingly irrelevant.

These attitudes do meet resistance, sometimes from young people themselves. Comparing the effects of 2008's plummeting economy on young people to youth growing up in the Great Depression, a widely read *New York Times* article predicted a reversal of prolonged adolescence. Emerging adults, negatively affected by the poor economy, are making a return to "Things That Matter," according to author Kate Zernicke—thus ending the ever-expanding carefree moratoria associated with adolescence. Even before the so-called Recession Generation, some upwardly mobile twenty-somethings (dubbed the "New Victorians") united behind a fierce commitment to marriage, parenting, and vocation early in life, "settling down" with families in their early twenties in a bid to choose adulthood as a way of life.[27]

These debates over how adolescence is changing raise two sets of core questions for the church. First, who is youth ministry for? In other words, in contemporary American culture, who "counts" as a youth and who doesn't? Second, should Christians protect young people from precocious adulthood, or should we encourage adulthood to start sooner? Does God call us to shield young people from the dangers of a predatory dominant culture by immersing them in an alternative "Christian" culture instead? Or, does God call us to liberate youth from the dominant culture's ideological shackles (including those imposed by the church) to assume their identities as Christian adults—even if they lack sufficient formation to know what "Christian" adulthood means?

We are using *youth ministry* as an umbrella term that refers to ministry to, with, and for adolescents and their families, focusing especially on young people from the onset of puberty through emerging adulthood. (We also refer to "teenagers" or "adolescents" from time to time, to acknowledge the age groups that churches most often have in mind.)[28] We recognize that the term *youth ministry* is problematic; societal changes and regional customs make the definition of youth itself something of a moving target. (Outside the U.S., *youth* commonly includes persons in their twenties and thirties, or persons of any age whose parents are still alive.) What we can say with certainty is that churches can no longer afford to limit *youth ministry* to teenagers who gather in the church basement. The research on adolescence, and our citizenship in a global village, require us to extend our reach.

Churches can no longer afford to limit *youth ministry* to teenagers who gather in the church basement. The research on adolescence, and our citizenship in a global village, require us to extend our reach.

The Challenges of a Changing Context

The changing adolescent lifestage is largely the result of changing sociocultural conditions in which young people are immersed. Since young people's cultural "screens" and psychological defense mechanisms are not yet fully formed, they are remarkably open to context, and are typically the first to feel the tremors of cultural shifts. Today's adolescents reflect what Savage and her colleagues call the three key coordinates of Generation Y's (born after 1980) culture: *globalization* and its effects on time and space, *electronic and information technologies*, and *consumerism*. Of course, these coordinates affect the entire church as well, but young people pursue these themes with such intensity that it is easy to forget that these engines of cultural change have pursued young people first.

> This may be a good time to remind ourselves that the bricks of the church and the bricks of the culture are made from the same mud.

This may be a good time to remind ourselves that the bricks of the church and the bricks of the culture are made from the same mud.[29] All anthropologists view religion as a critical component of culture, which means that the church needs the same redemption as other humanly constructed communities. But since Christians' first allegiance is to Christ—not to the state, the economy, the media, the educational system, the nuclear family, or any other lesser gods we might erect—the Holy Spirit nudges us to detach ourselves from competing allegiances and focus intently on Jesus in all that we do. This does, in fact, distinguish those followers of Jesus from those who fix their attention on other human horizons. Unlike worldly wisdom, for example, gospel wisdom calls youth and adults to

- care for the world God created and loves
- respect human freedom and finitude
- consume in ways that honor the earth and one another
- cultivate their relationship with God through personal and communal prayer
- tell truthful and graceful stories about our lives as God's children.

Attuning our lives to the gospel allows us to hear the dissonance between who we are, and who God calls us to be as followers of Jesus. But it is hard to detect this on our own. The community of faith is our tuning fork, and the power of the Holy Spirit is the vibration running through the church that helps us discern Christ's pitch over the din of cultural clatter. Here are some of the cultural issues making the most noise:

A New Sense of Place: The Challenge of Getting Grounded

Grace began volunteering at the foot clinic of Central Presbyterian Church's night shelter for homeless men as an eighth-grade confirmand.[30] Every

27

Wednesday night, Grace and the other volunteers offer guests a warm-water soak for tired, sore feet. Grace clips nails, treats infections, bandages cuts, and gives gentle foot massages. Somehow the act of washing restores dignity to the whole body. Even outside the foot clinic, Grace catches herself staring at feet sometimes, wondering where they have walked and what they might need. She feels deeply connected to the men she meets at the shelter. "It's like getting a new family," she says. "You get to know some of the regular guys by name. Sometimes they talk about their struggles with faith. Once I met a guy who was going through a really hard time. He asked me for advice, as though we were already friends."

For Grace, taking the street-worn feet of homeless men in her hands is an act of genuine humility. The word humility comes from *humus*, the Latin word for "dirt." Grace's act of footwashing connects her to the men in the clinic, to the feet she sees every day, to the city they share. It grounds her, the way feet ground us in a place—literally, connecting us to the dirt, locating us, giving us a place to stand. The foot clinic also is a place Grace stands her ground beside Jesus. His followers washed his feet and he humbled himself to wash theirs.

> "Place" no longer means what it once did; in a globalized world, "here" and "there" are increasingly detached from geography and redefined according to access.

Yet "place" no longer means what it once did; in a globalized world, "here" and "there" are increasingly detached from geography and redefined according to access. "Where are you going?" can refer to a location in cyberspace, a virtual visit, a faraway culture. Even rural teenagers, though more rooted to geography than their urban cousins, find their relationship to place complicated by the economic, technological, and cultural changes wrought by globalization. Scholars describe global culture using "liquid" images instead of "solid" ones.[31] For the majority of Americans, place is fluid; in the U.S., teenagers watch hometown factories close so that production can be outsourced to regions with cheaper labor. They know they are inheriting (and are already participating in) a global economy that is rapidly depleting natural resources, that objectifies human laborers, and that threatens myriad species with extinction—even as they leverage global systems to make the economy work. Allegiance to place is increasingly expendable; it is easier to make decisions that degrade local ecologies and compromise local lifestyles when the decision-makers don't live there.

Globalization makes instability a cultural norm, unhinging local attachments, which paradoxically intensifies our longing for "home." In this context, cultivating a community of care for people we do not know personally, and for the world God created and loves, becomes increasingly challenging—and necessary—for the church. The gospel calls us to balance concern for all of God's creation, near and far, with radical connections to the here and now. Christians maintain that the Word of God is a particular, not a generic, Word: it is God's

Word in Jesus Christ. The First Council of Nicea in 325 urged Christians to faithfully ground their hope in the particularity of Christ, while recognizing the church's witness in the wider world.[32] In no case does the church operate as a multinational organization. Each Christian community is a concentration of the whole church, not a branch office of some larger corporation.

> Globalization makes instability a cultural norm, unhinging local attachments, which paradoxically intensifies our longing for "home."

What this means is that those of us in youth ministry must learn to view "place" through binoculars, bringing near and far horizons into focus simultaneously. As the gathered church, we are bound together as a community of practice in a *particular place*.[33] A place has density and materiality—bodies and buildings, faces and livelihoods—that a location on a map does not. Whether we gather in an urban cathedral or a rural farmhouse, the church cultivates a fidelity to place often lacking in "the global village." Christian spirituality honors the particularity of its host culture. Churches over the centuries have always been united by their common focus on the person of Jesus Christ, relied on the same holy books, and engaged in the same special practices involving water, oil, bread, and wine—but other than that, a time-traveler might be hard-pressed to find similarities between eleventh-century Celtic monks up to their necks in ice water singing hymns, and twentieth-century Nigerian charismatics dancing through Sunday worship.[34] One of the miracles of the Christian community is that we still recognize it after centuries of local adaptation. Yet the church's binocular vision requires us to address both the neighbor beside us and the neighbor beyond us. Christ not only calls the church to take seriously its native soil; Christ also calls us to follow him beyond our provincial boundaries to become apostles as well as disciples, and witnesses in the world.

A New Sense of Time: The Challenge of Changing Tempo

Related to the challenge of displacement posed by globalization is the challenge of unbounded time posed by our "24/7" culture. The metaphor of global village conjures up an image of one large, cooperative community, united by the consumption of common products. But economically, the global village is not a cozy place. The pressure to compete for buyers fuels our determination to push our limits in order to remain competitive. While previous generations experienced the sweep of time using analog clocks, contemporary teenagers know time as a series of discrete, digital moments: now it's 3:34 p.m.... now it's 3:35 p.m.... and so on. Although physicists maintain that there is no such thing as perpetual motion (gravity and resistance eventually have their way in all matters of movement), global commerce has convinced us that time has no boundaries, and should be leveraged in the service of selling.

North American young people are formed by a culture where time and aspirations have come unhinged from their natural limits. Like Icarus, our bid to live unlimited lives makes us forget that our wings are made of wax—that being human means that we are made to live within bodies and time, to be present and fully alive in a particular moment. To ignore our moment in time is to squander a piece of our humanity.

> To ignore our moment in time is to squander a piece of our humanity.

As a result, most of us do not view time as a gift. We tend to think of it as a limit, a commodity to leverage, a product in scarce supply. We may or may not be working more hours than our grandparents did—reports vary, and younger workers are far more concerned (and intentional) about the work/family balance than their parents were.[35] What is certain is that technology has blurred the line between worktime and downtime; fewer and fewer people "leave the office" at the end of the day as technology makes it easier (and expected) for us to conduct our professional lives from home. A tsunami of emails and text messages—and the expectation of constant availability—creates low-grade anxiety as we do message-reply triage. We even blur the borders of waking and sleeping; sleep deprivation has been called America's top health disorder (the National Highway Traffic Safety Administration attributes more than 100,000 crashes and 1,500 fatalities a year to driver fatigue alone).[36]

Teenagers, of course, are programmed—by biology and by society—to test limits; they often push themselves in work and play beyond their capacities, often with the full cooperation of the adults who love them best. We urge young people to "seize the day," to fill their calendars with "productive activities" that will impress college admission counselors or will at least keep them "out of trouble." The result is a fusion of sacred time with ordinary time, a confusion of Sabbath and labor—which ultimately means a loss of holiness, the "set apartness" of God's people. In a pluralistic culture, Sunday is no longer an agreed-upon holy day, and the common worship hour is challenged by middle-class culture's avalanche of opportunities. Without a day of rest, some youth leaders build youth ministries around mission trips rather than Sunday fellowship gatherings in an attempt to leverage one week a year when young people will prioritize coming together with Christians (providing they plan far enough ahead).

Fred Edie, commenting on the time crunch faced by youth ministry, observes: "To ask, 'How can we find time to fit church into youths' lives?' is the wrong question. It is far better to ask, 'How can we offer youth the gift of time that God has created, redeemed, and continues to sanctify daily through Jesus Christ?'"[37] If the goal of human time is work and productivity, the goal of liturgical time is to enjoy God and imitate Christ. The church sets its clock by Easter, and Christianity's two most subversive timepieces, the liturgical calendar and the practice of keeping Sabbath, explicitly undermine our enslavement to the limits of time by boldly embracing the freedom of the resurrection. Christ has removed death as our human time limit. Easter offers concrete evidence that time belongs to God, who chooses to share eternity with us.

> "To ask, 'How can we find time to fit church into youths' lives?' is the wrong question. It is far better to ask, 'How can we offer youth the gift of time that God has created, redeemed, and continues to sanctify daily through Jesus Christ?'"—Fred Edie

The liturgical calendar gives young people a different way of telling time than the one dictated by the academic year or soccer season. The liturgical year is comprised of "a sequence of days and seasons, woven together in an order that tells the story of Christ and leads believers ever deeper into the mysteries of the Christian faith."[38] During Advent, we emphasize waiting (anathema to merchandizing). During Lent, we prepare ourselves to encounter Jesus' betrayal, crucifixion, and resurrection, a decidedly different approach to spring break than the one proposed by MTV. God gave Sabbath to the Israelites to remind them that their enslavement in Egypt was over. No more 24/7 workweeks: "[For] six days you shall labor and do all your work. But the seventh day is a sabbath to the LORD your God; you shall not do any work" (Exodus 20:9-10). It was a commandment designed to subvert business as usual, to help the Israelites—and to help us—experience the freedom of life-giving boundaries. Sabbath offers young people a way to say "No" to the slavery imposed by an endless cycle of producing and consuming, and "Yes" to feasting, worship, and playful re-creation.[39]

Of course, the real challenge of embracing liturgical time with young people is to become committed Sabbath-keepers ourselves.[40] "Teach us to count our days," the psalmist implores, "that we may gain a wise heart" (Psalm 90:12). If time is God's gift, a rhythmic reminder that genuine freedom is always circumscribed by human finitude, then our best shot at teaching young people to receive the day as a blessing instead of a burden is by modeling Christian time-keeping—a rhythm of life punctuated by Sabbaths, and that trusts that time belongs to God.

A New Sense of Stuff: The Challenge of Living Generously

Every Wednesday night, teen volunteers at the Agape Community Kitchen in Westfield, New Jersey, prepare and serve a nutritious meal to 250 people in the nearby town of Elizabeth. Teenagers started (and continue to lead) this soup kitchen ministry, which also provides a clothing closet for guests to receive blankets, clothes, and shoes. What began as a Presbyterian youth group's hands-on service activity has become a weekly, way-of-life priority that for almost a decade has attracted a very diverse corps of teenage volunteers. Young people are drawn to an activity that matters, that makes a difference in the world. Over time, Agape "forms" participants by engaging them in gospel practices of hospitality, bread-breaking, and justice-seeking. Stories and images of Christ emerge organically as youth stir chili, wash dishes, and listen to the testimony of guests. After serving, sharing dinner with, and cleaning up after their guests, young people debrief the evening with a pastor: Where was Christ most clearly present tonight?

To be human means to consume. Consumption is an identity-shaping practice; as the saying goes, "You are what you eat." Eating together with Jesus gradually shaped a group of fishermen and tax collectors into Jesus' disciples, just as eating at Jesus' table today profoundly shapes us into disciples as well, as we consume—and are ourselves consumed by—grace. At the communion table, there is always more than enough to go around.

> Consumption is an identity-shaping practice; as the saying goes, "You are what you eat."

It is ironic that Christians, especially those born into a culture of plenty, buy into the scarcity myth: the fear that there is *not* enough to go around promotes gratuitous consumption at every level. Despite God's lavish and prodigal grace, which has showered creation with resources that promote the flourishing of life, sin allows the suspicion of scarcity to supplant our awareness of God's abundance. The scarcity myth destroys trust and leads people to hoard rather than share life-giving resources. Whether it is an Israelite squirreling away more than his share of manna or a teenager amassing more after-school activities than she can ever invest in, we humans have perfected the art of distrusting God's providence. We try to protect ourselves against the future. It always backfires.

In Christian practice, the Eucharist (also called the Lord's Supper or Holy Communion) is our rhythmic reminder that our futures are not in our hands. Paul urged Christians to celebrate the Eucharist in order to enjoy God's gifts and remember that our sustenance comes at the price of another's sacrifice. Grain and grapes were crushed so that we have the benefits of bread and wine; Jesus died so that we might live. The Eucharist helps young people distinguish between feasting (which celebrates abundance) and binging (motivated by food insecurity that leads us to hoard). Paul encouraged every new community of Christians to center its common life around shared meals, and to invite Gentiles as well as Jews to Jesus' table. Wherever house churches sprang up during those first centuries, dining rooms were expanded to accommodate larger tables for feeding the faithful and especially the poor.[41] Wherever communion is served today, young people get a glimpse of God's expansive grace that invites all people to be nourished by the gospel together, challenging the hypnotizing drone of consumer culture.

> The Eucharist helps young people distinguish between feasting (which celebrates abundance) and binging (motivated by food insecurity that leads us to hoard).

A New Sense of Self: The Challenge of Branding

Paradoxically, cultures of consumption are fueled by a detachment from things. If I'm attached to a favorite coat I've worn for years, I won't run out to buy a new one. At some level I need to be dissatisfied with what I have so that I'll crave something else and go shopping. Marketers work hard to cultivate this dissatisfaction and then to forge a relationship between people and products via *branding*, getting people to identify with a particular corporate brand. Their goal is to embed products so deeply into my identity that I cannot imagine being me without it.[42] Branding cultivates cradle-to-grave product loyalty among consumers, from Mickey Mouse underwear at six to Disneyworld honeymoons at twenty-six, even as the product itself becomes "new and improved."

> The seductive power of branding becomes stronger when relational bonds between people become weaker.

The seductive power of branding becomes stronger when relational bonds between people become weaker. When friends disappoint, when families feel fractured, when we feel disconnected and apart, brand loyalty offers a sense of identity confirmation and continuity. "Love may let you down, but I'll always be here for you," a brand-name product seems to whisper. When teenagers feel excluded, a brand-name product reassures them that they belong to a worldwide community of product users. Wherever they happen to be in the world, a brand becomes a familiar face in an anonymous, uncaring crowd (especially convenient for U.S. citizens, as our national economy now produces more popular brands than tangible products).[43]

Advertising images rarely present and defend truth claims; they rely on suggestion and inference, the power of a story half-told. To finish the story, we must buy into it (literally). Before a product can save us, we must purchase it. Of course, the power of suggestion is not limited to consumer products. Governments instill patriotism; magazines advocate styles of dress, hair, and music; sports teams fan team loyalty; churches develop youth activities to target teens who are "sold" on particular "brands" of piety (spiritual? social? wholesome? pious?)—all suppress diversity in an effort to build loyalty around a particular point of view. And, once categorized, teenagers gravitate toward others who have adopted similar "brands" that, paradoxically, adults have imagined for them. Even "youth" itself functions as a brand in American culture. Celebrity stereotypes commodify young people and youthfulness, reducing young stars to "perpetual youth-hood" as we invest them with perfections, powers, and other airbrushed attributes. There is only one rule: do not age.

The church confers identity by a cleansing bath rather than by attaching a label. Baptism washes away our fake I.D.s and reveals our worth before God—worth that is independent of purchasing power, personal style, or nation-state affiliation. Through baptism, we become part of a body where every*body* counts and no*body* is disposable—where in fact weaker members are given greater honor (1 Corinthians 12). If the practice of celebrating communion is one way the church redirects young people's understanding of consumption, the practice of baptism represents the church's attitude toward branding. Christian identity is a gift from God, not the upshot of our relationship with a product.

> Baptism washes away our fake I.D.s and reveals our worth before God—worth that is independent of purchasing power, personal style, or nation-state affiliation.

A New Sense of Story: The Challenge of Telling the Truth

The church interrupts the flood of consumer messages with a story, not a sound byte, which proclaims salvation as a person, not a product. Sound bytes may charm or entertain us, but human beings are known through our stories. In a culture that relies on snippets and statistics, chronic alienation among American young people should not surprise us. Without a story to stick to, they have no way of being known, even to themselves. Author Katherine Paterson remembers a therapist who treated troubled teenagers, and who told her he had decided to end his practice. It had been his habit, upon meeting a new patient, to invite the young person to "tell me his or her story," which then gave him clues for how to proceed with treatment. "But that doesn't work anymore," he told her sadly. "I keep meeting with teenagers who look at me perfectly blankly when I ask them about their stories. 'I don't have a story,' they'll say. I'm not sure I know how to work with children who have no stories."[44]

Writing in the mid-twentieth century, novelist Flannery O'Connor already noted the devaluation of story in a modern culture increasingly enamored with data and facts: "There is a certain embarrassment about being a storyteller in these times when stories are considered not quite as satisfying as statements and statements not quite as satisfying as statistics," she wrote, adding: "But in the long run, a people is known, not by its statements or its statistics, but by the stories it tells."[45] Writer and youth minister Sarah Arthur concurs: "While journalism purports to tell us what happened, story tells us what happens."[46] Truth, not historicity, is the aim of story. We may amass data, but we are known by our stories.

> We may amass data, but we are known by our stories.

From the beginning, the Jesus movement that became the church was known by the stories it told. The early church had so many stories about Jesus that the Bible finally included four different versions of his life, death, and resurrection. Each gospel account—Matthew, Mark, Luke, and John—portrays Jesus in a different light, suggesting that multiple perspectives on Jesus are necessary. No one can tell the whole truth about Jesus that captures all we need to know about him.

So perhaps it is not surprising that the so-called "modern church" always seemed like something of a forced fit. Postmodernity, on the other hand, requires us to reconsider the modern era's confidence in data and truth claims. The dilemma facing postmodern young people is not the absence of truth claims, but the abundance of them; with so many truths, so many products, so many styles vying for young people's attention ("Choose me! Choose me!"), it is hard to blame youth for their exasperated "Whatevers!"—a sure sign of overload, not ideological tolerance. Overwhelmed, young people retreat inward. Unable to discern truth from Truth, unable to adjudicate between the thousands of messages bombarding them daily, they retreat to the authority of their own subjectivity.[47]

> The dilemma facing postmodern young people is not the absence of truth claims, but the abundance of them; with so many truths, so many products, so many styles vying for young people's attention, it is hard to blame young people for their exasperated *"Whatevers!"*—a sure sign of overload, not ideological tolerance.

Challenges Ahead: Serving Christ in a Post-Christendom Church

A persuasive case can be made that Americans have replaced the church's authority with the authority of personal experience—the "infallible gut," as Mary Belenky and her colleagues call it in their research on feminine epistemology.[48] This shift toward the authority of personal experience has been called a "disestablishment" of Christianity, meaning that the church has lost its power, privilege, and authority in the dominant culture. Theologian Douglas John Hall, for example, believes that we have reached the "end of Christendom," or the end of that period in history in which churches were actually supported by culture—if not officially, as in Europe, then unofficially, through customs and practices, as in America.[49] Despite the fact that America's founding patriots were mostly deists, many people still assume that America was founded on a hard bed of "Christian values" that led to a *de facto*

"Christian" nation.[50] Christianity—and specifically, Protestantism—became "established" in American culture, not by law, but by habit.

Referring to the emperor who legalized Christian worship in 323 C.E., ethicist Stanley Hauerwas reminds us why Americans still tend to think of the U.S. as a "Christian" nation, despite pluralism and skepticism:

> Constantinianism is a hard habit to break. It is particularly hard when it seems that we do so much good by remaining "in power." It is hard to break because all our categories have been set by the church's establishment as a necessary part of Western civilization.[51]

While religious affiliation has significantly declined among most religious groups since 1990 (in 2009, 15 percent of Americans listed their religious affiliation as "none," the largest religious affiliation next to Catholics or Baptists),[52] Hauerwas is right that churches—and church people—have difficulty relinquishing cultural power (think buildings, titles, operating budgets). The loss of young people in the pews—and young leaders in the pulpit—has been chronicled, and lamented, for more than half a century, and cries for ecclesial change abound.[53] But institutionalized habits die hard.[54] Like all social institutions, churches have a strong tendency to repeat themselves, with little alteration, from one generation to the next.

> The most serious challenge facing youth ministry in the twenty-first century church may simply be our uncertainty about how to go about *being* the church in an era that no longer grants cultural privilege to Christianity.

At the same time, it is clear that the cultural hegemony of Christianity in North America is fast evaporating. Today, we cannot count on the presence of a "Christian" culture to support the church's ministries—*even in congregations*. The Christian story is one of many truths available to young people, which is why "post-Christendom" seems daunting to some and defeatist to others (our own editorial team divided over this one). Yet in a post-Christendom context, Christian teachings and ethics stand in opposition to those in the dominant culture—a situation that, in Hall's view, calls for "creative indirectness," enacting God's word as well as telling, befriending as well as proclaiming.[55] The church's story is not a modern, objective one; it is an intimate, subjective one—a love story that calls, invites, and involves us. The point is not to know the story; the point is to know *Christ*, intimately and relationally, through his story, and in so doing come to know ourselves.

Hall views "disestablishment" as a promising predicament for the postmodern church. It is a contemporary form of what the medieval church called purgation, a way of ridding ourselves of competing allegiances to Christ in order to regain clarity about the business churches are in. Hall calls this "disengaging-in-order-to-engage," and thinks young people have a critical role in disentangling the gospel from its cultural captivity.[56] Pointing to the church's dire need for catechesis, especially for a generation numb to theological language, Douglas John Hall comments, "There are no shortcuts: *We must begin with basics.*"

> We have two or three generations of people in and around the churches now who are, most of them, not only unfamiliar with the fundamental teachings of the Christian traditions but ignorant even of the Scriptures.... Until a far greater number of church-going Americans and Canadians have become more articulate about the faith than they currently are, we cannot expect the churches to stand back from their sociological moorings far enough to detach what Christians profess from the mishmash of modernism, postmodernism, secularism, pietism, and free-enterprise democracy with which Christianity in our context is so fantastically interwoven.[57]

Disestablishment requires practices of catechesis to familiarize newcomers with the core stories of Christian identity, and with core practices that enact it like discernment, justice-seeking, and truth-telling, to name a few. By realigning communities of Christians with the gospel, these stories and practices help churches gain clarity about their mission in the world. As Episcopal priest and organizational consultant Loren Mead puts it:

> Congregations must build themselves up as religious communities, as bases from which ministry is done. They need first to get clear that this is their primary business. They are in business to help people find God and be found by God, to build a community in which God's Word is studied and reflected upon, a community in which people are nurtured, healed, and fed.[58]

Taken together, Hall, Mead and others suggest a new role for youth ministry in the twenty-first century church: helping Christians reconceive the church for a post-Christendom world. Practices of catechesis and disestablishment are inscribed in youth ministry's DNA. Teaching Christianity's stories of origin and practices of community are part of every youth ministry curriculum, and teenagers are only too glad to point out where Christian communities need to become realigned with the power of Christ instead of the powers-that-be. Hall sees this realignment as requiring people who seek moral authenticity, develop meaningful communities, search out transcendence and mystery and meaning—a description that reads like a profile of adolescence. He advocates a new language for the story of Jesus Christ to be heard in a post-Christendom culture—one that sounds less like speech and more like prayer, less like words and more like dance, less like reason and more like joy[59]—a language, in other words, that sounds much like the communication of the young.

Practices of catechesis and disestablishment are inscribed in youth ministry's DNA.

Learning to Be Church (Again)

Of course, these daunting challenges to youth ministry are challenges facing the whole church, and not young people alone. Youth ministry tends to function as the church's "research and development" wing, where congregations explore new ways to relate to culture with minimal resistance in the pews.[60] Many people enter youth ministry partly because it is one place where ecclesial change seems possible, even as we hand on a sacred story from one generation to the next. Youth ministry offers a theological laboratory for exploring difficult questions like:

- What happens to the church when the postmodern accent on personal experience trumps communal traditions?
- What does a church look like that is genuinely inclusive, starting with youth?
- In sharing faith across the generations, are we conveying cultural messages that unwittingly undermine the church's own story?
- In what ways might a robust ecclesiology help teenagers (and all people) entertain doubt?
- What kind of church makes sense to young people (and all people) who never darken the door of a church building, who are just trying to survive?

> Youth ministry tends to function as the church's "research and development" wing, where congregations explore new ways to relate to culture with minimal resistance in the pews.

All of this leaves youth ministry in a somewhat unanticipated position—as unlikely leaders in a postmodern, post-Christendom church. Youth ministry offers the wider church tools for making disciples who take a global, participatory culture for granted. Rewind to Thomas, the teenager I mentored through confirmation. We met for dinner at his favorite pizza place to discuss the statement of faith he is required to submit to the church session (the governing body of a local Presbyterian church) to be confirmed. The conventional, programmatic aspect of confirmation bothered Thomas. It seemed domesticated and accommodating. I tried to point out that, in the U.S., where we often don't examine or question Christianity, confessing our faith is easy to take for granted. It's a luxury that believers in many other parts of the world do not have. "If you were being confirmed in a country where Christian faith is a scandal or illegal…" I began. Thomas finished my sentence. "Then I'd do it in a minute," he said, "because then it would count for something."

In the end, Thomas decided not to be confirmed. He continued to attend worship and youth activities, and still participates in the Bible study before school. On Youth Sunday, he composed the following prayer and read it after communion:

God of Eternal Glory, we have been united with all Christians, living or dead, in your Son. Our stomachs are filled with the bread of life and our thirst for you quenched with the cup of salvation. Help us show in our daily lives the thanks we give for the life of Jesus Christ. Amen.

It's a remarkable prayer, really. Using simple words, Thomas confirmed that we can still participate in Christ, even when filled with doubts. Steeped in the changes swirling around his development as an adolescent, his cultural context, and the church itself, Thomas' decision to formally "join" the body of Christ of his own accord is a far more complicated decision than it might have been fifty years ago. His journey did not end with confirmation; it isn't clear where it will end. There are no guarantees in youth ministry. Young people ultimately must find a faith that authentically bears witness to Christ in the contexts of their lives. Their ability to do so, we must humbly confess, often has distressingly little to do with us.

Yet while we must stay alert to issues posed by youth ministry's developmental, cultural, and ecclesial contexts, the gospel transcends these challenges. Some themes in youth ministry have stood the test of time in spite of these changes, and therefore predict promising possibilities for ministry with young people in the future. The next two chapters outline some of those themes, and introduce reasons we have for hope.

Further Reading on Themes in This Chapter

Arnett, Jeffrey. *Emerging Adulthood: The Winding Road from the Late Teens through the Twenties*. New York: Oxford University Press, 2006.

Bass, Dorothy C. *Receiving the Day*. San Francisco: Jossey-Bass, 2000.

Borgmann, Albert. *Power Failure: Christianity in the Culture of Technology*. Grand Rapids: Brazos Press, 2003.

Cavanaugh, William. *Being Consumed: Economics and Christian Desire*. Grand Rapids: Eerdmans, 2008.

Graham, Philip. *The End of Adolescence*. New York: Oxford University Press, 2004.

Hall, Douglas John. *The End of Christendom and the Future of Christianity*. Eugene, OR: Wipf and Stock, 1997. For a condensed version of Hall's argument directed toward youth ministers in particular, see "Where in the World Are We?" and "Finding Our Way into the Future," *For Such a Time as This: Princeton Lectures on Youth, Church and Culture* (Princeton, NJ: Princeton Theological Seminary, 2006); available online at www.ptsem.edu/iym/index.aspx?id=3904 (accessed April 13, 2009).

Kett, Joseph. *Rites of Passage: Adolescence in America 1790 to Present*. New York: Basic Books, 1978.

Richter, Don. *Mission Trips that Matter*. Nashville: Upper Room Books, 2008.

Savage, Sara, et al., *Making Sense of Generation Y: The World View of 15-25-Year-Olds*. London: Church House Publishing, 2006.

Smith, Christian and Patricia Snell. *Souls in Transition: The Religious and Spiritual Lives of Emerging Adults*. New York: Oxford University Press, 2009.

White, David. *Practicing Discernment with Youth: A Transformative Youth Ministry Approach*. Cleveland: Pilgrim Press, 2005.

Williams, Rowan, Graham Cray, et al., eds. *Mission-Shaped Church*. London: Church House Publishing, 2004. Available online at www.cofe.anglican.org/info/papers/mission_shaped_church.pdf.

CHAPTER THREE

ENDURING THEMES

Praise the LORD, all you nations!...
For great is [the Lord's] steadfast love toward us,
and the faithfulness of the LORD endures forever.—Psalm 117:1-2

Perhaps we are asking the wrong questions.—The Matrix *(1999)*

The last time I (Kenda) saw Peter—if you don't count the "save the date" wedding postcard that came this weekend—he was a senior in high school, all red hair and exuberance.[1] At the time, Peter was president of the East Ohio Conference Council on Youth Ministry, a United Methodist outfit that was formative in my own life as a teenager, and I was the preacher at annual conference, a regional gathering where Methodist pastors and teenagers were out in force. After worship on Sunday, Peter approached me with a coterie of flip-flop-clad companions. Would I be able to join the youth for Bible study on Tuesday night? Peter thought I might want a couple days' notice.

Of course, this is the kind of invitation youth pastors live for. To be *invited* by *teenagers* for a *Bible study!* I picked a passage, threw some thoughts together, and on Tuesday evening, trudged up the hill to the youth dorm.

That's when I remembered.

When I showed up at the dorm, Peter greeted me, handed me a songsheet, and pointed me to a foyer humming with teenagers. I suddenly realized that I was the most expendable person in the room. Peter had asked me to *participate* in the Bible study—not to lead it. The youth already had the leadership under control. I was greeted by a perky platoon of welcoming sophomores. An eighth grader prayed. A couple of seniors led the scripture discussion; a few others seemed to be in charge of scouting out reluctant participants and encouraging them to give it a go. A motley assortment of musicians led singing (you could tell who sang in choir); others arranged the room for the Lord's Supper. Adults joined in an easy camaraderie with the young people, stepping in and out of various roles (one played piano with the musicians, a pastor officiated at communion). Adults were clearly valued members of the congregation here, clearly in touch with the youth, but also clearly Not in Charge of the Program.

When I was a high school student twenty-some years earlier, this group had been my spiritual home. When I left Ohio to begin my life as a pastor in Maryland, I thought all youth ministry worked this way. Youth served as primary leaders and peer ministers for congregational and conference events, programs, and mission activities; adults played outfield, offering spiritual guidance, mentoring, organizational help, and occasional last minute assistance. The adult advisors approached youth ministry like driver's ed, riding shotgun while teenagers did the driving. When, as a pastor, I attended my first youth conference in Maryland—an event designed and led by a team of passionate adult volunteers who poured themselves out for the sake of the teenagers who came—it came as a jolt. In Maryland, the adults did ministry *for* teenagers. Worship, service projects, curriculum, skits, the camp itself were done (very well) by adults doing ministry *for* teenagers—rather than with them.

> The adult advisors approached youth ministry like driver's ed, riding shotgun while teenagers did the driving.

That night in the dorm, I watched Peter and his friends orchestrate a Bible study with the ease that comes from doing something because "this is how it's done." I had forgotten. I began to think of the tracks these practices had laid, in me and in hundreds of teenagers since then, and I marveled at their durability. Little wonder that young people who take part in youth organizations like CCYM—even if they leave their home church or denomination—tend to enter service professions, and professional ministry, in droves. After all, hadn't we grown up *doing* ministry? Hadn't we been helping lead Christ's church all along? Isn't that what Christians do, guide one another as we row together toward God? Peter is now a youth pastor in Cleveland. No one is surprised.

Some Things Last: Christ's Call to Discipleship

One of the ironies of youth ministry is that God calls us to help young people claim a faith that endures while they are in a stage of life that (optimally) does not. By definition, teenagers are people in transition, "betwixt and between" our increasingly porous understandings of childhood and adulthood. It is not too much to say that the most enduring quality of youth ministry is flux. The pace with which young people change developmentally, socially, and culturally is so swift that it masks our own rapid turnover as leaders. Between the ages of twelve and seventeen, even if family status and geography remain virtually unchanged, teenagers' bodies, emotions, minds, social lives, spiritual sensibilities and, often, physical surroundings undergo a series of revolutions. The conditions that shape young people as seventh graders move so quickly that by senior year they can justly say to us, "Really, you have *no* idea." They're right, of course; but somehow the church must keep up.

> The most enduring quality of youth ministry is flux.

At the same time, some things last. People who stay in youth ministry for decades will tell you that, as adults, "keeping up" with the warp speed of cultural change shaping the lives of contemporary adolescents is a losing battle—and beside the point. Keeping up *with the teenager* is the point, staying the course with young people throughout life's dips and peaks, suffering with them, enduring the death of half-formed identities that can no longer hold all that they are becoming. Despite the changes inherent in adolescence and the ever-shifting sands of cultural context, some aspects of youth ministry are constants. While Christ binds himself to particular expressions of "church" in specific moments in time, the Holy Spirit also invites us into a story of redemption that is relevant in every place, and in every moment in time.

> Some themes are on the pastoral "to do" list of every Christian community, especially where young people are concerned. It's an uncomplicated list. Include them. Accompany them. Point them toward God's grace in the world.

Some themes are on the pastoral "to do" list of every Christian community, especially where young people are concerned. It's an uncomplicated list. Include them. Accompany them. Point them toward God's grace in the world. The list endures because it emanates from the earliest descriptions of Christian discipleship that we have. The word "disciple" in the New Testament suggests being both a learner and a follower. A disciple is much like an apprentice. Every disciple has a master, every master hands on a tradition to a disciple.[2] Rabbinical students in Jesus' day were disciples; they learned the rabbi's way of thinking and way of living by following him around for an extended period of time.

> Following Jesus earns no stature—and what's more, Christian apprenticeship has no term limits. Jesus' disciples follow him all the way to the cross.

Jesus called people to follow him too, but he turned the practice of rabbinical discipleship inside out. Most followers choose their master; Jesus chose us. Traditionally, the disciple-master relationship centers on teaching; but Jesus' relationship with his disciples was more personal than pedagogical; he shared his life as well as his teachings. The Pharisees bragged about the burden of discipleship, but Jesus viewed discipleship as a blessing and urged his followers to cast their cares upon *him*, for his "burden is light" (Matthew 11:30). Traditionally, the objective of discipleship was for the follower to achieve the status of his or her master once the apprenticeship ended. But following Jesus earns no stature—and what's more, Christian apprenticeship has no term limits. Jesus' disciples follow him all the way to the cross.

Thumb-lines in Youth Ministry

Belonging: Including Young People in the Community of Faith

Accompaniment: Joining Young People on the Journey of Faith

Grace: Strengthening Young People for the Life of Faith

The Sign Potential of Community
The Sign Potential of Imagination
The Sign Potential of Adolescence

"Being in Time"

Thumb-lines in Youth Ministry

In jazz, the thumb-line is the underlying, recurring phrase played on the piano by the thumb of the left hand. We don't usually notice the thumb-line right away, but it persists. It is a theme that holds a song (and often multiple instruments) together, freeing the right hand to improvise and respond to other instruments without compromising the song's structure or integrity. It acts as a song's rudder, steadying and steering it while the surface melody responds to the other instruments in the room.

Theological thumb-lines do the same thing for youth ministry. They allow for faithful improvisation while tethering us to a guiding story of faith. These thumb-lines in youth ministry free us to invest more of our energy in creative responses to the situation at hand. The three thumb-lines described in this chapter—inclusion, belonging, and participating in means of grace—have undergirded discipleship formation from the New Testament church forward. Their durability proves their value. It is impossible to faithfully innovate in youth ministry, on the one hand, without maintaining one's allegiance to these broad gospel themes, on the other.

Belonging: Including Young People in the Community of Faith

On the first day of the week, when we met to break bread, Paul was holding a discussion with them; since he intended to leave the next day, he continued speaking until midnight. There were many lamps in the room upstairs where we were meeting. A young man named Eutychus, who was sitting in the window, began to sink off into a deep sleep while Paul talked still longer. Overcome by sleep, he fell to the ground three floors below and was picked up dead. But Paul went down, and bending over him took him in his arms, and said, "Do not be alarmed, for his life is in him." Then Paul went upstairs, and after he had broken bread and eaten,

44

he continued to converse with them until dawn; then he left. Meanwhile they had taken the boy away alive and were not a little comforted. (Acts 20:7-12)

Homiletician Anna Carter Florence maintains that the story of Paul and Eutychus is a play "that gets produced in more local congregations than any of us would like to think."[3] This is not a compliment. What she means is that churches risk young people's *very lives* when we marginalize and anesthesize them, instead of embracing them in the name of Jesus Christ. In the Acts passage, Paul overcomes the dire consequences of boring preaching by giving Eutychus a life-giving, Spirit-inspired hug. The thumb-line of belonging grows out of the conviction that *Christ calls the church to include young people as primary (not peripheral) participants*—which means, of course, that we must invite them into the middle of our life together, even if they don't come to church.

Christ calls the church to include young people as primary (not peripheral) participants.

The scene in Acts 20 sounds eerily familiar: a preacher drones on and *on* while young people zone out at the margins, until they finally fall out of church altogether. Eutychus tumbles out the window to the ground three stories below, where he is "picked up dead"; our young people slip out the back door of the church, never to be seen again. Florence refuses to let the passage serve as a smug commentary on long-winded preaching. She sees it as a "text of terror" because it is the *church* that places Eutychus at risk. The church must take responsibility for Eutychus' fall, and for the falls of other youth on the margins of worship. We are the ones who have allowed them to stay on the periphery when in fact "their safety and well-being—indeed, *their very lives*—depend on their alert participation in the community's proclamation."[4]

The tragedy, of course, is that many congregations fail to pay attention to young people until they aren't there. Nobody noticed Eutychus or the danger he was in until he fell out the window and died. Teenagers naturally assume that the church's story is not for them; if they do not know the church's story, and do not speak the church's language—and if nobody bothers to teach it to them so they can participate in a gospel conversation—they understandably conclude: "I am not part of this." As Florence points out, unless we share the language of the church with young people (and fast), "the only way off this windowsill [for young people] is to quit coming to church."[5]

The tragedy, of course, is that many congregations fail to pay attention to young people until they aren't there. Nobody noticed Eutychus or the danger he was in until he fell out the window and died.

Discipleship formation begins with the invitation to belong. The Acts passage opens by illustrating a persistent *mis*understanding in youth ministry—the separation of young people from the church as a whole, what has been dubbed the "one-eared Mickey Mouse model of youth ministry" (*see Figure 3.1*).[6] The congregation meets in the sanctuary, the youth meet in the youth room; the congregation worships, the youth group does devotions; the congregation has a budget, the youth group has a bake sale. Come graduation, young people who may have been active in youth ministry find nothing in the "adult" church that looks remotely like the Christian community they experienced in youth ministry. Florence illustrates the point with preaching: "We have separated preaching and youth, both literally and figuratively, in the church and in the academy. We have separated them into distinct ministries, and then we have not talked about it, so that our silence perpetuates the problem and maintains a mute, marginal caste of Christians in our own churches." Paul's sermon may have seemed enthralling to the adults in the front row, but it is well past midnight and, over by the window, a sleepy teenager perched on an open ledge is an accident waiting to happen. "Why does no one notice?" Florence demands. Why don't we interrupt the sermon or pull Eutychus into the center of the room? What will Paul say (what would *we* say?) to the boy's parents after he falls off the grid—parents "who thought that because their son was at church he was safe?"[7]

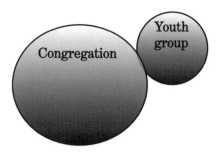

Figure 3.1

The One-Eared Mickey Mouse Model of Ministry

Youth ministry insists that the church counter the *separation* of young people from the congregation as a whole by heeding God's call to *include* young people as participants in the faith community, not in the church basement or on a third-floor classroom windowsill, but at the very heart of the Christian community. Throughout the Bible, God seems to exercise a "preferential option for the young," calling unlikely youth—David, Jeremiah, Mary, Timothy, unnamed slave girls and unprepossessing young men asleep at the switch—to proclaim God's salvation.[8] As young people *take part* in proclaiming the good news of Christ's salvation, rather than watch from a remote corner in the back of the room as others proclaim it, they *become* God's witnesses—participants, not onlookers, in God's story.

If Paul indirectly contributed to Eutychus' unfortunate fall, Paul also illustrates a constructive way forward for churches that fail to notice young people until too late. First, Paul stops preaching at them. When we realize young people are dying in our midst, "*everything* has to stop," insists Florence. "We must take a good, hard look at what's going on"—and why—before the church can even think about resuming business as usual.[9] To Paul's credit, once he realizes the problem, he takes immediate, decisive, extravagant action on Eutychus' behalf. He does not tiptoe around the issue, or address it in increments ("Let's look into this, and appoint a committee") or waste time rationalizing ("I shouldn't have preached so long") or blaming ("The kid was an idiot, sitting in an open third floor window!").

Instead, Paul acknowledges the crisis, and holds nothing back—*nothing*—in restoring Eutychus to the community. Paul goes outside the church, looking for the boy, pursuing him. When he finds Eutychus sprawled on the pavement, he falls upon him, embraces him, wakes him up, *does whatever it takes* to bring Eutychus back. The text tells us that Paul hurled himself onto the young man in an undignified manner, the way the prodigal father flung himself at his wayward son who returned home.[10] "Paul understands that it is more important to find life than to find fault in the youth," Florence observes. Though Eutychus fell to his death, Paul proclaims that "his life is in him."[11] The moral of the story for Florence is that the church must urgently pursue the young people we lose, embrace them, and celebrate whatever speck of God-given life is in them—and then restore them to the community's shared life of faith, giving them seats in the center of the room.

> The church is called to urgently pursue the young people we lose, embrace them, and celebrate whatever speck of God-given life is in them—and then restore them to the community's shared life of faith, giving them seats in the center of the room.

Eutychus illustrates adolescents' vocation as bellwethers for the church's overall spiritual health. For decades researchers have recognized that adolescents' well-being is a benchmark for the health of an entire community; likewise, the spiritual vitality of young people in a faith community serves as a sign of overall congregational vitality.[12] The story of Eutychus reminds us that bringing young people to life in congregations has the effect of bringing the church to life as well. But to do this requires our undignified embrace of young people at the margins, whose inclusion emboldens us with the unabashed, unfiltered witness of adolescents themselves.

Accompaniment: Joining Young People on the Journey of Faith

> As they came near the village to which they were going, [Jesus] walked ahead as if he were going on. But they urged him strongly, saying, "Stay with us, because it is almost evening and the day is now nearly over." So he went in to stay with them. When he was at the table with them, he took bread, blessed and broke it, and gave it to them. Then their eyes were opened, and they recognized him; and he vanished from their sight. (Luke 24:28-31)

Solvitur ambulando, roughly translated, means "it is solved by walking"—or, as we might say today, "We will find the answers as we go."[13] Emmaus was a three-hour trip in sandals, but the events of the week had been so staggering, and the day itself had been so utterly bewildering, that Cleopas and his companion needed to walk it out. We can imagine them saying to one another, "Maybe a walk will clear our heads." Maybe the mystery of recent events will be "solved by walking." "We had hoped that he was the one to redeem Israel," Cleopas and his friend lament to the stranger who joins them on the road (Luke 24:21). And then they told him about the women, talking of resurrection. What were they to make of these events? Surely a walk would help.

Talking only gets us so far in the life of discipleship. Eventually, notes practical theologian Shauna Hannan, we must walk—we must get up and do the things Jesus did, whether we fully appreciate them or not. That is when the church starts to take shape.[14] It was not until Cleopas and his companion did what Jesus did—they invited a stranger home for dinner, and shared bread and table with him—that they recognized that Christ had been with them: "Their eyes were opened, and they recognized him; and he vanished from their sight" (Luke 24:31). In what almost passes as a Homer Simpson moment, Cleopas and his companion lock eyes across the table (*Doh!*): "Were not our hearts burning within us while he was talking to us on the road, while he was opening the scriptures to us?" (24:32). And straight back to Jerusalem they went, three more hours of walking, to tell the others.

> Talking only gets us so far in the life of discipleship. Eventually, we must walk—we must get up and do the things Jesus did. That is when the church starts to take shape.

It is no coincidence that Cleopas undertook this walk of faith with a companion, or that Jesus met them on the road, on the way to discovering that Jesus, in fact, is the salvation God promised. Instead of encountering Cleopas and his companion as the Cosmic Answer, Jesus accompanied them as a fellow traveler, journeying with them, sharing their conversation along the way. If a red thread can be found in Christian discipleship from the early church until now, it is the thread of spiritual accompaniment, the grace-conducting presence of those who walk beside us as we try to decode the divine in the events of our lives. The spiritual accompanist is a millennial version of the ancient spiritual guide. We walk alongside young people, in formal and informal settings, artfully prodding them to reframe the events of their lives in light of God's promise of resurrection and return. Spiritual direction offers a formal version of this role—but youth ministers are far more apt to be spiritual accompanists, cojourneyers who remind young people of God's promises as we walk. Spiritual accompaniment requires intentionality, discipline, humility, sensitivity, prayer, and discernment: pointing out divine fingerprints here, surfacing a spiritual tussle there. At its best, youth ministry surrounds young people with spiritual friends from multiple arenas (coaches, grandparents, stepparents, probation officers, teachers, youth ministry volunteers, confirmation sponsors, and so forth). Youth ministry consultant Mark DeVries advocates a ratio of one youth ministry volunteer for every five youth. But that's not all: he also recommends identifying five adults in the congregation for every teenager in order to immerse them in a community of spiritual companions who offer prayers, care, and a gentle ministry of noticing in and beyond the life of the congregation.[15]

The art of accompaniment is a thumb-line for youth ministry. The assumption that communicating Christ requires us to employ his methods—in other words, to operate "incarnationally" in deference to God's preference for entering the world through human beings—comes close to functioning as dogma in the practice of youth ministry. As our lives and our hearts become more closely aligned to Christ's, young people experience Christ's suffering love for them through us. Youth ministry literature is close to univocal on this position. The Incarnation has received more attention in youth ministry education than any other theological theme. Just as God came to us in human form, the church is called to "imitate Christ" by translating God's good news into human forms as well. The goal of "incarnational" or "relational" ministry is not to *be* the savior for young people, but to be *transparent* to the real Savior whose love shines within us, and is enacted through us. It is a fallible plan, to be sure; God has more confidence in it than we do. Most of our "crash and burn" stories as youth leaders can be traced to our failure to point young people beyond ourselves to Jesus, or our failure to recognize how filthy our theological windshields have become, as our best efforts to be transparent to Christ run afoul. Unsure how to ground relational ministry theologically, we often revert to developmental theory as a default position, justifying our reliance on "relational ministry" as a strategy that addresses young people's developmental need for relationships, capitalizing on these relationships to convince youth of Jesus' importance.

> The goal of "incarnational" or "relational" ministry is not to *be* the savior for young people, but to be *transparent* to the real Savior whose love shines within us, and is enacted through us. It is a fallible plan, to be sure; God has more confidence in it than we do.

Spiritual accompaniment, of course, is more than this. Most of us are better acquainted with incarnational *strategies* than incarnational theologies, but in fact these strategies are only possible when they flow from Christ's own self-emptying presence. Christ calls us to view teenagers as fellow travelers toward God rather than as potential ideological converts. "Ministry...is not about 'using' relationships to get individuals to accept a 'third thing,'" practical theologian Andrew Root reminds us. "Rather, ministry is about connection, one to another, about sharing in suffering and joy, about persons meeting persons with no pretense or secret motives. It is about shared life, confessing Christ not outside the relationship but within it."[16] As chapter 6 points out, Root is one of many young scholars locating youth ministry in the discipline of practical theology, an approach that releases young people from being objects of well-meaning but unexamined pastoral strategies. The journey of faith is one we can share but never orchestrate. We are called to travel alongside young people, and "find the answers as we go."

Participating in Means of Grace: Strengthening Young People for the Life of Faith

> Then an angel of the Lord said to Philip, "Get up and go toward the south to the road that goes down from Jerusalem to Gaza." (This is a wilderness road.)...Now there was an Ethiopian eunuch, a court official of the Candace, queen of the Ethiopians, in charge of her entire treasury. He had come to Jerusalem to worship and was returning home; seated in his chariot, he was reading the prophet Isaiah. Then the Spirit said to Philip, "Go over to this chariot and join it." So Philip ran up to it and heard him reading the prophet Isaiah. He asked, "Do you understand what you are reading?" [The eunuch] replied, "How can I, unless someone guides me?" And he invited Philip to get in and sit beside him. (Acts 8:26-31)

Grace is the oxygen of ministry. In his theological dictionary *Crazy Talk*, theologian Rolf Jacobson describes means of grace as "the simplest stuff of every day through which the most profound event of eternity happens to you."[17] In other words, Christ enters our world and our bloodstreams through the "stuff" of our lives, bread and water and wine and Scripture and giving alms—and as we receive these blessings, Christ uses them to transform us into means of grace as well. This thumb-line of youth ministry assumes that *young people are strengthened for the life of faith through means of grace*, actions God uses to pour divine grace into the world. Means of grace are "living signs" that God is with us, strengthening our faith, empowering our hope, transforming us into the witnesses God has called us to be.

Grace is the oxygen of ministry.

Christians view means of grace as signs of God's presence and promise, outward expressions of the grace God has given us within to sustain and encourage our faith. God is fully present in these signs, but cannot be contained by them. Signs have a surplus of meaning; they both reveal and hide God's presence with us, which means that we are usually knee-deep in divine grace before we know it. Means of grace function as holy portals, doorways through which Christ enters human experience, thresholds on which we recognize God personally whether God meets us in church or in traffic.

Philip's encounter with the eunuch is awash in such means of grace. The story culminates with the eunuch's baptism, but other signs of God's grace pave the way for this moment: the divine messenger, the reading of Scripture, the holy conversation itself. Philip's day job was distributing food to the poor as a deacon in the church of Jerusalem. But after hours, Philip was moonlighting as an evangelist, and a good one; when the angel shows up, Philip is in the middle of preaching an all-out revival in Samaria. Yet God has a new plan for Philip. In a move worthy of a Methodist bishop, the angel gives him different instructions and sends him to a new ministry in the middle of nowhere: "Get up and go to the road that goes down from Jerusalem to Gaza—not the interstate, the desert road." The road less traveled. Not exactly a place Philip can hone his preaching skills.

Enter the Ethiopian eunuch, a man whose skin tone, dress, and out-of-state plates clearly mark him as an African royal official. He was traveling this same desert road by carriage, trying to decode Scripture alone. He had traveled more than a thousand miles (six weeks by carriage) to pray in Jerusalem—but Jewish law prohibited eunuchs from worshiping in the Temple (Deuteronomy 23:1). Eunuchs could be "gate proselytes" (uncircumcised Jewish sympathizers who feared God) but they could not be fully Jewish. So the eunuch had received no help from the assembly in understanding God's promise. Now, heading home, he is left to figure out God's word on his own. But the story makes no sense. "Who is it about?" he asks Philip. The eunuch doesn't realize that God's promise is practically standing in front of him in the Isaiah text. He doesn't know that in three short chapters Isaiah will proclaim God's embrace of eunuchs in particular. Without someone to guide him, he doesn't know who the passage is about, or that God's grace includes him.

With no one to guide them other than media and marketers, young people don't know that God's grace includes them, either. They don't know who the prophets foretold or that the gospel shows God's special concern for the young. Fortunately, the Holy Spirit does not wait for us to help them ask for grace. The Holy Spirit creeps into the cracks of young people's lives unbidden, shoving grace under the door, entering the world through means of grace like water and bread, meeting adolescents "on the road." Meanwhile, God taps us as interpreters, often when we're in the middle of doing something else we thought was important.[18]

Christ encounters human beings through material signs and repeatable actions of the community of faith. These means of grace are "sacramental" but they are not necessarily sacraments.[19] Even youth ministers from nonsacramental backgrounds frequently employ sacramental imagery to describe God's action with young people. The word "sacrament" comes from a Latin translation of the Greek word for "mystery" (Eastern Christians still call sacraments the "Holy Mysteries").[20] While churches understand sacraments differently, what catches young people's attention is the mystery of it all—God's willingness to "happen to us" through the earthy materials of human life, while remaining mysteriously and eternally beyond us. Such signs let us participate, mysteriously and concretely, in the dying-and-rising life of God, making God's grace-giving action visible. "Look, here is water!" crows the eunuch as he grasps the good news of Jesus Christ. "What is to prevent me from being baptized?" The eunuch may not have found salvation in Jerusalem—but here, on a desert road at high noon in the middle of nowhere, with Philip pointing to God's promise in Scripture, Jesus "happened" to him.

> Youth ministry strengthens young people for the life of faith by immersing them in means of grace, actions God uses to pour divine grace into human communities.

Means of grace rest on the assumption that God *does* things, and that God does things *through us*. Means of grace strengthen us for the life of faith; in them, Christ "happens" to us personally. Chapter 4 explores the importance of Catholic "sacramentals" and Protestants' faith "practices" (which include but are not limited to sacraments "proper") for ministry with young people. What matters is not the form these grace-bearing actions take but their ability to shape our identity as Christians, empower us for witness, and point to a way of life in which God continues to "happen." Youth ministry (and Christian life generally) is made possible by God's gift of sanctifying grace that God makes present in these human but holy actions. Some aspects of youth ministry serve as particularly potent signs of God's presence with us, and offer vehicles through which Christ strengthens young people's faith in particularly visible ways. Here we will mention three that are closely tied to the experience of adolescence—and that are especially likely to be overlooked for their sign potential.

The Sign Potential of Community

For Christians, community enacts *communion*—being "one with" Christ and one another. Apart from the presence of God's sanctifying grace, of course, such oneness is not possible. Communion with God means more than sharing bread and wine together; it implies a willingness to lay down our lives for one another, as Christ laid down his life for us. "Community" is a youth ministry imperative, and when young people encounter its Christian form, they experience love willing to share one another's burdens, love willing to suffer on their behalf. Without such communion, countless young people would be stuck in the back of a carriage trying to figure out God's word on their own—never knowing that Christ is right in front of them, unaware that God's grace includes them.

Youth ministers view "community" as one of a very few nonnegotiables in the church's ministry with young people. As we have noted, it is in the experience of community that we learn to recognize the incarnational, transfigurative, and crucified nature of divine grace. "In communities of faith," wrote Luther, "each of us should become a Christ to the other. And as we are christs to one another, the result is that Christ fills us all and we become a truly Christian community."[21] In the intense relational webs of Christian community, the gospel is re-told in embodied form. Nate, a youth pastor I know, told me how his mentor Merv—also a youth pastor, twenty years his senior and technically his superior—became a means of God's grace for him, and how this grace transformed their relationship.

> We had breakfast together once a month or so, and it could last five hours. There was no agenda, just a sense that he was further down the road than me, and that he was okay that I wasn't very far down this road at all. It was absolutely not an answer-driven relationship; Merv had no answers for me. If he had a story that connected to mine, he would tell it; if he had advice to share, he would give it. But mostly, we just shared life. I drove away from those meetings questioning what we did there. Was there some specific point when he was no longer my conference youth pastor, but a colleague? Was he just there because he was paid to be there? Merv choked up the last time we were at a youth service together; he said: "And so, we've become good friends."

Pausing for a moment, Nate spoke for countless youth ministers by saying: "That's why I do this. I want to give others that same life, that same presence."

The evidence that a community is a means of grace is participants' willingness to "suffer love" for one another. The emphasis here is on love, not suffering—but as any teenager will tell you, true love is worthy of sacrifice. True love is worth dying for. Through acts of suffering love, we become "little incarnations" of God's self-giving love in Jesus Christ. Unexpectedly, as we follow Christ together, we find ourselves reflecting God's glory in "little transfigurations." When others risk themselves for our sake, we experience "little crucifixions" on our behalf. As a community, we re-constitute the body of Christ in actions that re-member (*anamnesis*, or put back together) Jesus' life, death, and resurrection.

> "In communities of faith each of us should become a Christ to the other. And as we are christs to one another, the result is that Christ fills us all and we become a truly Christian community."—Martin Luther

The Sign Potential of Imagination

An equally potent mediator of divine grace—especially in a culture increasingly marked by creativity and collaboration—is a holy imagination. One of the most disturbing conversations I ever had was with Cuyler Black, youth pastor-by-day and cartoonist-by-night. At the time, Cuyler was toying with the idea of applying to seminary to pursue ordained ministry. (Okay, I was recruiting him.) Meanwhile, his career as a Christian cartoonist was taking off. We had both been to a seminar on cultivating our callings, and Cuyler confessed his divided heart: God had gifted him for more than one kind of ministry. His gifts for ordained ministry seemed indisputable to me; theologically passionate, smart, bold, creative, gentle. He seemed to exude qualities of leadership that postmodern churches are crying for. But it was equally clear that God had given Cuyler a snappy sense of humor and profound artistic talent as well. Why not use that talent as a member of the clergy? I asked him, thinking what a breath of fresh air his ministry would be. "Because," he said, with sad eyes I will never forget, "I'm afraid that if I go into ordained ministry, I'd have to surrender much of my creativity."

> He said, with sad eyes I will never forget, "I'm afraid that if I go into ordained ministry, I'd have to surrender much of my creativity."

Cuyler is still a lay youth pastor in Connecticut and the artist behind a successful (and funny) cartoon series (check out www.inheritthemirth.com). I understand why he stayed in youth ministry; it is one of the church's best opportunities for helping young people develop what practical theologian Fred Edie calls "artistic knowing."[22] God's overwhelming, self-giving love defies human logic. It can only be approximated by stories and symbols, metaphors and imagery—human containers for truths too large to tell in full. The surplus meaning of these symbols and metaphors nourishes the kind of imagination that is capable of perceiving the divine grace they convey.[23] A holy imagination makes mysticism, the "raw material of all religion," possible.[24] When we stoke young people's imaginations with the stories, symbols, and images of Christian tradition, we equip them for the kind of artistic knowing that helps them, like the Ethiopian, "know what they are reading."

Edie believes that artistic knowing is essential to Christian faith—as essential as cognitive and social knowing—because God uses human imaginations to be recognized.[25] The issue is with the antennae, not the broadcast; God does not *need* art to communicate divine mystery and grace, but *we* need art to recognize and appreciate them. Nowhere is this artistic knowing more necessary than in the interpretation of scripture. Theologian Garrett Green points out: "To call the Bible scripture is to claim that it enables its users rightly to imagine God and the world."[26] Yet our chances of "rightly imagining" God and the world are becoming slimmer; American churches face "astounding illiteracy and inarticulacy of the mainstream populace regarding theological and biblical concepts," and research describes teenagers themselves as "incredibly inarticulate" about Christian faith.[27] Without artistic knowing, young people lack the tools to recognize themselves in the Christian story, or to perceive Christ's mysterious, pulsing presence through it.

> Artistic knowing is essential to Christian faith—as essential as cognitive and social knowing.

Youth ministry's reliance on symbol, metaphor, story, and art helps young people hone sacred intuition, the kind of imagining that recognizes God from behind, through indirect means that acknowledge a sacred role for bodily knowing and participatory engagement, and that pursues creativity as a playful form of divine discovery. Young people's desire for primary—and primal—experience makes them voracious participants in the arts. They disproportionately comprise what has been called society's "creative class," a tendency accentuated by today's participatory culture, as young people self-consciously produce global cultural content.[28] Nearly all research on assets for youth development identifies an important role for the arts. Art prompts visceral responses, "sighs too deep for words" (Romans 8:26), prayers that both utilize and transcend human modes of communication. God is profoundly present in the elements of daily life, but God is also decidedly and mysteriously free from them. God comes to us in ways that are both *kataphatic* and *apophatic*—in ways that can be perceived through the senses, and in ways that defy explanation, that exceed our imaginations.

So artistic knowing, which is necessary to perceiving God's revelation, is at once necessary, ambiguous, and generative. The ineffable nature of faith (i.e., it can't be described in words) requires an embodied telling. We need mystics and artists—"the saints and the poets," as playwright Thornton Wilder put it—to serve as intermediaries and interpreters, translators and storytellers, priests and youth ministers who have been to the mountaintop and can testify to God's glory in imaginative, nondiscursive ways.

> To reclaim the imagination's vital role in spiritual formation, youth ministers must "become bards: poets charged with the tasks of imparting the stories, language, and beliefs of a culture."—Sarah Arthur

Sarah Arthur blames young people's inability to experience Scripture as a divine encounter on the church's *"colossal failure of the imagination regarding both the claims and the demands of the gospel."*[29] To reclaim the imagination's vital role in spiritual formation, Arthur calls youth ministers to "become bards: poets charged with the tasks of imparting the stories, language, and beliefs of a culture."

We are *wordsmiths*, as the ancient meaning of the poet implies: "speech-weavers" who take the many texts of our hearers' lives and thread them through the warp and weft of the Christian narrative until patterned meaning emerges.[30]

Ultimately, the church is a troubadour of hope, and the Bible is the loom that weaves young people's lives into a pattern that has purpose and meaning. Arthur turns to author Madeleine L'Engle, who asks, "Why does anyone tell a story? It does indeed have something to do with faith, faith that the universe has meaning, that our little human lives are not irrelevant, that what we choose or say or do matters, matters cosmically."[31] Adolescents are story people, entrusting us with their stories of faith and unfaith, tacking back and forth between the Church's story and their stories, cobbling together hope that there is meaning in the world after all, and purpose, and significance.

The Sign Potential of Adolescence

This last means of grace in youth ministry is, perhaps, too obvious to mention; then again, it may be the sign that churches most frequently overlook. God employs young people themselves as signs of God's grace in the faith community, and in the world they inhabit. Much has been made of adolescents' unique vulnerability to culture, and to teenagers' receptiveness to the spirit of their age. Adolescence has been called "the human condition on steroids:"[32]

> Young people have always served as barometers of the human condition, indicators of rising and falling pressures on the human psyche.... Because adolescence itself is a modern invention that weds social location with psychological development, young people inevitably "act out"—acutely—what is required for being human in their particular moment in history.[33]

At the same time, young people seem to embody Irenaeus' conviction, "The glory of God is a human being fully alive."[34] Because adolescents are human beings in "acute" form, they point to the glory of God in their unswerving commitment to feel life deeply and experience life fully, even when that means experiencing—with unfiltered intensity—suffering as well as joy.

Young people seem to embody Irenaeus' conviction, "The glory of God is a human being fully alive."

Pastoral theologian Roland Martinson hypothesizes that the first third of life is "paradigmatic" for God's plan for us to be fully human. Jesus suggested as much:

> People were bringing even infants to [Jesus] that he might touch them; and when the disciples saw it, they sternly ordered them not to do it. But Jesus called for them and said, "Let the little children come to me, and do not stop them; for it is to such as these that the kingdom of God belongs. Truly I tell you, whoever does not receive the kingdom of God as a little child will never enter it" (Luke 18:15-17).

We tend to trot out this text for Christian Education Sundays in order to demonstrate that churches like children ("Jesus wanted children to come to him, and we do too"). But none of the synoptic accounts of this moment are value statements about children; they are value statements about *adults*. The paradigmatic human beings in God's kingdom, the ones adults are meant to emulate, are not wise or even self-consciously faithful; they are *young*. Little wonder that one measure of church vitality is the presence of young people in the pews. The church is more fully alive through them.

"Being in Time"

These thumb-lines of youth ministry tether us to a tradition so that we can freely improvise ministry with young people while maintaining the basic shape of discipleship with the other. In this way, youth ministry is like jazz itself, which trumpeter Wynton Marsalis calls "the art of negotiating change with style."[35] The description could just as easily describe the church's ministry with young people. Marsalis grew up around the "jazzmen" of New Orleans, and admired Coltrane, Davis, Monk, and Armstrong as a young musician. But he saves his loudest praise for the shop musicians of New Orleans who could take a thumb-line and improvise. For Marsalis, improvisation requires three skills: (1) being able to honestly express your feelings; (2) being able to genuinely listen as other people express theirs; and (3) being committed to "working it out" together. Unlike some forms of music that require a common level proficiency for musicians to play together, jazz bands would stand a ten-year-old boy beside a sixty-year-old man, as their instruments "learned" to talk to each other. Marsalis remembers: "To be heard demanded that we...listen to one another. Closely. And to sound good we had to trust one another."[36]

> Youth ministry is like jazz, which trumpeter Wynton Marsalis calls "the art of negotiating change with style."[37] The description could just as easily describe the church's ministry with young people.

As a result, Marsalis recalls, jazz players were people who could help you out in a tight spot: they could come up with the right words at the right time and the right notes at the right time. They could talk and they could listen. This ability to listen to the underlying theme of a song and respond is what Marsalis calls "being in time."

Swing is a matter of manners. When you are in time you know when to be quiet, when to assert yourself, and how to master the moment with an appropriate or unusually inventive response....To be in time requires you to make the subtlest kinds of adjustments and concessions to keep everyone in a groove. And your colleagues have to be willing to do the same for you....Being in time...gives you the confidence to take chances.[38]

But Marsalis noticed something else too. The most meaningful phrases in jazz were not the most difficult ones. They were almost never technically challenging.

Anyone could play them. They anchored a song because they "were succinct phrases that would run right through you, the way profound nuggets from Shakespeare's plays can both cut through you and linger; all those words in *Hamlet*, but you remember 'To be or not to be' or 'to sleep perchance to dream.' Something in those types of phrases reveals universal truth."[39] As in jazz, the thumb-line of our work with young people, the notes that tether youth to Jesus' call to make disciples, are as straightforward as they are enduring: help young people belong in a community of faith, accompany them on the journey of faith, immerse them in means of grace that strengthen them for faith. Anchored by these thumb-lines of discipleship formation, the promising possibilities of youth ministry can begin to take flight.

Further Reading on Themes in This Chapter

Arthur, Sarah. *The God-Hungry Imagination.* Nashville: Upper Room, 2007.

Bass, Dorothy and Craig Dykstra. *Practicing Our Faith.* San Francisco: Jossey Bass, 1998.

Beaudoin, Tom. *Virtual Faith: The Irreverent Spiritual Quest of Generation X.* San Francisco: Jossey-Bass, 2000.

Carotta, Michael. *Sometimes We Dance, Sometimes We Wrestle: Embracing the Spiritual Growth of Adolescents.* Orlando, FL: Harcourt Religion Publishers, 2000.

Cummings-Bond, Stuart. "The One-Eared Mickey Mouse," *Youthworker* 6 (Fall 1989), 76.

Dean, Kenda Creasy. *Practicing Passion: Youth and the Quest for a Passionate Church.* Grand Rapids: Eerdmans, 2004.

Edie, Fred. *Book, Bath, Table and Time: Christian Worship as Source and Resource for Youth Ministry.* Cleveland: Pilgrim Press, 2007.

Florence, Anna Carter. "A Prodigal Preaching Story and Bored-to-Death Youth," *Theology Today* 64 (July 2007), 233-43.

Green, Garrett. *Imagining God: Theology and the Religious Imagination.* Grand Rapids: Eerdmans, 1998.

Jacobson, Rolf. *Crazy Talk: A Not-So-Stuffy Dictionary of Theological Terms.* Minneapolis: Augsburg, 2008.

Mercandante, Frank. *Growing Teen Disciples: Strategies for Really Effective Youth Ministry.* Winona, MN: St. Mary's Press, 2002.

CHAPTER FOUR

PROMISING POSSIBILITIES

Forget the former things; / do not dwell on the past. / See, I am doing a new thing! /
Now it springs up; do you not perceive it? / I am making a way in the desert / and
streams in the wasteland.—Isaiah 43:18-19, NIV

You're only given a little spark of madness. You mustn't lose it.—Robin Williams

Bruce Main, executive director of UrbanPromise, in Camden, New Jersey, remembers Albert as a neighborhood kid who practically grew up in the ministry. After-school programs led to summer camps, which led to employment as a "street leader" (a teen leadership program), which led to a scholarship to Eastern University. After graduation Albert wanted to give back to his old neighborhood. He moved back as the director of the North Camden After School Program, one of UrbanPromise's many youth ministries in the "murder capital" of America. "People came from all over the world as volunteers to help me," Albert liked to say. "I made it; now [these kids] can see how they can make it too."

But now, a new drug operation had moved outside the church that hosted the after-school program, and Albert was worried. Junkies were "shooting up just where kids could see what was going down," he recalled. He asked Bruce to help him figure out what to do. They debated about confronting the drug dealer. Calling the police would only bring retribution, but doing nothing would be detrimental to the kids. Finally Albert decided: "I'm going to have a talk with that guy who runs that operation." Bruce tells the rest of the story:

> Later that week Albert burst into my office. "Bruce, Bruce, I talked to the guy who runs the corner.... I asked him if he could move his operation somewhere else. I told him how I was trying to set an example for the little kids in the community." Albert paused. "Right away the guy started to yell at his crew to clear the corner. Apologetically he told me that he would have them out of there by two o'clock." Albert then looked at me and asked curiously, "Bruce, did we ever have a guy named Jeff work here—about 15 years ago?"

Bruce dug back into his memory. Yes, Jeff had been an intern from Southern California. He had spent a number of years with UrbanPromise before going into teaching. Everybody liked him. "Why do you ask?" Bruce wondered.

Albert paused. "That dealer asked me if a guy named Jeff still worked at UrbanPromise.... The dealer [said] he had been part of UrbanPromise when he was in fifth grade, and Jeff was his favorite counselor."

As Bruce reflected on this strange coincidence, he wondered how two boys in the same ministry could turn out so differently. Albert graduated from college and came back to serve his community. Why didn't the other boy have a story like Albert's? "Instead," Bruce mused sadly, "this nameless twenty-seven-year-old had slipped through the cracks and ended up a drug dealer—yet a dealer who chose to apologetically shut down his operations so that young kids could safely enter our After School Center." Bruce ends the story with quiet determination, a kind of fire that explains how a skinny white guy from Vancouver came to be trusted—even revered—in the toughest neighborhoods in Camden:

> I don't yet know that drug dealer's name. But I will find out. Then, hopefully, and by God's grace, I will have a chance to bring him up to date on the good things happening in Jeff's life, and how those things could happen in his. For I believe the end of this sad story, this perplexing, brief encounter, has not yet been fully written. Our God continues to move in mysterious and exciting ways and writes miraculous stories.[1]

The Madness of Ministry with Young People

Youth ministry is replete with ambiguous endings. Is Bruce's tale a happy one or a sad one? Does it chronicle youth ministry's success or failure? It's not hard to find people who believe that a touch of madness is an asset for working with teenagers; and if investing in teenagers is not madness, then surely investing in Jesus is. How many people stake their lives on something as outlandish as resurrection? Nothing about the empty tomb makes sense. As the curtain rises on the closing scene of the Gospel of Mark, we see Mary Magdalene, Mary the mother of James, and Salome trudging toward Jesus' tomb at sunrise, ready to perform that final task of love: anointing the body. Just as they wonder aloud about the logistics of removing the stone from the tomb's entrance, they stop, stunned. The huge stone at the mouth of the tomb is gone. A young man in a dazzling white robe startles them: Jesus is not here; he is risen! Shooing them on, the young man says, "Go, tell his disciples and Peter that he is going ahead of you to Galilee; there you will see him, just as he told you" (Mark 16:7).

> Youth ministry is replete with ambiguous endings.

The women bolt, but not to tell the disciples the good news—at least, not in Mark's Gospel. Mark's Gospel leaves us hanging.[2] The women fled "for terror and amazement had seized them; and they said nothing to anyone, for they were afraid" (Mark 16:8). That's it. The end. No telling, no fish fry on the beach, no Emmaus Road encounter, just fear and silence. Jesus is ahead of them in Galilee; they will see him, just as he promised. Yet their fear and amazement are well-founded. What they have heard is ludicrous—it is a mad, unfathomable, ridiculous promise. And it is the hope of the church.

Jesus is ahead of us. There is no place young people can go, no place we can take them, that Jesus hasn't arrived first. Even death is old hat to Jesus. As Mark tells it, the end of this perplexing story has not yet been fully written. Just as God continued to write miraculous stories of witness after the resurrection, God continues to write surprise endings into young people's lives today. The question we have to ask when we enter a pastoral situation is *not* "What can I get going here that would be good for these kids?" but "What is Christ already up to with young people that I can get in on?"[3]

> The *most* promising possibility in youth ministry is the promise that Jesus has gone on before us, and that one day he promises to let us catch up to him.

The *most* promising possibility in youth ministry is the promise that Jesus has gone on before us, and that one day he promises to let us catch up to him. Jesus is already at work in the young people we love (and, to be sure, in those we don't)—"Christ is on the loose," as biblical scholar Don Juel put it.[4] God gets to our churches, to our communities, and to young people themselves long before we can, kneading stiff necks, softening hard hearts, closing some doors and opening others, kicking up some hope. The dangling ending to Easter in Mark's Gospel reminds us that, crazy as it seems, God's story is not over yet. Christ will not rest until his story includes us.

Promising Possibilities for Youth Ministry

The Theological "Turn" in Youth Ministry

Dick and Jane Go to Church: The Hunger for a Worthy Adventure

The Missional Church: Following Jesus into the World
Redefining Community: From Connections to Communion
Sacred Practices: Aiming for Embodied Faith
      1. Practicing the Presence of God
      2. A Curriculum of Sacred Practice
      3. The Importance of Parents

Beyond Training Events: New Possibilities for Forming Leaders

Streams in the Wasteland

The Theological "Turn" in Youth Ministry

One of the most promising signs of ministry with young people is that we are becoming far more theologically self-aware. As we have seen, the most enduring themes in youth ministry are theological ones, reflecting Christ's call to young people (and to us) to become disciples. The hopeful signs for youth ministry's future flow from this theological consciousness as well. As we acknowledge young people's witness to and on behalf of the broader church, youth ministers are growing more systematic in our thinking, more deliberate about our purposes, and more self-critical about our practices—to the point that youth ministry has begun to cohere into something resembling a "field of study" within the larger discipline of practical theology. (Skip to chapter 6 if you want to know more.) By grounding youth ministry in the mission of the church, ministry with young people becomes less "hit and miss" and more integrated into the witness of the faith community. We can now discern patterns in youth ministries that thrive, and in those that struggle—patterns that cluster around the presence, or the absence, of certain practices that help young people and their families encounter Christ in the texts and traditions of the Christian community.

> Theologically engaged youth ministry is patterned after the life, death, and resurrection of Jesus Christ, as young people learn to interpret their lives through the texts and traditions of the Christian community.

All of these patterns signal what Andrew Root has called the "theological turn in youth ministry"[5] —a shared consensus that youth ministry should stop lingering over logistics ("Who will roll the stone away? How will we keep kids interested on Sunday night?") and start looking for signs of resurrection instead, knowing that Christ is already in young people's lives ahead of us. Theologically engaged youth ministry is patterned after the life, death, and resurrection of Jesus Christ, as we learn to interpret human experience through the lenses of the Christian story, mediated through the texts and traditions of the church. The promises and possibilities for youth ministry all develop relationships that enact Christ's suffering love as we follow Jesus into the world. Mad though it may seem, Christ is ahead of us, waiting to write us into the stories of young people we have yet to meet.

Dick and Jane Go to Church:
The Hunger for a Worthy Adventure

"The challenge of discipleship—of following Jesus—is the heart of the Church's mission. *All ministry with adolescents must be directed toward presenting young people with the Good News of Jesus Christ and inviting and challenging them to become his disciples.*"[6] These words from the 1995

National Conference of Catholic Bishops' *Renewing the Vision* document, outlining the goals for the Catholic church's mission with young people in the twenty-first century, capture the heart of youth ministry for most churches. Pope John Paul II, a successful youth minister in Poland after World War II, minced no words in describing the way the church must meet this challenge of discipleship: by offering young people "a *world-shaping vision* that meets their hunger for the chance to *participate in a worthy adventure.*"[7]

As a teenager in the American South in the 1980s, I (Amy) did not think going to youth group was an adventure; it was not even remotely countercultural. Everyone I knew went to church. The values of the church and the priorities of my school and community seemed to be in complete agreement; stores closed on Sundays and schools closed around Christian holidays. It never crossed anyone's mind to schedule a soccer game on Sunday morning (though scheduling games during Friday Shabbat was common). Nor did it occur to us to use the pulpit for cultural critique. Attending Sunday night youth group meant participating in the script of a predictable story: work hard in school, be a good citizen, join the church of your parents, do what your family and peers expect of you. The good people in my congregation considered this Christian formation, but what my church really offered me was a part in a *Fun with Dick and Jane* story—neat, homogenous, and uncomplicated, with bright pictures and no plot.

> The good people in my congregation considered this Christian formation, but what my church really offered me was a part in a *Fun with Dick and Jane* story—neat, homogenous, and uncomplicated, with bright pictures and no plot.

Dick and Jane remain alive and well in American churches. Very few young people seem to view religious involvement as a worthy *adventure*. The good news from the (2005) National Study of Youth and Religion is that it jarred many youth ministers, and a few congregations, into reassessing discipleship formation as more than a passive rite of church membership. The overwhelming absence of a theological vocabulary among American teenagers suggests a disturbing distance between the concerns of the church and the concerns of young people. By "theological vocabulary" I do not mean technical doctrinal jargon or facile "Jesus-speak." In interviews, teenagers simply do not articulate their experience using theological categories (for example, being thankful to God, having a purpose in life that may follow Christ's example, sensing God's presence at key moments in one's life), which suggests that Christian teaching is either unfamiliar or irrelevant to them—or both. Meanwhile, teenagers are consistently very articulate about other abstract or meaningful subjects, especially those taught in school or discussed in the media.[8]

What this tells us is not only that most teenagers, including churchgoing ones, seem to feel uncomfortable discussing religion in public. It also suggests that they have little opportunity for, exposure to, or inclination toward theological reflection. Nor are they practiced at drawing on Christian tradition to inform their daily lives and decisions. It is no surprise that teenagers are hesitant to wear their religious stripes in the "judge-not-lest-ye-be-judged" public square, where religious affiliation often carries political freight. What *is* surprising is that *churches themselves* seem to have avoided theological or spiritual engagement with young people, leaving teenagers to grapple with faith privately, without a language to connect their lives to the stories of the Christian community, and without practices that allow them to take this faith with them into the world.

Perhaps we should have seen this coming. In 1950, for example, the Methodist Church, eager to downplay its evangelistic reputation, identified the following as the desired outcomes of Methodist Youth Fellowships (MYFs) in a statement that was soon replicated by other denominations:

- to build Christian character
- to provide young people a chance for self-expression
- to train leaders
- to develop friendships
- to promote the welfare of the church.[9]

In the 1950s, many pastors welcomed these goals as a way to move beyond Christian provincialism. In a broad ecology of Christian socialization, where tending the youthful soul was the task of multiple overlapping social institutions (e.g., families, congregations, faith-based community groups, and religious schools), youth ministry could afford to serve as a broadening agent, since teenagers received basic religious formation elsewhere.[10] In the 1950s, families, congregations, parochial schools, and Christian colleges all offered opportunities for religious formation, and were contexts where young people could reflect on their lives and the broader world in light of faith.

Thirty years later, a decisive change in this ecology of religious formation had occurred. In 1980, sociologist Dean Hoge and his colleagues demonstrated a dramatic shift away from theological formation in youth ministries.[11] Hoge's team compared the top outcomes sought by youth ministry in six denominations before and after 1980 (*figure 4.1*). While youth ministry before 1980 placed a high priority on engaging young people in faith-shaping spiritual practices, after 1980 spiritual formation become nearly invisible in youth ministry's priorities. By 1991, a Carnegie Council on Adolescent Development study found that the largest religious denominations/communities in the U.S. (Protestant, Catholic, and Jewish) shared two parallel goals in religious youth work: fostering faith identity (or sense of belonging in a faith community) and providing young people with safe passage into adulthood.[12] In 2000, more than two thousand youth ministers once again identified spiritual development as one of several desired outcomes for youth ministry.[13] Here is what these studies found:

BEFORE 1980 (a) (Hoge *et al.*) *Desired* outcomes in youth ministry *A young person...*	AFTER 1980 (a) (Hoge *et al.*) *Desired* outcomes in youth ministry *A young person...*	1990 (b) (Dean) *Desired* outcomes in youth ministry *A young person...*	2000 (c) (Strommen *et al.*) *Achieved* outcomes in youth ministry *A young person...*
Sees prayer and reflection as worthwhile	Has healthy self-concept about his/her value/worthiness as a person	Obtains a faith identity	Develops spiritually
Sees God as demanding a personal surrender to God's will	Takes a responsible view toward moral questions such as drug abuse and sex behavior	Obtains safe passage into adulthood	Has a sense of ownership in youth ministry
Lives each day with a sense of divine forgiveness	Understands sexual feelings and has responsible ways of handling them		Experiences strengthened family relationships
Has a daily prayer life	Is acquiring knowledge about human sexuality and has formed a responsible Christian approach in sexual matters		
Values the Bible as inspiration for personal spiritual growth	Distinguishes between the values of the popular culture and the church		
Has personal relationship with Jesus Christ			

(a) Denominations studied: Catholic, Southern Baptist, United Methodist, Episcopalian, Presbyterian, Church of God/Anderson, IN.
(b) Interviewed denominational youth leadership for the ten largest Protestant denominations in the U.S., the National Conference of Catholic Bishops, and Reformed, Conservative, and Orthodox Judaism in the U.S.
(c) Interviewed 2,000 individual youth workers, identified through national youth worker training events.

Figure 4.1
Desired Outcomes in Youth Ministry before and after 1980[14]

For youth ministry to be *ministry*—bearing witness to Christ's self-giving love in the church and in the world—it must primarily provide a context for spiritual engagement, where a lively, intimate communion between young people and God is nourished through the texts, traditions, and communities of the church. To be clear: in Christian tradition, theological engagement nourishes Christ-like interpersonal relationships and profound social responsibility. Yet unless young people can frame these relationships and responsibilities in light of faithfulness to Christ, youth have no choice but to interpret them using the only tools they know—usually the habits and worldviews they receive from their families, peers, and the global media.

> Dodging theological content in youth ministry impairs teenagers for accepting their identities as God's beloved and stunts their participation in a faith community.

Some churches, of course, have long traditions of theologically engaging young people (even churches in the denominations studied above). After several decades of well-meaning avoidance (i.e., "the Bible turns teenagers off"), we now know that dodging theological content in youth ministry actually impairs teenagers for accepting their identities as God's beloved and stunts their participation in a faith community that "speaks Christian," as Stanley Hauerwas puts it.[15] A number of developments in current trends aim to deepen young people's participation in identity-forming Christian practices, engage more fully with Christian texts and traditions, and reflect on their lives, and on the world as a whole, from an explicit theological point of view. This chapter will consider three promising possibilities: attention to mission, attention to communities of belonging, and attention to sacred practices.

The Missional Church: Following Jesus into the World

It would be hard to overestimate the importance of mission for the church in a post-Christendom age. Mission (from the Latin *missio*, "to send") does not mean proselytizing. In fact, missional theologians are anxious to avoid the imperialistic and exclusivist claims associated with "mission" in previous centuries, reminding us that the church's original identity was as people sent by God into the world. "As the Father has sent me," Jesus told his disciples, "so I send you" (John 20:21). The church's job is to confess, not convince.[16] Mission was never intended to become the job of a few individuals sent to some faraway place to persuade others to join the Christian movement. God sends the *whole* church, youth included, into the world to confess Christ, which means two things for youth ministry: (1) we don't have to go very far to engage in mission, and (2) congregations are themselves "missionary"—eliminating the need for many denominational and even pastoral "middle managers."

66

The growing emphasis upon the local congregation is accompanied, in churches of the Western tradition, by the diminishing importance of regional and national church structures. They are both getting smaller and are being redefined.... As they decrease in size and authority, denominational structures in the North Atlantic context increasingly affirm the local congregation as the prime unit of mission.[17]

One significant shift in our understanding of mission has been the view that North America—and the North American *church*—are themselves loci of mission communities in need of the good news of the gospel. Missional theologians like Darrell Guder argue that reorganizing the church does not go far enough to restore the church's true identity as an agent of Christ's mission in the world. What is required is nothing short of conversion, "the continuing conversion of the church."[18]

> Churches are not gatherings of "the saved" but are communities of "the sent."

The missional church movement is a bid to disestablish churches from their dominant culture captivity.[19] The term *missional church* (a phrase that strictly speaking is redundant) does not mean a vigorous campaign to convert people to Christian faith but rather a church that participates in God's healing and transforming purposes in and for the world. The phrase "missional church" was coined by a group of scholars who took seriously the consensus statement of Vatican II: "The church on earth is by its very nature missionary since, according to the plan of the Father, it has its origin in the mission of the Son and of the Holy Spirit."[20] To understand this statement means we must first admit what mission is *not*. It is not one of many church programs; it is not a matter of sending a few Christians into a foreign culture to convert unbelievers; it is not about dispatching a van full of youth on a mission trip to Appalachia or Mexico on behalf of the rest of the congregation. To be a missional church means, first and foremost, that everything we do bears witness to God's reconciling mission for the world. Being missional requires us to understand that churches do not exist for the benefit of our own members. Mission is the business the church is in. A church that is not missional is not a church in the first place.[21]

To be sure, most young people disenchanted with their churches do not form a "missional church"; they just quit. In the U.S., 11 percent fewer people said they are Christians in 1990 than in the decade before. "When it comes to religion," writes Cathy Lynn Grossman, reporting the results of 2008's American Religious Identification Survey, "the USA is now land of the freelancers."[22] The study concludes: "The challenge to Christianity...does not come from other religions but from a rejection of all forms of organized religion."[23]

1. Vocation and Mission

The missional church offers young people a "worthy adventure" through the vocation of discipleship. Churches are not gatherings of "the saved" but communities of "the sent"—people called and sent by God into the world as envoys of Christ's saving grace. Missional churches do not view the Christian story as a vehicle for socializing young people into better church members or more wholesome citizens. For them, to follow Christ is to take part in a great adventure story—more *Lord of the Rings* trilogy than *Fun with Dick and Jane*. Youth ministry that takes seriously the church's missional identity invites young people into a way of life that reflects the dying-and-rising rhythm of baptism, as they step into an adventure with great risks and greater rewards.

> To follow Christ is to take part in a great adventure story—more *Lord of the Rings* than *Fun with Dick and Jane*.

But to become a worthy adventure, youth ministry must invoke gospel madness, the inside-out logic in which the last shall be first and the first shall be last. David White explains, "Youth ministry, at its best...engages youth as partners in the Kingdom of God, mobilizing the skills, practices, and attitudes to sustain a countercultural Christian faith beyond adolescence into adulthood."[24] In other words, missional churches introduce young people to their vocations as full-fledged witnesses to the gospel. Forget the stereotypes of "witnessing" as knocking on doors, handing out tracts, or preaching on the street corner. All Christians are called to serve as witnesses—not just those who volunteer to serve on the evangelism committee, not just adults, not just those with enough interpersonal *chutzpah* to risk ridicule at school. Theologian Karl Barth proposes that our very identity as Christians is found in our calling to serve as witnesses: "[Christians], with their whole being, action, inaction and conduct, and then by word and speech,...have to make a definite declaration to other[s].... The essence of their vocations is that God makes them witnesses."[25]

2. Through the Roof and through the Window

There is no right way to go about youth ministry in a missional congregation. As a youth minister in Virginia explained, "I aim for mission and kind of hit youth ministry along the way," which suggests the kind of ministry we read about again and again in the gospel.[26] In Mark 2, we meet a group of friends so determined to bring a companion to Jesus that they carry their paralyzed buddy on a stretcher to the house where Jesus is staying—only to find it "standing room only." Purpose, creativity, and determination make these friends missional. They adapt to their context in ways that some might call ingenious, others might call destructive, but that changes the *status quo* for the sake of allowing someone on the margins to encounter the healing ways of Christ. These friends are not willing to wait for the crowds to disperse, any more than our youth are willing to wait for the church to evolve into something they can relate to after graduation. Like the paralyzed man's roof-scaling friends, teenagers are impatient. They are creative. They are persistent and bold and unconventional. The paralyzed man's friends opt for a top-down approach: one hole in the roof and down he goes, stretcher and all, to see Jesus. Jesus acknowledges the friends' faith, forgives the paralyzed man of his sins, heals his body, and sends them all home.

Some Christian communities go to great lengths to carry out a missional mindset, breaking holes in the roofs of tradition so that young people can encounter Jesus. Founders of the "emerging church movement"—a loose collective of Christian communities who adapt their practices for the mission field of postmodern culture—believe that most churches have become so culturally bound to modernism that alternative practices must be developed to address postmodern young people, whose cultural experience makes traditional expressions of Christianity completely alien. Emerging churches often "poke holes" in the modern church roof, challenging its institutional structures, its systematic theology, its professional clergy, its propositional teaching methods, and its preoccupation with bringing people into the church rather than with bringing the church to people to transform their lives and contexts.[27] As a result, emerging churches have developed countless creative ways for lowering stretchers into the church, helping young men and women, who might not otherwise see Jesus, get into a room, where they can encounter the transforming presence of God.

Other missional communities forego the hole in the roof in favor of opening a window, providing alternative entry points into the church that, in turn, offer alternative perspectives on Jesus. The front door still works for some youth; but going through the window provides fresh theological angles, benefiting traditional church members as well. Congregational mission and service trips are perspective-changing examples. For a teenager to experience mission as a witness to Jesus Christ is quite different from experiencing "missional tourism"—trips that make no long-term claim on us, do not invest in real community or compassion, though they may help young people feel good about themselves and fulfill high school service requirements. Practical theologian and educator Don Richter encourages mission planners to include prayerful, reflective practices that awaken young people to systemic injustice, open them to the witness of others, and overcome the tendency to relegate "community service" to an annual experience that bears no relationship to their daily lives.[28]

Of course, missional churches—like all churches—must be critiqued as well; as theologian Ted Smith points out, since consumerism capitalizes on the new and the different, being countercultural hardly protects us from being co-opted by dominant culture values.[29] Yet the missional church conversation offers the church different endings to the Easter story we read in Mark, helping us imagine how we might run from the tomb to a world that is wildly unprepared for good news.

Three Missional Churches

Outreach Red Bank (ORB) in Red Bank, New Jersey, began as a ministry to disenfranchised homeless youth who hung out in a local park. Young adults had a simple vision for the ministry's beginnings: since teenagers weren't going to church, these adults brought the church to them. They ate together, sang together, and talked about God. As ORB grew, other adults in the community caught the vision and got involved. Today, ORB is an intergenerational congregation, but it retains its original missional purpose: to bear witness to Jesus Christ among young people, especially those on the margins, in the Red Bank community. www.theorb.org

BroadStreet Ministries, on the Avenue of the Arts in Philadelphia, is a new church development initially supported by mission dollars from local Presbyterian Church (USA) congregations. Meeting in a once-abandoned Presbyterian church building, the congregation was formed by young adults who wanted to be Christ's witnesses to people in the neighborhood—many of whom were artists with few (or negative) church experiences. In addition to developing youth ministries, mental health initiatives, and a variety of programs to serve homeless Philadelphians, BSM builds bridges between the arts and Christian spirituality by sponsoring CD release events, concerts, a film and speaker series, art exhibits, and other public events for local artists and by having a Curator of Experiential Arts on staff. www.broadstreetministry.org.

Oconnee Presbyterian Church in Watkinsville, Georgia, was formed around a vision of a church that is radically inclusive of all generations. If you were to visit on Sunday, you would find children and youth participating in worship, worshipers being asked to greet someone twenty years younger or older (who is not a family member!), and first and second graders reading Scripture or leading in some other fashion. To encourage multiple generations in worship, soft cushions are placed around the sanctuary in case anyone wants to sit on the floor; multi-sensory elements are included in sermons and the liturgy; and the community gathers at other times besides Sunday morning. During the week, teens and adults work together to provide meals and shelter for those in need. At church suppers, guests are frequently seated by birthday month, so that table conversations may include several adults, a few teenagers, a three-year-old, and a ten-year-old, all of whom share April birthdays. http://opcusa.org/.[30]

The Emerging Church

Emerging churches "emerge" around the mission of serving Christ in a postmodern context. Nadia Bolz-Weber is the "mission developer" for **House for All Sinners and Saints** in Denver, Colorado. She describes House for All Sinners and Saints as "an urban liturgical community with a progressive yet deeply rooted theological imagination." It is also, according to her blogspot, an "Emerging Church *a la* Luther."[31] In a post on March 19, 2009, she offers her take on the emerging church:

If I had a dollar for every person who has asked me "So, what IS the emerging church?" we could meet our budget this year. Here's my own definition, and it is just that—my definition. Not the definition. When I use the term "emerging church," here's what I mean by that...(I feel like I'm walking into a minefield, but here we go...)

Emerging Church: *Christian communities that emerge out of very particular cultural contexts where the traditional church is basically irrelevant. These cultural contexts are more often than not urban, youngish, and postmodern.*

Emerging church is not a worship style. I know emerging churches that do traditional liturgy with jazz (Mercy Seat), who use electronica (Church of the Beloved), who are a cappella Gregorian chant (House for All Sinners and Saints), and who do nothing but old-time Southern gospel (House of Mercy).

So, when trad churches in the suburbs are wanting to attract young people (with all the good intentions in the world) and they ape some kind of worship style they read about in a Zondervan book by starting an "emerging" worship service, it's a bit ironic.

Ok, now before you leave me angry responses, let me say: this is not saying that there is something wrong with the traditional church. Trad church is often a faithful expression of Christian community. But my friends would have to culturally commute from who they are to who the trad church is. This is why I want to make a t-shirt that says, "Light all the candles you want to; they are not coming." The back of the shirt would say "It's OK to be who you are (traditional, suburban, small town, conservative, Methodist...whatever it is. Be it.)"

For the record: I wanted to start a church in a context that I am native to. I am not "targeting a population" nor have I at any point had to ask myself, "What is it they want"? They being postmodern urban young adults. I am they.

Redefining Community: From Connections to Communion

Every youth worker knows that to "belong" is a sacred trust for teenagers. The need for community is part of young people's developmental circuitry; one frequently cited early report on brain development declares adolescents "hard wired to connect."[32] Today's emerging adults place a greater value on community than their parents do.[33] Yet the ways in which millenial young people belong are quite different than was the case for their Boomer or even their Xer parents. Millennials are less likely to join organizations and more likely to seek out communities and networks. If their experience of the church is positive, they are less likely to think of it as a place and more likely to experience it as a system of relationships.

In many ways, the impulse to become part of a community or network taps into gospel forms of "belonging" more faithfully than many youth ministry fellowship programs. Communities do not come into being for their own sake; they tend to emerge from a group of people who focus together on common interests and objectives. Anyone who has ever planned an evening for teenagers to "get to know each other" quickly realizes how shallow forced fellowship feels. On the other hand, experiences of risk, vulnerability, creativity, and meaning-making all evoke organic bonds between all who share the experience. Serving in a soup kitchen, discussing theology in a restaurant, repairing porches in Appalachia, playing in a band all strengthen group sinews among young people in congregations. When thousands of young people stream into Taizé, France, each summer to work and pray with the tiny ecumenical monastic community there, nobody plays icebreakers. Instead, points out practical theologian and educator Jason Santos, the Brothers of Taizé practice the radical welcome of Jesus Christ—and as youth participate in these Christ-centered practices, they consistently experience a new, compelling, and transformative way of being human.[34] Christian community is less an end in itself than the joyful by-product of people focusing on Christ together. In our common focus on Jesus Christ, the church becomes *koinonia*—a fellowship created not by you and me but by Christ who draws all people to himself.

1. New Ways to Belong

Millennial young people are restructuring the coordinates of community, experimenting with ways to connect that were not possible even a decade ago. Web 2.0 technology offers young people visibility, mutual vulnerability, participation, and a sense of common purpose that transcends time and geography, which are essential for belonging in a networked, globalized society. In fact, some educators believe technology makes these avenues of belonging more readily available than churches do.[35] The "flat" world of globalization exponentially expands the number of communities available to teenagers. Belonging is horizontal as well as vertical, wide as well as deep, virtual as well as actual, near as well as far. The technological engines of globalization (the internet, transportation systems, cellular technology, the entertainment media, and so on) make intercultural contact normative, giving teenagers a "planetary perspective" that lets them pick and choose from an endless array of potential communities of belonging. Community is not a given; it is constructed from the possibilities of a global culture. No people group, no part of the planet is off limits.[36]

Add to the mix another dimension of belonging for adolescents: participation. "Teenagers belong where they participate," observes practical theologian and educator Andrew Zirschky. "Web 2.0 is all about participation."[37] A 2008 Harris Interactive poll underscored teenagers' increasing dependence on cell phones (40 percent of teenagers surveyed said they "would die" without one) and demonstrated how these technologies enable young people to create communities in which they have legitimate power.[38] The participatory culture of the twenty-first century offers a context where young people have become creators of cultural content and not merely consumers of it.[39] While churches largely follow the traditional American institutional script of restricting full teenage engagement, participatory culture welcomes young people's contributions to the "formation" of culture itself. While most teenagers cannot vote, lack meaningful work, and have limited transportation, in the online world they can and do publish, trade stocks, build businesses, provide services, and engage with other youth and adults on an endless array of topics and causes.

2. Communion, Not Connections

An interesting sidebar accompanies the multiple communities and connections available to young people. Despite these communities' virtual forms, young people consistently prefer face-to-face interaction with friends (beeper studies show that teenagers are happiest when partying or when they are with a romantic partner).[40] By 2009, media analysts like Danah Boyd and Anastasia Goodstein reported "social networking fatigue" among young people, although youth have not yet moved to other media platforms, and they still depend on social networking sites for community-shaping activities like conversation, coordinating social plans, sharing photos, and so on. Still, adolescents crave interpersonal interactions and "the call of 'real life.' "[41] The intimacy young people seek is a deep and spiritual sense of belonging and being known—an intimacy enacted in the Christian practice of communion:

> Culture offers connections, but it can't offer communion.... Coming together in church over bread and wine involves human technologies too—humanly made elements of bread and wine—until the Holy Spirit shows up and transforms them. Communion comes as a result of the Holy Spirit in our community.[42]

> "Culture offers connections, but it can't offer communion....
> Communion comes as a result of the Holy Spirit in our community."
> —Andrew Zirschky

As Zirschky points out, the church is called to cultivate *communion* and not just connections with young people. Being a face-to-face community is not enough; the church must be a communion (and not just serve it from time to time). We must become a community looking in the same direction, at the same God, seeking union with the Holy Spirit, offering the life-for-life intimacy of being known, the safety of mutual vulnerability, and the agency of participation in a community that transcends time and geography. Many young people seek such intimacy online, and feel more open and understood by virtual friends than by those they see every day. Yet the church concretizes belonging, giving it embodied form in the sacrament of the Lord's Supper. The Eucharist is the "outward sign" of God's gift of inward grace, which is what makes communion—literally, "one-with-ness"—possible in the first place. When the church becomes a community of belonging, we embody "communions"—one-with-ness in every form—that imperfectly but authentically becomes the body and blood of Christ as we remember him.

Sacred Practices: Aiming for Embodied Faith

The importance of communion for youth ministry (both in the sacramental and in the communal sense) points to a third promising theme in youth ministry: a renewed interest in sacred practices, as mentioned in chapter 3.[43] Maria Harris's 1981 *Portrait of Youth Ministry* anticipated the practices paradigm by calling churches to reappropriate ancient curricular forms like teaching, prayer, communion, advocacy, and troublemaking in our ministries with young people. Two decades later, youth ministry emerged as the church's testing ground for a "practices approach" to faith formation that takes seriously calling, preparing, and sending young people (and the rest of us) into the world as Jesus' disciples.

Practices are the ongoing actions of the Christian community that the Holy Spirit uses to mark us as, and shape us into, followers of Jesus Christ.[44] Practices are simultaneously formative and performative; they are actions that God uses to change us and, through the church, to change the world. Christian tradition allows a good deal of latitude for contextualizing faith practices for particular flocks, but because each practice imitates Christ in large or small ways, adapting them does not alter their essential, cruciform shape. We somehow still recognize Christ through the dying-and-rising patterns brought to life in faith practices, as God uses them—uses *us*—to enter the world. Practical theologian and educator Craig Dykstra explains,

> Christian practices are not activities we do to make something spiritual happen in our lives. Nor are they duties we undertake to be obedient to God. Rather, they are patterns of communal action that create openings in our lives where the grace, mercy, and presence of God may be made known to us. They are places where the power of God is experienced. In the end, these are not ultimately our practices but forms of participation in the practice of God.[45]

Practices, therefore, function as embodied beliefs. Remember those sponge bath toys you had as a child, the kind that came in small, compressed pellets? Add water and—presto!—they grew into three-dimensional ducks and dinosaurs. Christian practices are like that. Doctrines are Christian teachings in their flat, compressed form, but practices make these doctrines spring to life in the three-dimensional experience of following Jesus.

> Practices are the ongoing actions of the Christian community that the Holy Spirit uses to mark us as, and shape us into, followers of Jesus Christ.

1. Practicing the Presence of God

Practices, like signs and sacraments, are human actions that point to the promise of God, and that often serve as a context for divine-human encounter. Because sacraments allow us (quite literally) to "practice the presence of God," as Brother Lawrence (1614–1691) famously put it, they function as means of grace that invite our participation in the life of God. Sacraments like baptism, for example, enact this participation explicitly. Yet sacraments "proper" are not the only human actions that serve as opportunities for divine-human encounter. For Brother Lawrence, every practice of Christian life amounted to a form of prayer, and every "common business" was a medium of divine love.[46] Youth ministry includes many other means of grace that outwardly signify the divine grace that fuels the Christian life. For young people accustomed to a participatory, image-driven culture, the power of outward signs—active, tangible, and personal—is significant.

> For young people accustomed to a participatory, image-driven culture, the power of outward signs—active, tangible, and personal—is significant.

Young Catholics, for instance, are rediscovering *sacramentals*, which practical theologian Tom Beaudoin describes as "miniature, personal signs of God and God's grace in the world."[47] For Catholics, sacramentals may take any number of forms: prayer, the use of holy water, salt, and other blessed foods, the avowal of faults in Mass, the giving of alms, or priestly blessings involving candles, ashes, or palms, to name a few. Sacramentals emphasize faith's personal dimensions, especially God's presence in daily life, which heightens their power for young people who tend to view personal experience as the ultimate test of "what counts as religious."[48] Beaudoin explains sacramentals' appeal to Generation X (born roughly between 1961–1981): "Grounded in accessible, quotidian practices, sacramentals help Xers see their own experience as religious. The divine may be present in the artifacts that attend Xer quests for the religious life."[49]

Meanwhile, Protestant youth ministry tends to emphasize actions that imitate Christ more than material signs of God's grace, though sometimes these actions are indistinguishable from sacramentals. Martin Luther, for instance, considered confession, absolution, and reading and hearing the gospel sacramental. John Wesley defined means of grace as actions that God uses to strengthen us for "holiness of heart and mind," and divided them into two categories: works of piety (i.e., prayer, searching the Scriptures, holy communion, fasting, Christian conferencing, and healthy living) and works of mercy (i.e., doing good, visiting the sick, visiting the imprisoned, feeding and clothing those in need, earning/saving/giving all that one can, and seeking justice).[50] In Wesley's view, practices were not only signs that help us grow in faith; they were the Holy Spirit's means of equipping and sending God's people into the world.

2. A Curriculum of Sacred Practices

Because God uses these sacred actions to transform the church (starting with us), "practicing the presence of God" provides a curriculum for participating in the life of Christ. Faith is not formed through the heady dispensation of data, but by the gift of the Holy Spirit imparted in relationships through which Christ is known. By inviting young people to participate in the practices that have bound Christian communities to Jesus Christ for two thousand years, young people come to know themselves as Jesus' followers, both because they act like other Christians and because through these relational practices, God transforms us into people who resemble Jesus.

> "I may have been fooling around, but Jesus wasn't. My heart may not have been in it, but Jesus' was."—Barbara Brown Taylor

Sacred practices offer young people concrete ways to participate in an ancient tradition of faith, while simultaneously creating space for holy encounters that are immediate, personal, and transformative, even when we do not consciously look for them. Recalling a half-hearted prayer in college that put her on a lifelong pursuit of Christ, Barbara Brown Taylor recalls: "I may have been fooling around, but Jesus wasn't. My heart may not have been in it, but Jesus' was."[51] Sacred practices do not just pass along information about Jesus; they immerse young people in an embodied version of the Christian story, taking part in God's action in the world here and now.

3. The Importance of Parents

In the "Concluding Unscientific Postscript" to *Soul Searching*, sociologists Smith and Denton mull over ways that churches might deepen teenagers' engagement with their faith traditions. Besides reiterating the importance of adult-youth relationships and religious practices for adolescent discipleship, they contend that adults need to stop thinking of teenagers as a separate species and start practicing faith along with them:

- The best way to get most youth more involved in and serious about their faith communities is to get their parents more involved in and serious about their faith communities.
- Parents and faith communities should not be shy about teaching teens.
- Religious educators need to work harder on helping young people articulate faith.
- Religious communities might themselves think more carefully and help youth think more carefully about the distinctions among (1) serious, articulate, confident personal and congregational faith, versus (2) respectful civil discourse in the pluralistic public sphere, versus (3) obnoxious, offensive faith talk that merely turns people off.
- Regular religious practices in the lives of youth (beyond those in and of collective weekly congregations) seem to be extremely important.[52]

It is strange to hear such recommendations from social scientists; they are commonly heard—though seldom heeded—in youth ministry. Yet without this research, youth ministry has often been stuck at the level of "lore," habits of thinking that attribute lively faith in young people to some mysterious alchemy between youth ministers' training and leadership skills and the peer relationships and practices of youth themselves. Research is abundantly clear: *if we want young people to have faith, we must attend to the faith of their parents and congregations.*

> "The best way to get most youth more involved in and serious about their faith communities is to get their parents more involved in and serious about their faith communities."—Christian Smith and Melinda Denton

The National Study of Youth and Religion is one of dozens of studies that identify parents as the most important influence on the religious lives of their children. Longitudinal research from the NSYR reveals the significance of parents' religiosity for emerging adults, as well; youth between the ages of 18-23 who remain devoted to religious faith after the high school years are overwhelmingly young people whose parents were highly religious while their children were teenagers—and, for young people without religious parents, congregational relationships with other Christian adults often compensated.[53] The 2004 Exemplary Youth Ministry study links thriving faith in teenagers to congregations' capacities to theologically engage parents and other adult leaders. While theologically prepared leaders and peer relationships were regarded as enormously significant, the EYM study found adolescent faith maturity to be most evident in churches that immersed teenagers in congregational life, and that cultivated partnerships with parents for the faith formation of their children (see *Appendix A*).[54]

Beyond Training Events:
New Possibilities for Forming Leaders

Most churches know that the stereotype of a young, hip youth leader who plays the guitar and makes it cool to be for Jesus is a cartoon (not that they wouldn't hire this person if they found him—or less often, her). That didn't stop one search committee, phone-interviewing several graduating M.Div. students from the seminary where I (Kenda) teach, from asking each candidate to please play a "youth ministry song" on the guitar (over the phone) as part of the interview, to assess his or her readiness for the position.

As new possibilities for the future of youth ministry present themselves in the early twenty-first century, leaders must be prepared to leverage them. In chapter 6, we will discuss how the professionalization of youth ministry in the past three decades has catapulted ministry with young people into a completely new sphere of proficiency and theological preparation—but it has not solved every problem in youth ministry. Statistics are hard to come by, but even with the move toward professionalization, the vast majority of youth ministers are not professionals—they're volunteers, with day jobs and busy lives. In a 2002 report commissioned by the Evangelical Lutheran Church of America, 84 percent of churches said their high school youth ministry's primary leaders were adult volunteers; 27 percent reported a lay, paid youth minister as one of their youth ministry's primary leaders—and fewer than 5 percent reported having an ordained, paid youth minister as a primary leader. Most long-term youth ministry training and degree programs (undergraduate and graduate), focus on these last two categories.[55]

One of the downsides of professionalization seems to be churches' tendency to hire youth ministers to "take care of" the church's young people—suggesting that faith formation is a job for professionals, not for families and communities. Most churches still expect youth pastors to use their personal charisma and boundless energy to attract teenagers to the church, and once there to keep them busy, happy, and out of trouble. It is an impossible standard to uphold whether you are a guitar-playing twenty-something or a middle-aged mom. Furthermore, most professional youth ministers agree: the days of the solo, lone ranger youth director are over, which should indicate that the days of preparing youth ministers as individual repositories of talent are over as well. Slowly, churches are beginning to recognize that youth ministry leadership must be shared by the entire congregation rather than assigned to one superhuman paid youth worker. More churches are coming to believe that ministry with young people should be incarnational, and more youth ministers are developing methodologies for spiritual formation with young people that echo the relational strategies practiced by Jesus himself.

Yet models for leadership formation that both acknowledge the communal nature of Christian formation *and embody it* are hard to come by. Despite our profound commitment to the formative power of relationships in the lives of young people, an incarnational approach to forming *leaders* in youth ministry has largely eluded us. The "youth ministry training event" model—an event featuring speakers and workshop leaders that requires youth ministers to parachute in for a day and sit passively while being inspired—has become nearly ubiquitous, making leadership formation in youth ministry (1) highly focused on individual leaders, (2) abstracted from actual situations of ministry, and (3) largely concentrated in "one off" events—one-hour presentations, one-day seminars and workshops, or speaker/seminar series ("one off" events in the sense that once completed, they are not repeated).

Youth ministers are typically so hungry for training that they appreciate whatever youth ministry education is available to them, so well-meaning efforts are not wasted, and they offer short-term benefits and, sometimes, meaningful networks of colleagues for isolated youth workers. Yet the disconnect between the way we prepare leaders, and our increasingly intentional theologies and practices in youth ministry. All of the research we know in youth ministry—*all of it*—advocates *shared, incarnational* forms of leadership, not individuals with "skills." And all of the research we know from educational leadership—*all of it*—maintains that genuinely influential teacher training is *communal, repeated, ongoing,* and *situated.*[56] Add "Spirit-led" to that list (since, after all, the goal of Christian formation is to cooperate with the promptings of the Holy Spirit) and you get a helpful acrostic to guide youth ministry leadership formation:

Communal
Repeated
Ongoing
Situated
Spirit-led

Figure 4.2

Dimensions of Leadership Development
for Youth Ministry

Incarnational Leadership Formation Is Communal

Communal leadership formation is a shared proposition at many levels: it aims to shape both congregational leaders (including youth ministers) and congregations, developing a framework of support for youth ministry throughout the entire congregational system. Developing leaders in this way means that leadership education must come alongside both the leader *and* the congregation as ministry is being practiced. Communal models of leadership education ask questions like, Does every member of the congregation see himself or herself as a youth minister? Does the congregation acknowledge the importance of constellations of supportive adults in a young person's life, in addition to the presence of the youth pastor? Does the church have a plan for dealing with the stresses that youth ministry places on other congregational systems? Has the congregation put time into tilling the soil of youth ministry—developing deep layers of volunteers, identifying stakeholders in youth ministry's mission and vision, equipping parents, creating a congregational culture that welcomes and extends Christ's love for young people (including the ones we never see)? In short, does the church understand youth ministry as a shared mission that requires leadership development for the entire congregation, and not just for the volunteers who show up on Sunday nights?

Old habits die hard, but some congregations are beginning to realize that youth ministry cannot be functionally outsourced to a hired hand. Young church leaders increasingly gravitate toward leadership teams and equipping ministries, nudging congregations toward models of youth ministry that involve multiple leaders, in differing capacities, and that utilize all the gifts of a congregation. Communal leadership formation involves partnerships of many kinds linking practitioner training with academic programs, developing learning communities (with peers as well as experts), creating venues that facilitate both horizontal (peer-to-peer) and vertical (teacher-to-learner) learning. The most promising approaches distribute support for youth ministry throughout the entire congregational system, while providing education and spiritual growth opportunities for youth leaders themselves.[57]

Incarnational Leadership Formation Is Repeated and Ongoing

As we noted earlier, single youth ministry training events inspire hope, and often launch important friendships (especially among the people leading them), but they do not develop leadership skills, nor do they form people theologically. Developing habits of leadership—and not just knowledge about habits of leadership—requires ongoing focus and attention. If we know from organizational research that it takes 10,000 hours of practice to become good at something (anything), and ten years to become an expert in a field (any field), then it is safe to say that a single exposure to any aspect of ministry is insufficient. Engaging in ongoing, repeatable practices, on the other hand, have enormous transformative potential—especially those that explicitly connect us to others in the Body of Christ, open us to the Holy Spirit's presence, and conform our lives to Jesus' life, death, and resurrection.

Effective leadership formation utilizes Jerome Bruner's concept of a "spiral curriculum," which insists that people of all ages learn by following tracks that have been laid by prior learning, but at increasingly complex levels.[58] For example, every level of youth ministry involves some kind of incarnational relationships, but our relational skills as a rookie youth minister should be different from our relational skills as a veteran. By naming what distinguishes an accomplished first-year youth pastor from an accomplished fifth- (or fiftieth)-year youth pastor we begin to hold people accountable to appropriate strategic and theological standards while discerning whether these standards are being met. A spiral curriculum offers an ongoing, incremental approach to learning, so that congregations, academic institutions, and continuing education opportunities all play an irreplaceable part.

Incarnational Leadership Formation Is Situated

The advantage of situated learning is what some educational theorists call "legitimate peripheral participation"—a kind of actual participation in a community that gradually moves learners from the margins of belonging to full participation in a community as the learner acquires the language and skills needed to take part in more significant ways.[59] Situated learning maintains that learning comes from actively participating in communities of practice, utilizing advice from mentors and coaches to become more proficient and confident in the community's defining practices. Despite the dominance of situated learning models in the corporate world, they are quite scarce in youth ministry. Although many congregations "apprentice" teenagers to adults who can model the faith journey for them, apprenticeship relationships in leadership formation are scarce—though where they do exist, they are often cherished. More often, we associate situated learning with "coaching models" of leadership formation, in which corporately minded congregations contract consultants to come alongside them for several months, usually to address some area of concern in the ministry.

> Camping ministries have a long tradition of developing leaders through situated learning; many camp counselors and directors once were campers themselves who moved through the ranks (newbie, experienced camper, junior counselor, counselor) as they mastered the camp's culture.

The irony is that, historically, situated learning is not a product of corporate culture; it is based on observations of how humans are integrated into social groups. When worshipping communities identify leaders within the congregation and groom them for particular roles, they are employing some of the

81

principles of situated learning. Camping ministries have a long tradition of developing leaders through situated learning; many camp counselors and directors once were campers themselves who moved through the ranks (newbie, experienced camper, counselor-in-training [apprentice], counselor) as they mastered the camp's culture. African American churches offer another example. Many African American churches "raise up" new leaders from within, identifying mentors from the membership to walk alongside congregants who aspire to Christian leadership, as they assist with ministry itself. Academic programs sometimes provide "micro-versions" of situated learning (field education, internships, simulations, micro-teaching, immersion experiences, and other "laboratory" experiences are common). In short, while situated learning is not the norm for leadership formation in youth ministry, it offers great potential for educating church leaders, starting with youth leaders and young people themselves.

Incarnational Leadership Formation Is Spirit-led

The church's unique contribution to leadership formation, of course, is attentiveness to the Holy Spirit, who—if Scripture is any indication—routinely transforms "bad risks" for leadership (Moses, Mary, Paul) into towering spiritual giants (Moses, Mary, Paul). New metaphors for leadership in youth ministry in the early twenty-first century—bards, witnesses, Godbearers, place-sharers, spiritual guides—indicate a shift in the way we imagine our task with young people, as we try to cultivate divine attentiveness as much as on cultural or developmental awareness.[60] Metaphors have power; they guide our thinking and our practice, but above all they shape our imaginations. All of these popular metaphors for youth ministry are helpful in bringing certain theological priorities to the foreground.

What they also reveal, however, is a persistent bias in our thinking in the direction of individual leaders—a sense that God is most likely to transform young people in the crucible of a relationship with a single adult, calling into question the role of the church as a whole. To be fair, no one writing in youth ministry today would advocate such a reductionistic (or theologically questionable) view of leadership formation. Still, churches who hire youth ministry professionals (and even those who invest in volunteers) tend to translate our guiding metaphors into individuals who "do" youth ministry. While the adult-youth relationship is pivotal, pointing young people to Christ and equipping them for ministry in the world is a community affair—which only underscores the importance of "C.R.O.S.S." training for postmodern youth ministry education.

> New metaphors for leadership in youth ministry in the early twenty-first century—bards, witnesses, Godbearers, place-sharers, spiritual guides—indicate a shift in the way we imagine our task with young people, as we try to cultivate divine attentiveness as much as cultural or developmental awareness.

Streams in the Wasteland

The madness of youth ministry, of course, is the story we proclaim: the stone is rolled away, the tomb is empty, and Christ is on the loose. He is ahead of us, bringing new life to young people and to the church: "See, I am doing a new thing! / Now it springs up; do you not perceive it? / I am making a way in the desert / and streams in the wasteland" (Isaiah 43:19, NIV). As we learn to approach youth ministry as a form of theological engagement, by necessity the church becomes a worthy adventure where what is at stake is death versus life, wastelands versus pastures, despair versus hope. Anything less would defy the gospel. The promise of missional churches, communities of belonging, and faith practices is that they invite young people to imagine the church in new (though not necessarily original) ways. Such imagination inevitably demands that youth ministry leaders develop competencies that participate in these promising possibilities—competencies that are the subject of chapter 5.

Further Reading on Themes in This Chapter

Buckingham, David, ed. *MacArthur Foundation Series on Digital Learning—Youth, Identity, and Digital Media Volume.* Cambridge, MA: MIT Press, 2008.

Dean, Kenda Creasy and Ron Foster. *The Godbearing Life: The Art of Soul-Tending for Youth Ministry.* Nashville: Upper Room, 1998.

Guder, Darrell L. *The Continuing Conversion of the Church.* Grand Rapids: Eerdmans, 2000.

Jones, Tony. *Postmodern Youth Ministry.* Grand Rapids: Zondervan/Youth Specialities, 2001.

Martinson, Roland, et al. *Across the Generations.* Minneapolis, MN: Augsburg Fortress, 1991.

Peterson, Eugene. *The Contemplative Pastor: Returning to the Art of Spiritual Direction.* Grand Rapids: Eerdmans, 1989.

Renewing the Vision: A Framework for Catholic Youth Ministry. Washington, DC: National Conference of Catholic Bishops, 1995.

Root, Andrew. "Youth Ministry as an Integrative Theological Task: Toward a Representative Method of Interdisciplinarity." *The Journal of Youth Ministry* 5, Spring 2007, 33–50.

Strommen, Merton, et al. *Youth Ministry That Transforms.* Grand Rapids: Zondervan, 2001.

Ward, Pete. *God at the Mall: A Youth Ministry That Meets Kids Where They're At.* Peabody, MA: Henrickson, 1999.

Westerhoff, John H. *Will Our Children Have Faith?* Harrisburg, PA: Morehouse Publishing; Toronto, Canada: Anglican Book Centre, 2000.

Yaconelli, Mark, ed. *Growing Souls: Experiments in Contemplative Youth Ministry.* Grand Rapids: Zondervan, 2007.

CHAPTER FIVE

EMERGING COMPETENCIES

Let no one despise your youth, but set the believers an example in speech and con-
duct, in love, in faith, in purity. Until I arrive, give attention to the public reading of
scripture, to exhorting, to teaching. Do not neglect the gift that is in you, which was
given to you through prophecy with the laying on of hands by the council of elders.
Put these things into practice, devote yourself to them, so that all may see your
progress. Pay close attention to yourself and to your teaching; continue in these
things, for in doing this you will save both yourself and your hearers.
—1 Timothy 4:12-16

I know God will not give me anything I can't handle. I just wish that He didn't
trust me so much.—Mother Teresa

Growing up as a pastor's kid (that's right, I Rodger am living proof that you can grow up as a pastor's kid and still love Jesus), I remember waking up in my elementary school years and going downstairs in the early morning hours. There in the living room sitting by a solitary lamp was my Dad, reading his Bible. It is one of my earliest and most abiding memories. I remember him greeting me as I made my way to the kitchen to get a bowl of cereal with my mother and other brothers. Every morning without fail, Dad would read his Bible. On those early weekday mornings before going off to school, I do not remember Dad ever telling me that he was reading the Bible. I do not remember Dad ever stopping to point out what he was reading or sharing some new insight or question from Scripture. Certainly there were other times when he would share those things with us either in church from the pulpit or even during times of family devotions. As an adolescent, I came to dread those family devotion times; but now, in my adulthood, I realize that through all those moments, Dad was teaching an important truth. I learned that my father loved the Bible—and that he would never be finished reading it or studying it or loving it.

The Apostle Paul's words to his young friend Timothy ring true. As leaders in ministry, we are to set an example for others through our speaking and, perhaps even more important for youth ministry leaders, in our doing. Paul urges Timothy and all who are called to lead in any form of ministry to live in such a way, reading Scripture, exhorting or admonishing or encouraging others, and teaching so that others see our progress.[1] This is one of the reasons ministry with young people is as wonderful as it is precarious. Young people are in a tenacious search for relationships that are worthy of their trust. In my experience, this worthiness comes when they encounter persons whose words consistently match their actions. Parker Palmer calls this "living lives of wholeness...of integrity."[2]

Setting the Believers an Example (or Not)

Several years ago I was invited to speak to a gathering of young people from congregations in the San Francisco Bay area. It was a gray, rainy Sunday afternoon and nearly four hundred youth and adults were crowded into a church gym. I remember the room smelled like wet teenagers. One of the local youth pastors was leading the crowd in a series of group-building activities. The place was too small for the group and the sound system was inadequate. The pastor shouted into the microphone trying to be heard over the noise. His instructions were convoluted, and we were all trying to understand what he wanted us to do and cooperate. Eventually we clustered up in circles of fifteen or so and tried to hear each other's names and churches. Then the pastor called out some objects that we were to try to find within our own group (a cell phone, an iPod, car keys, and so on—he must have expected a wealthy group). If we had them, we were to send a runner to him as quickly as possible. My group was one of those on the farthest edge of the gym; we could barely hear him, much less get to where he stood. Eventually, we gave up and just started telling more about ourselves and trying to get to know one another.

Finally, the pastor rearranged the groups, sending us to the four corners of the gym. He told us to run to the opposite corner as fast as possible when he called "Go!" You have to picture this. So here we are, with about one hundred youth and adults shoved into each of the four corners of the gym, trying simultaneously to get to the opposite corner when he says so. Some of the bigger guys took this as a challenge and ran like offensive linemen through the crowd. Some of the smaller and younger kids were nearly trampled. The wiser ones just avoided the mayhem in the middle and skirted the edges. After doing this a couple of times, the pastor had us all sit down. He asked us to tell him why it was great to be a youth pastor. Some kids did not understand that the question was rhetorical and tried to answer. He ignored them and answered his own question: "Because you get to make people do stupid stuff like you just did, instead of having to do it yourself!" And then he laughed. The group started booing him. I have to confess: I joined them. The pastor did not get it. He needed to read Paul's letter to Timothy.

The call to youth ministry is the call to set an example not just by our words but also by our lives. The call to youth ministry is to lead with integrity so that our words are commensurate with our actions. The word *integrity* means unbroken, uncompromised, whole. People with integrity lead undivided lives: their hearts and their minds and their bodies and their wills are united. They live comfortably in their own skins, which allows them to be completely present to people who are less comfortable in theirs. Their leadership flows organically from who they are and is not easily reducible to what they do. They lead exactly as they are, and that is enough.

> The call to youth ministry is the call to set an example not just by your words but also by your life—and not just for young people, but for all people.

According to Paul, what is the result of practicing and devoting ourselves to leadership with integrity? People see how we progress and grow. Paul reminds Timothy (and all of us who are leaders, young and old alike) that when we live integrated, faithful lives, we grow and others see the Holy Spirit growing in us. The young people we work with see it, the parents we haven't had time to meet see it, our colleagues in ministry see it—even our own children see it on their way to breakfast before school in the morning.

Leading with Integrity: Still Learning

I teach at a seminary and I love what I do. I feel tremendously privileged to journey with these women and men through their years of study as they reflect upon and engage in various expressions of ministry even as they prepare for a further call to ministry. I enjoy the fact that school has a clear starting point (the beginning of each school year in the late summer) and an ending point (the end of the academic year in the late spring). This kind of rhythm fits my soul.

But here's the problem: graduation. The great majority of our students, when they finish their work, are conferred the *Master of Divinity* degree. Even on our best days that is an audacious claim—*Master of the Divine*. And some of them, I can tell, actually believe it. They're the ones who make me the most nervous. If I had my way, as soon as they receive that parchment with their name and the degree with the gold seal on it, I would be standing there to scribble something like "in process" or "by the grace of God" or better yet "as if!" on the edge of their diplomas. That seems to be what Michelangelo had in mind when, in his eighty-seventh year, this Italian Renaissance painter, sculptor, architect, poet, and engineer is said to have written the words *ancora imparo* in the margins of one of the sketches.[3] *Ancora imparo* is Italian for: "And still, I am learning."

This chapter proposes the rather simple thesis that leaders called to youth ministry must echo Michelangelo's words: we are still learning. There is never a point in ministry when we have arrived and can sit back contented and sated. To respond to God's call to lead is to engage in the lifelong task of exploring new contexts for youth ministry and the new questions and skills that accompany them. We have spent a great deal of time on questions, challenges, underlying themes, and hopeful possibilities that await us in ministry with young people. What follows is a discussion of some of the emerging competencies that will help us lead in these circumstances—capacities the church needs in those who seek to be faithful in ministry with young people, especially for the church and culture of the early twenty-first century. These discussions are brief and, to be sure, far from complete, but hopefully they offer a glimpse of what it means to speak and live out Michelangelo's affirmation that, no matter what our age, we are all learning still.

Emerging Competencies in Youth Ministry

Setting the Believers an Example (or Not)

Leading with Integrity: Still Learning

Searching the Scriptures: Transformation in Bible Study
Inviting Wholeness: Identity and Integrity in Teaching
Stilling the Soul: The Practice of Presence
Soul Doctors: Nurturing Hope amidst Suffering
Spectators No More: Creating Church versus Consuming It
Choosing Life: Discerning Vocation with Young People

Benedict of Nursia, Youth Guy

Searching the Scriptures: Expecting Transformation in Bible Study

I was sitting in the back of a large auditorium filled with more than a thousand high school young people. It was the last day of a week-long summer conference and there were two young women on the platform presenting an impromptu skit encouraging the group to attend next year's conference. The skit was cleverly done. They were "texting" each other. Behind each one was a screen that displayed their texts and two voices were also reading out loud the words they were sending to one another. One of the young women was trying to convince the other to come to the conference.

"It will be fun," she wrote to the other.

"Well, what do you do?" asked her friend.

"It's totally cool. There are lots of fun things to do and cute guys. You'll like it," she assured her.

"But I've never been to a Christian camp before," her friend wrote back. "I mean I don't even own a Bible. Do I have to bring a Bible?"

Quickly her friend replied: "A Bible? No! This is a *Presbyterian* church camp. We don't use the Bible!"

I remember the auditorium broke out into laughter and applause. I didn't think it was that funny. Sadly, Christians tend to approach the Bible in one of two ways. Some churches are literally stuck in the Bible. Young people in these churches are unable to move and sometimes barely able to breathe, as if the Word of God were wet concrete, something we step into and never move again.

Not surprisingly, the only way to get out of this kind of theological suffocation is to break out a jackhammer, which makes for a noisy, destructive escape with lots of shrapnel. Other churches act as though they can live without the Bible, reducing it to a quaint relic, abandoning it as a source of God's revelation and as a guide to holiness. Young people in these churches think of the Bible as philosophically interesting but certainly not authoritative, and certainly not for them.

Nothing could be further from the truth. From the days of the early church, Christians have understood Scripture as a place God meets us—not as a historical figure or a philosophical muse, but as the living, saving God in Jesus Christ, who is active in the world. Reading Scripture is an activity of cosmic significance. The Holy Spirit bursts into our lives, kneading our souls, turning our soil so we will be receptive to the Word of God that falls on us. When that happens, the Holy Spirit kicks into high gear, helping us understand God's meaning. Luther taught that the Word of God was unintelligible unless the Holy Spirit showed up to illuminate it.[4] As we mentioned in Chapter 4, Luther, Wesley, and many other reformers understood Scripture sacramentally, as a "means of grace" that ushered God's salvation into the world. For Wesley, the Spirit was active and present whenever God's Word was read, "making alive the truth that is already in the text of Scripture" so that the hearer could apply it.[5]

Reading Scripture is an activity of cosmic significance.

Somewhere in their bones, adolescents already know that if Scripture is to bear witness to God, then reading the Bible must be an opportunity for divine encounter and not just a text. What young people need and seek in the Bible—and what *we* need and seek in the Bible—is not the Bible, but *God*. Barbara Brown Taylor remembers responding to her congregation's desire for a Bible study by offering a series conducted by local seminary professors. Despite the high-powered leadership, attendance was lousy. "Finally," she says, "I got the message. 'Bible' was a code word for 'God.' People were not hungry for information about the Bible; they were hungry for an experience of God, which the Bible seemed to offer them."[6]

Young people are not dying for Bible studies, but they are dying for God, and approaching Bible study as transformation prepares them for this holy encounter. Throughout our history, Christians have claimed that the Bible is the power of God. We have confessed the Bible as central to our life and our mission. We are to know its stories. We seek to hear its words of comfort and challenge and wisdom. We wrestle with its claim upon our lives as the Bible forms our very identity as God's people. In its pages we struggle to hear not just *about* God, but *from* God. So we must wonder, how is it possible that we have understood the Bible as rigid? How is it possible that we have conveyed the message that the Bible is optional?

Old Testament scholar John M. Bracke and Christian educator Karen B. Tye remind us that the goal of teaching the Bible is transformation rather than just information.[7] When we teach the Bible for information, as little more than a series of ancient stories, for instance, we fail to realize that we are actually in these narratives and that these stories are not disengaged from our own experience. At the same time, without denying that facts and information are important, Bracke and Tye argue that "Bible study" as we usually approach it simply ends there, as we wrongly assume that when you know the information in the story, you somehow have taken the text and made it part of your own identity, part of your own story. No wonder, in an information age in which young people have become numb to moment-by-moment bombardment of facts and figures, the Bible becomes one more thing to take in momentarily and then discard.

Transformational Bible study, on the other hand, borrows the insight of the church fathers and mothers and the reformers alike that the Holy Spirit is present in every reading and experiencing of the holy narrative. Because this is true, we must approach Scripture with humility, anticipating that somehow we are about to be confronted with the Maker of the Universe who is drawing us in and changing us in ways beyond our imagining. For North American Christians, this posture of humility presents a particular challenge. Ethicist Stanley Hauerwas writes:

> No task is more important than for the Church to take the Bible out of the hands of individual Christians in North America. North American Christians are trained to believe that they are capable of reading the Bible without spiritual and moral transformation. They read the Bible not as Christians, not as a people set apart, but as democratic citizens who think their common sense is sufficient for the understanding of scripture.[8]

Hauerwas has it right. We usually read Scripture to "get something out of it" by our own means and through our own understanding. We do this because we have been trained to think this way—to rely, as Hauerwas writes, on our own "common sense." We do not approach Scripture with humility, as a source of wonder and mystery. As a reminder of the correct posture for Scripture reading, one youth group I know does every Bible study barefoot. Before the reading of Scripture begins, the youth leader asks people to take off their shoes and sandals, as Moses was instructed to do in Exodus 3 when he encountered Yahweh in the wilderness through a burning bush. "It's a tangible reminder," the youth leader explained to me, "that when we read the Bible, we are doing something that is special for our community. This is not just another activity. We anticipate being changed and called out just as Moses was changed and called out by God."

> Before youth ministry can contribute to the mission of the twenty-first century church—before discipleship formation is possible—young people must recognize that the power of the Word of God is placed in their hands through Scripture.

Before youth ministry can contribute to the mission of the twenty-first century church—before discipleship formation is possible—young people must recognize that the power of the Word of God is placed in their hands through Scripture. Bible study, therefore, has explosive potential. Leaders in youth ministry must embody not only an anticipation of being transformed as they read Scripture, they must also embody a love for and a competence about it. When young people know we regularly and faithfully take time to read Scripture, we are doing precisely what Paul encouraged Timothy to do—to lead by example. When we share our excitement for what the Holy Spirit is teaching us in our own study of Scripture, we show young people what it is like to take the narrative into one's own being. Increasingly we are learning that this kind of teaching has less to do with pedagogical technique than with the person of the teacher, which leads to our next emerging competency.

Inviting Wholeness: Identity and Integrity in Teaching

In the early years of youth ministry education, youth ministry literature focused on "right method." The objective of youth ministry resources was to offer formative techniques and educational strategies for the classroom or the youth room. This philosophy convinced us, for a time, that if we had the right program or used the right activity, young people would come and would "get Jesus." What happened as a result (and we should have seen this coming) was a dangerous emphasis on education—and indeed ministry—as *entertainment*, which led to a bizarre escalation of ever more outlandish and frenetic techniques. Churches, trying to compete with schools, civic organizations, and one another for adolescents' increasingly limited time and attention, found themselves doing everything from renting inflatable carnival rides to raising thousands of dollars for trips to exotic locales, convinced that these experiences would help their young people know what it means to be a disciple of Jesus. What happened? Pretty much the opposite. Teenagers learned two things exceedingly well: that youth ministry can be fun, and that the church is no different from any other group begging for their time and energy.

I am not saying fun is irrelevant to good youth ministry leadership. There is a proper and crucial role for play in youth ministry. But twenty-first-century youth leaders are starting to remember that our job is not to compete with other forms of entertainment (if we even could) but to offer the truth of a gospel that genuinely and authentically demands much and delivers even more. Our methods as educators grow out of reflective practices that enact our core values and being, and are developed to be suitable for "this particular case." Quaker educator Parker Palmer says it this way: "Good teaching cannot be reduced to technique; good teaching comes from the identity and integrity of the teacher."[9] For Palmer, the role of the teacher is to connect the student to the subject. For youth leaders, this means that our task is to connect young people to the gospel of Jesus Christ—a connection conveyed by the identity and integrity of our discipleship, and by our faithfulness as pastors and educators.

> "Good teaching cannot be reduced to technique; good teaching comes from the identity and integrity of the teacher."—Parker Palmer

For Palmer, identity refers to one's whole self—differentiated, defined, and deeply connected to others, embracing all of who we are physically, emotionally, intellectually, spiritually, and experientially. Parker believes that too many leaders, motivated by fear, try to hide parts of their identity or compartmentalize these dimensions of the self. Integrity, therefore, refers to coherence between the leader's soul and role, the congruence between inner and outer self, the ability of the teacher to bring all of the dimensions composing his or her identity into an integrated and coherent whole.

Of course, this does not mean that when we teach or lead or counsel or speak we open our guts and plop them in the middle of the youth room for all to see. But it does mean that every interaction, every conversation springs out of our identity and our integrity as we do our best to be honest with God and with ourselves about our vulnerabilities, limitations, hopes, and dreams. Historian Stephen Rosen, of Harvard's Derek Bok Center for Teaching and Learning, offers a useful rubric for professional conduct in teaching that youth ministers can adapt for teaching with integrity:

• Know (and love) our material
• Know (and love) our learning environment and context
• Know (and love) our students
• Know (and love) ourselves.[10]

To these four guidelines, youth ministers and Christian educators must add a fifth: "To know (and love) God, our true teacher and subject matter."

To minister from the depths of our integrity instead of from the breadth of our knowledge requires practical wisdom—the kind of knowing that can discern the appropriate choice in a given situation that comes from years of experience, or from being steeped in a tradition formed by centuries of practice. As leaders, however, this kind of integrity carries the risk for exposure. At the seminary where I teach, the community often holds a service for wholeness and for healing. During that service, there is an opportunity to go forward and speak quietly with those leading the service about a particular need or concern, and to be anointed and prayed over. At one point last year, I was struggling through some painful decisions and went forward. I found to my own surprise that I could not even speak what was breaking my heart at that point. After a few moments of trying, I gave up and just sat there with tears streaming down my cheeks. The two students who were sitting at that particular station simply placed their hands on my head and prayed for me and then anointed my forehead with oil, making the sign of the cross. Later, I saw one of them on campus. I was a little embarrassed by my own lack of control in that service.

She smiled and said she had been praying for me. I thanked her. Then she thanked me and said it meant a lot to her to see me act so honestly and vulnerably—that even in that moment, I had shown her a way to live when she was out serving a parish as a pastor.

The safest space on earth is at the center of God's will. Because of this, youth ministry offers young people space for mutual vulnerability—a shared openness to one another and to God. Being open to the "other" means allowing ourselves to be moved by another, not opening up a guilty vein and spewing forth. Yet when the church provides a context for mutual vulnerability, it allows us to receive others wholly, as they receive us, and to allow ourselves to be moved by them, as we are moved by God.

> Being open to the "other" means allowing ourselves to be moved by another, not opening up a guilty vein and spewing forth.

Palmer writes that too often we, as teachers and leaders, try to protect ourselves from vulnerability, and we end up constructing elaborate structures of separation from students, from our own selves, even from the gospel. When we do this, we deny both our own identity as well as the hope of integrity. Palmer reminds us that there is a proper role for techniques that ultimately connect us rather than separate us from one another. Techniques and activities that reveal rather than conceal our identities as persons created in the image of God help us teach and lead with integrity. Remember the youth pastor who ridiculed us after leading us? It was a teachable moment, all right. He showed me how to use youth ministry techniques and activities to separate myself from the rest of the group and to demonstrate my own need for power. What is so disheartening is that he might have used that teachable moment to convey a very different message: that Christ-following leadership springs from being joined to the Holy Spirit, who joins all of us together. This attention to the Holy Spirit reinforces another emerging competency for youth ministers: contemplative practice.

Stilling the Soul: The Practice of Presence

Before I became a seminary professor, I served for a number of years as the director of the youth ministry division for the Presbyterian Church (U.S.A.). One of my major responsibilities was to lead a series of summer conferences for young people. These week-long conferences gathered youth and their adult leaders from all over the church. Early in Week Three one summer, two leaders from a church in New Orleans approached me. They asked when the morning speaker or evening preacher was going to issue an "altar call." I explained that some speakers offer such public invitations, inviting teenagers to either commit their lives to Christ for the first time or rededicate their lives to Christ in a new way, but I was not sure about this year. I spoke with the morning speaker and the evening conference preacher and neither planned to issue such a public invitation.

When I reported that to the group leaders, they were disappointed. "Well, then," they asked, "how are we supposed to find out where our young people are with their faith in Jesus Christ?"

"Why don't you ask them?" I responded.

"Can we do that?" they replied, stunned.

I admit, that sounded like a no-brainer to me. But I offered my opinion. "Actually, it seems to me that since you are the adults who have traveled here with them and spent the week with them and will go home with them, you are the persons *best* suited to ask that wonderful question of your young people." When they asked how I thought they should go about this, I knew a longer conversation was in order.

I set up a time to meet with all the adult leaders and suggested some ways they might start the conversation. At the end of the week, I heard from one of the leaders that they had indeed talked with each of the young people and the conversations had been rich and rewarding. "This has been the best week we've ever had," he told me with excitement. "It has been incredible to talk with our young people and to hear their stories and their questions. We're returning home like we are a whole different group."

Mark Yaconelli contends that if we want young people to live lives of faith, "we need to live in the presence of Jesus....We have to share not only the teachings of Jesus but more importantly the presence of Jesus."[11] By "presence" Yaconelli means a number of things: "being open and available to others with as much of ourselves as possible...to be awake to the Mystery of God within each moment...[and] relating to youth in the way Jesus related to people—with authenticity and transparency."[12] The best way to do this, believes Yaconelli, is to spend time in the presence of Jesus ourselves, which for him means participating in ancient contemplative disciplines of prayer and discernment, updated somewhat for contemporary Christians, and inviting young people to join us. (Yaconelli would agree that serving the poor, working for justice, and other forms of active spirituality also place us in the presence of Jesus; his work focuses on contemplative spirituality primarily as a corrective for our over-scheduled, often spiritually vacuous, lives and ministries.) "Who would we become if we spent time in the presence of Jesus?" he asks. Then he identifies the real issue holding us back:

> The central problem in sharing the Christian faith with young people doesn't concern words; it's deeper than that. The real crisis facing those of us who seek to share faith with youth is this: We don't know how to be with our kids. We don't know how to be with ourselves. We don't know how to be with God.[13]

He is right, of course. As veteran youth minister Mike King reminds us: "The most important thing we bring to our youth ministry is a heart seeking the face of God and a life that is truly lived in God's presence."[14] Yaconelli's work on young people and contemplative spirituality has led youth ministers to explore what it means to be with our young people, with ourselves, and with God as spiritual learners and leaders. As we have noted repeatedly throughout this book, ministry with young people requires more than group-building activities or fun outings or mission trips or even Bible study. It requires us to do more than help youth become good moral citizens or conscientious consumers. Youth ministry aims, above all, to build up young people as disciples of Jesus Christ, calling them into an alternative rhythm of life that practices the presence of God.

> "The most important thing we bring to our youth ministry is a heart seeking the face of God and a life that is truly lived in God's presence."—Mike King

The competency of *presence* stands as a direct challenge to ministry (any ministry) that tries to compete with soccer or Starbucks or band or business or you name it. Practicing the presence of God, as Brother Lawrence put it, invites young people, and invites us, to slow down and to place God at the center of our lives. It is an emerging competency because so few of us are good at it yet. For a church seeking to take a prophetic stance against practices of cultural excess, including the need to be more places and to have more time, practicing "presence" offers an alternative to trying to out-program consumer culture. Interestingly, in the early days of Yaconelli's research, he found that young people did not resist contemplative youth ministry; adults did.

> In the early days of Yaconelli's research, he found that young people did not resist contemplative youth ministry; adults did.

Young people whose lives are already so programmed and driven yearn for an opportunity to step out of the race and slow down. In this they act as prophets in our midst, calling the church to step out of a culture that idolizes busy-ness. Our editorial team shared some of our struggles on this point. Kenda recalled a recent "car conversation" with her sixteen-year-old daughter, Shannon. Kenda was complaining about a spate of church-related deadlines she had agreed to. "It's like Whack-a-Mole," she grumbled. "As soon as I get rid of one deadline, another one pops up."

"So," Shannon said simply, "stop putting in quarters."

Of course. While we are being seduced by the "just say yes" culture of accomplishment, teenagers like Shannon see immediately that the way out is to declare Sabbath, to practice Godly presence instead of dutiful compliance. When faith becomes one more thing to do, teenagers understandably (1) opt out or (2) misunderstand Christ as someone who demands their work, rather than hopes for their being. Presence-centered youth ministry refuses to reinforce the frenetic pace at which young people already live; on the contrary, it subverts this pace. The challenge for adult leaders is to live lives that demonstrate this alternative rhythm of life—no easy task, obviously, for hyperscheduled youth ministers. Yet small steps matter: for instance, listening to young people more than talking to them, or honing our own engagement with ancient practices of prayer, meditation, and discernment.

Contemplative practices do not naively disconnect us from daily living; in many ways, they allow for more honest ways of seeing the world, freeing us for unworried lives of joy and freedom. This reorientation also helps us see clearly, and face squarely, the pain and suffering of young people so that our presence can share their burdens, lightening their load. For all of our skills as teachers, leaders, counselors, and life coaches, what young people need us most to become is their pastor (and if we don't do this, who will?). And of course, in this process of shepherding, this act of accompanying them into the world and home again, young people accompany us as well.

Soul Doctors: Nurturing Hope amidst Suffering

There are some young people you meet that you immediately enjoy. Sarah was one of these. She was one of the high school leaders of a weekend retreat where I was speaking in the Santa Cruz Mountains in California. Barely sixteen, she laughed easily, smiled often, and gave energy. She and the other youth and adult leaders had arrived at the conference center early and set up the place. When hordes of youth and adults began to arrive, Sarah was out front greeting them and directing them to cabins or dorm rooms. When one young girl arrived, struggling with her backpack, duffel bag, sleeping bag, and pillow, Sarah grabbed the duffle bag and walked with her to her cabin, chatting and asking questions of the young girl. It was obvious she transformed the girl's first few minutes of the retreat.

At the evening session, Sarah and the other student leaders led us in several probing group-building activities. I noticed that it was Sarah who reached out to include some of the youth who were on the edges of the room. She ran up to one guy, a big, athletic-looking young man who was easily a head taller than she was, introduced herself and stood next to him, encouraging him to participate while other young people led an activity. In no time, he was sitting on the floor in a small group, smiling and enjoying himself. I leaned over to one of the pastors and asked about Sarah. He told me she was one of their best leaders, effervescent and yet humble. He was hoping she would go to seminary following college. I hoped the same. She was just the kind of person I would want for my pastor.

The next day, Saturday afternoon, after I had finished speaking, I was delighted when Sarah asked if she could talk with me. We sat down outside at a picnic table and Sarah told me her story, a story that revealed a depth of pain that called upon everything I had ever read in psychology and addiction.

She asked me to pray for her, and especially for her little sister Maddie. Sarah and Maddie lived with their grandparents, who had become their legal guardians because the courts declared their mother an unfit parent. A drug addict, her mother had often left Sarah and Maddie to fend for themselves and, in fact, had allowed one of her boyfriends to abuse Sarah a few years earlier. I realized that some of Sarah's gifts, including her desire to please, had evolved to help her cope with living in a household riddled with addiction and abuse. Now her grandparents had retired and were thinking about moving. Sarah and Maddie hoped to stay put because they loved their schools, their church, and their friends. As Sarah shared her story, she began to cry quietly. I took her hands, and we prayed together. What struck me was the way Sarah prayed:

> I know you have a plan for me and for Maddie (her little sister), and I am so grateful for grandpa and grandma, and I know it's been hard on them raising us but Lord, I am wondering if it would be possible in your plan for us to stay somehow because it seems that you have given us such a wonderful place to be and a wonderful community that helps us know what it is to live as a family. I know your family is all over the world and that you are at work in it and even in Mom's life. I just want to be faithful to you, so please help me to listen to you.

It was a jaw-dropping holy moment, one of those breathtaking interludes when you just want to thank Christ for the privilege of being in his presence as he shone through this young person. When we finished praying together, Sarah looked up and smiled and wiped the tears from her face. She apologized for crying and for taking up my time. I told her how honored and humbled I was to be with her. Then I asked if we could read some Scripture together. ("Sure.") "Do you know Jeremiah 29:11?" (She wasn't sure.) So we read it together:

> For surely I know the plans I have for you, says the LORD, plans for your welfare and not for harm, to give you a future with hope. (Jeremiah 29:11)

After we read it, Sarah said, "Wow." I told her this passage came to mind because of the way she prayed. I also told her how grateful I was for the way she framed her life experience through her relationship with God. "You're a fine theologian," I said to her. When she objected, I insisted, "I am learning a lot from you today, and I am the one who is grateful for your time."

That's how it is with fine theologians. Theologians help us see our whole life experience, both joys and pain, through our relationship with God. Today, it is all too easy to compartmentalize our school world or work world or family world and play world as separate and unrelated. Developmental psychologist David Elkind says the result is a "patchwork self"—a sense that our lives are a series of unrelated moments that have no effect on one another.[15] A patchwork self is assembled by appropriating the feelings, thoughts, and beliefs of others. As a result, the young person has no inner sense of coherence, no integrating core, and is therefore wildly susceptible to outside pressures and the inner whims of emotion and indecision. Christian theology offers a different understanding of self. Theologians do not deny that there is pain and suffering in the world; in fact, they help us understand God's presence in those moments of despair. These *dark nights of the soul*, painful as they are, can become new sources of spiritual growth and wonder, providing a more profound sense of God's presence and a deeper grasp of God's ways.[16]

> Theologians help us see our whole life experience, both joys and pain, through our relationship with God.

Adolescents are by no means immune to pain and suffering, and their anguish strikes at the very core of their being. Young people need, as pastoral theologian Robert Dykstra puts it, "physicians of the soul," people attuned to the spiritual as well as the psychological and physical dimensions of pain.[17] A 2008 YouTube video of an old (1994) Foreigner song makes the point:

I need to see the soul doctor before the fever begins.
You know I'm searching for the soul doctor when love is wearing thin.
Doctor Soul is in.

Drawing on the tradition of the ancient church, in 1958 pastoral theologian Seward Hiltner argued against reducing pastoral care to psychological healing; rather, he said, the church's job was to assist the Great Physician in the "care and cure of souls," which has the effect of making every pastor a "soul doctor," called to leverage every available resource—psychological and theological—in order to address human suffering.[18] Hiltner's emphasis on the theological as well as psychological dimensions of pastoral care represented one of the first responses to the twentieth-century tendency to shrink spiritual care into modern, secular categories.

Dykstra, too, reminds us that the church doesn't always "get it right" when it comes to addressing suffering. Fully acknowledging that many young people are in crisis, Dykstra says youth ministers, like all Christian leaders, are "heirs to and stewards of the sometimes healing, sometimes destructive doctrines and rituals of the Christian heritage" and that our major work is to discern the "Spirit's stirrings" and to honor and refashion the mysteries and wisdom of faith for a new generation. Essential to this process is the Christian doctrine of hope. Faith in the cross and resurrection of Jesus Christ inspires Christians to a kind of "hope against hope"—a crazy hope, stemming from our amazement at finding the tomb empty, that despite all appearances to the contrary and against all odds clings to God's promise to make all things new.[19]

Spectators No More: Creating Church versus Consuming It

It was an impressive worship service. I was visiting an independent "megachurch" in the Midwest and had worshiped at one of their "seeker-friendly" hour-long services. It unfolded like clockwork, technologically perfect. Not one moment dragged. The service moved seamlessly from the music to a video introduction of the theme for the day. The presenters were clear and energetic. The video clips were clever and perceptive. Several greeters approached me as I made my way to the worship center. The signage was welcoming and communicative. Like I said, it was impressive.

I walked out shaking my head, remembering some other worship services I had attended that were making an earnest effort at including some media, but the screens were too small, words were misspelled, video clips were unintelligible, PowerPoint slides appeared too early or too late so that we could not sing along. I thought about services where the music was too slow or too fast and services that were lifeless and obtuse. No wonder, I remember thinking to myself, that there are hundreds of bright young adults here.

As I headed to the parking lot, I overheard a conversation between the three young adults who were walking in front of me. One of them asked his companions what they thought about the service. A woman said she liked it. "That," she said, "was really a great show."

Now, I don't usually interrupt complete strangers having a conversation in the church parking lot, but I wanted to be sure I got that right. I apologized and explained that I was a visitor too, and asked her what she meant by "show." Forgiving me for eavesdropping, she said, "Well, I guess I was entertained. Not in a totally bad way—but it was really different from what I thought church was supposed to be like. It's sorta like when you go to a concert and walk out saying it was good. That's sort of what it was like." This woman liked the church service the way she liked a good concert.

The next day I returned to the church for an appointment with one of the pastors. I told him about my conversation in the parking lot. He smiled. "It's not like we're trying to entertain here, but the comparison is not bad. We work really hard at making worship as engaging as possible." I asked him about the difference between "engaging" and "entertaining." He said he thought they were related. That's as far as the conversation went.

That's a problem.

Let's be clear about a few things here, since I am well aware that I am walking into a minefield. First, the word "entertain" comes from the French *entre* + *tenir*—to bring together. Entertainment brings people together. This is a good thing. Originally worship brought primitive people together to perform a play as an offering to appease the gods (theatre and worship share the same origin). Christians borrowed this pagan notion in developing the first church liturgies; the idea was to worship for God's pleasure, not ours—which of course makes God the audience, and the congregation one of the leads. In fact, street theatres got started in the early Middle Ages because the church no longer welcomed entertainers (acting was considered "deceit"). So plays stopped being religious performances to please the gods and started to be popular performances to please the people, thanks largely to the church's decision to exclude certain kinds of people from worship (a bad move, always).

Christians also patterned worship after their Hebrew heritage, in which worship meant coming into God's presence with humility—not groveling, sniveling, "yes master" kinds of humility, but grateful, honest gladness that we are not God, but are human and beloved by God. "I do not call you servants any longer," Jesus told his disciples, "because the servant does not know what the master is doing; but I have called you friends, because I have made known to you everything that I have heard from my Father" (John 15:15). We get to come into God's presence as friends. Friends do not need to be appeased; but they do need to be thanked. Christian worship, then, offers God thanks simply for being who God is.

So we do not need to make worship meaningful; it is already meaningful. An encounter with the living God, coming into God's presence, is as meaningful as this life gets. "Worship," as homiletician Tom Long writes, "is about awe, not strategy."[20] So when worship is awful instead of awe-full, we have a problem. We come into the presence of God, not because God commands us to, but because—as any love-struck teenager will tell you—being present with our beloved is everything and enough.

> Worship is a lot like falling in love. When someone falls head over heels for another, adoration flows naturally from the lover toward the loved one. This adoration is not primarily about anything else, nor does it serve any utilitarian purpose outside the love relationship. Indeed, in the presence of the loved one, the lover cannot help but adore, and apart from the beloved, nothing can provoke adoration—not perfume or soft music or dim lights or wine and roses.[21]

What matters is *not* whether worship or ministry in general uses technology or ancient chants; these are merely ways we show our adoration, like perfume and wine and roses. What *does* matter is that we fall in love with God, who is head-over-heels smitten with us. And falling in love is not a spectator sport.

> What matters is *not* whether worship or ministry in general uses technology or ancient chants; these are merely ways we show our adoration, like perfume and wine and roses. What *does* matter is that we fall in love with God, who is head-over-heels smitten with us. And falling in love is not a spectator sport.

The days of spectator ministry are gone, thankfully, since it was never theologically sound ministry to begin with. In those bygone days, leaders expected young people to sit passively while they filled them up with information and knowledge. When ministry became boring or irrelevant for new generations, passionate church leaders threw themselves into addressing the problem—by coming up with better, more professional, more up-to-date ways for people to be a passive church. A generation later, the cycle started (and will start) over.

The problem is analogous to the one activist Paulo Freire noticed in education. Friere described "the banking method" of education. He describes a classroom where the students sit like "containers," empty receptacles waiting to be filled by the teacher. The more completely the teacher fills the receptacles, the better teacher she is. The more meekly the receptacles permit themselves to be filled, the better students they are. Instead of educating, the teacher makes "knowledge deposits" which students passively receive, memorize, and recite. The problem, of course (besides sheer boredom), is that students never discover how to actively learn on their own.

The rise of participatory culture directly challenges banking models of education—and youth ministry. In fact, people who are in ministry with young people stand at the helm when it comes to developing new competencies for Christian leadership in participatory culture, where interactivity rather than passivity is the new learning culture of young people. To be sure, worship is a spectator sport in traditional churches as often as in megachurches (maybe more often), and participatory worship emanates from all corners of Christian tradition. In many corners of the church (Eastern Orthodox, Pentecostal, and emerging churches all come to mind), worship has never *not* been primarily participative. For young people who make "playlists" instead of buying compilations of songs produced for them, who create collaborative Wikis instead of appropriating the definitions supplied by others, who write their own blogs rather than admire Pulitzer-prize-winning columnists, participatory culture means making our own decisions from multiple options, and creating cultural content and not just consuming it. In a "karaoke" culture, as futurist Leonard Sweet calls it, music is not music (art is not art, education is not education, religion is not religion) unless one can perform and participate in it if one chooses.[22]

Proficiency in participatory culture is both intoxicating and intimidating for most of us.[23] On the one hand, it offers a way to counter the conformist nature of teenage faith (adolescents in the National Study of Youth and Religion mirrored their parents' patterns of religious devotion—or lack thereof—to a profound degree).[24] When young people contribute to worship or offer creative venues for reconciliation or service, the church is not only less anachronistic to participation-oriented teenagers; we are also far more faithful to the Christian community's call to all of us to bring our offerings to God.

> The church, by definition, is a participatory community; in some ways, our best preparation for participatory culture as adults is to simply be the Christian community Christ calls us to be, a community where every gift is exercised to its fullest for the glory of God.

On the other hand, proficiency in participatory culture quickly overwhelms those of us who do not think of ourselves as "natives" to such a culture. Yet the church, by definition, is a participatory community; in some ways, our best preparation for participatory culture as adults is to simply be the Christian community Christ calls us to be, a community where every gift is exercised to its fullest for the glory of God. Becoming familiar with the native culture of young people is always important, the way learning the language of another culture is important; it honors those who speak it. But more important still, to young people and to Jesus Christ, is to be the church, people who participate in God's re-creation of culture—whether we know how to use iMovie or not.

Choosing Life: Discerning Vocation with Young People

Suzanne is a bright, attractive young adult and an aeronautical engineer working at Boeing. We sat down for coffee at Starbucks one Saturday, where I congratulated her on her new promotion. She looked down and smiled. "I guess that's what's on my mind," she said. She went on to explain that she was rising quickly at work, gaining new responsibilities with a steady increase in pay. Then she looked at me and said, "I have been praying and thinking. I appreciate the recognition and the good salary at work. What I am wondering is if this is it—if I am really doing what God created me to do."

Suzanne was a child of the church. She grew up in a faithful family, worshiped every Sunday, loved youth group and went on mission trips and conferences. In college, she was part of the Asian American Campus Fellowship. She led Bible studies and now was a youth group advisor and a deacon. "For awhile now," she said, "my energies have been around school, getting my Master's in engineering. But when I think about doing the work that I am doing—not even for the rest of my life, but just for the next few years—I can't stand it."

As we talked for the next couple of hours, I began to get this sinking feeling in the pit of my stomach. I remembered when she graduated from high school as an honors student. I remembered when she graduated from college magna cum laude. I remembered when she gained admission to the competitive Master's degree program in aeronautical engineering. I remembered when she got her first job at Boeing. The church had affirmed her with each accomplishment. Then she named my growing discomfort. "You know what I have come to realize?" she said. "I have come to realize that my whole life I have been looking ahead...looking at the next step, the next task. I've never stopped to just listen to God and hear what I am supposed to be doing right now—not next, but right now. And I guess I am a little surprised because I don't remember anyone at church ever asking me to do that. I mean, isn't that what church is supposed to be about? Helping you find out what God wants you to be and do with your life?" That's when I almost lost my latte.

> Christ's call to us is remarkably straightforward: "Follow me."

One of the best known definitions of "vocation as call" comes from Christian poet Frederick Buechner, who says, "The place God calls you to is the place where your deep gladness and the world's deep hunger meet."[25] In truth, vocation is much simpler than this. The root for the word *vocation* is the Latin *vocare*, which is the verb "to call." But Christ's call to us is remarkably straightforward: "Follow me." What Christian young people want to know is: How? Where? To do what? (all of which are moving targets where Jesus is concerned). We want to know what God wants us to do *as* we follow Jesus—which usually means, what *work* God wants us to do—and the truth is that this just isn't a subject God weighs in on at all. Plumbers and pastors and parents and policemen and topiary specialists are equally delightful to God. What matters in Christian tradition is not the work we do, but the lives we live—and whether our work helps or distracts us from following Jesus. What Suzanne really wanted to know was whether being an engineer at Boeing would help her delight in, or distract her from, following Jesus.

Today the most common understanding of *vocation* refers to one's paid work. This is a secular understanding, not a theological one. You hear it in phrases like "vocational training" and "vocational school" or "vocational counseling." Sometimes we contrast *vocation* (paid work) with *avocation* (things outside of work that we do because we delight in them)—which only reinforces the idea that our *vocation* has to do with work and career. Some traditions turn this understanding upside down; Roman Catholics give *vocation* a distinctly religious connotation, referring to particular roles in church leadership (i.e., priests, monks, or nuns). Protestants—and teenagers—may use the term more broadly as a synonym for "calling," which generally means a subjective "feeling" that certain work suits them.

Perhaps that is why catechized adolescents often think that receiving God's calling is (a) a miraculous event (burning bush, anyone?) and (b) unlikely to happen to them. In truth, discerning our vocation is a lifelong process with dramatic results but a lot less day-to-day drama. Key to this process is a theological worldview that says we somehow participate in God's activity in the world by responding to God's call. Christian tradition understands all aspects of life as holy, even the mundane. (Martin Luther said that the labor of a cobbler and of a preacher are equally valued by God, if each is undertaken in faith.) So the idea of vocation infuses all of life with theological significance.

This theological understanding is important because it helps us discern what is and is not part of our God-given vocation. Some activities—stealing or violence toward ourselves or another, for instance—must be viewed as outside of God's will for our lives. Further, whether we talk about a general calling that is large and lifelong, or particular callings that are more specific and time bound, God is the one who calls. We do not call ourselves nor do we call each other. Familiarizing adolescents with qualities of God's call helps them distinguish between competing voices in their lives: Which voice is from my parents, wanting me to succeed? Which voice is from my culture, wanting me to conform? Which voice is from Christ, wanting me to flourish? Christian tradition suggests that discerning an authentic, divine call involves the following:

• *Dependence and relationship.* You are not in this alone; discerning a calling is not simply up to you. The community of believers who know you and love you exist to help you discern your call.

• *Gratitude to God.* Humility is an essential trait in pursuing a God-given vocation. Divine calls are not graded; some are not better or worse than others. God calls all of us to follow Jesus, and to build up the church in gratitude for God's amazing love, shown to us in Jesus Christ.

• *Obligation.* There is much concern these days about a growing sense of entitlement and privilege among young people. Helping young people recognize their grateful obligation to God deflates this tendency. This obligation does not put our salvation at risk; rather, it is a posture of gratitude, of being "beholden," a willingness to allow an other (or Other) to place a claim on us.

• *Meaning.* Ultimately, human beings are meaning-makers. We are made to seek meaning, which is what makes us human, and what leads us to seek God. A key task of vocation is to find purposeful work, to contribute to the world in a way that transcends our own pleasure or growth. Suzanne was on that search. Truthfully, we are all on that search.

For these reasons, practical theologian Brian Mahan reminds us that vocation is less about discovering our occupation and more about uncovering our preoccupations.[26] Because adolescents are at an extraordinary time in their lives, looking for their place in the world—and because they do not hear the theological language of God's calling anywhere else in their lives, not at school, not in the wider culture, and increasingly not at home—a critical emerging competency for youth ministry leaders is helping our young people discern God's call.

Benedict of Nursia, Youth Guy

Pope St. Gregory (540–604) wrote that if anyone wants to know about St. Benedict of Nursia's character and life, they should read the *Rule* that Benedict wrote to instruct the brothers how to live together.[27] Fifteen hundred years after Benedict's death in 547 C.E., Benedictine orders all over the world still depend on his "little rule for beginners." It contains directions for all aspects of the monastic life: from establishing the abbot as superior, arranging psalms for prayers, and correcting faults, to details of clothing and the proper amount of food and drink. Benedict believed that the love of Christ comes before all else, and clearly recognized the frail nature of human beings, encouraging even the abbot to "distrust his own frailty."

What we don't always realize about St. Benedict is that he was a youth minister: his work as an abbot included overseeing the youngest people in the monastery's care, who were boys—children and teenagers—given by their parents to be brought up as monks.[28] According to Pope St. Gregory, Benedict literally worked miracles with youth, raising a boy from the dead who had been crushed by an overturned wall (tradition has it that Benedict raised him and sent him back to work).[29] Benedict's *Rule* insists on including the youngest monks in the community's deliberations, because "the Lord often reveals what is best to the youngest."[30] So Benedict's rules are not only helpful for youth ministers because of their clarity and practicality; they also come from a place of deep affinity for the work we do. In many ways, our leadership with young people resembles Benedict's leadership of the abbey—which means that Benedict's second rule, on the qualifications of the abbot, include instructions that youth ministers can take to heart:[31]

- *Remember the One you represent.* Benedict calls upon leaders to remember first that you represent Christ since, like Christ was among his disciples, you are addressed as "abbot," a derivative of father. Therefore, all that you teach and command must comply with Christ's own teachings and commandments.
- *Remember to whom you are accountable.* An ongoing theme in his rules, Benedict calls upon leaders to remember that ultimately they bear responsibility to God for those whom God has entrusted to their care. Leaders are like shepherds who care for their sheep just as Christ was the Good Shepherd.
- *Remember how you are to guide and teach.* The best way to lead and to teach is by example more than by words. If you want it to be done, show them by doing it yourself. In the same way, if you do not want them to do something, then you should not do it.
- *Remember how you are to treat others.* Do not play favorites and do not act as if you are a better person than those whom you lead. The only way the abbot should be found better is in good works and humility.
- *Remember how your people best learn.* Benedict also calls upon leaders to remember that each person learns in different ways. Some respond best to verbal encouragement, others learn best by doing. Benedict says the abbot must know the learners well enough to adjust his teachings appropriately.
- *Remember what is expected of you.* Since as the leader more is entrusted to you and because you hold the place of Christ, more is expected of you. Live your life accordingly.
- *Remember to keep the important things central to your life.* Benedict tells the abbot to not show "too great concern for the fleeting and the temporal things." The challenge is to not be distracted from the primary task of glorifying Christ and caring for souls.

> We need neither romanticize nor be naïve to the responsibility we bear as leaders in youth ministry.

Benedict closes his discussion on the Qualities of the Abbot with yet another reminder, that "anyone undertaking the charge of souls must be ready to account for them...and indeed for his own as well." Clearly Benedict felt the weight of leadership profoundly—and there is great wisdom in this for us all. It was Jesus himself who warned his disciples: "If any of you put a stumbling block before one of these little ones who believe in me, it would be better for you if a great millstone were fastened around your neck and you were drowned in the depth of the sea" (Matthew 18:6). We need neither romanticize nor be naïve to the responsibility we bear as leaders in youth ministry. It seems fitting, then, to end this chapter where we started: with the reminder that we are still learning, and with Paul's message to Timothy ringing in our ears: Leadership in any of these competencies will show best through both words and example. Pay close attention to your own self, and to your own growth, and continue on, for by doing this, you will save both yourself and your hearers.

Further Reading on Themes in This Chapter

Apter, Terri. *The Myth of Maturity.* New York: W. W. Norton, 2001.

Benedict. *The Rule of St. Benedict,* ed. Timothy Fry. New York: Vintage Spiritual Classics, 1998.

Dykstra, Robert. *Counseling Troubled Youth.* Louisville, KY: Westminster/John Knox Press, 1997. For Dykstra's thoughts relating his work to youth ministry, see his lectures on www.ptsem.edu/iym.

Elkind, David. *All Grown Up and No Place to Go,* Revised edition. Cambridge, MA: Perseus Books, 1998.

Gregory, Pope St., I, and Terrence Kardong. *The Life of St. Benedict.* Collegeville, MN: The Order of St. Benedict, 2009.

John of the Cross. *The Dark Night of the Soul.* Grand Rapids: Christian Classical Ethereal Library, 1999.

King, Mike. *Presence-Centered Youth Ministry: Guiding Students into Spiritual Formation.* Downer's Grove, IL: InterVarsity, 2006.

Long, Thomas G. *Beyond the Worship Wars: Building Vital and Faithful Worship.* Herndon, VA: Alban Institute, 2001.

Mahan, Brian. *Forgetting Ourselves on Purpose: Vocation and the Ethics of Ambition.* San Francisco: Jossey-Bass, 2002.

Palmer, Parker. *A Hidden Wholeness.* San Francisco: Jossey-Bass, 2004.

CHAPTER SIX

A MATURING DISCIPLINE

We must no longer be children, tossed to and fro and blown about by every wind of doctrine, by people's trickery, by their craftiness in deceitful scheming. But speaking the truth in love, we must grow up in every way into him who is the head, into Christ, from whom the whole body, joined and knit together by every ligament with which it is equipped, as each part is working properly, promotes the body's growth in building itself up in love.
—Ephesians 4:14-16

You may strive to be like them, but seek not to make them like you....
You are the bows from which your children, as living arrows, are sent forth.
—Kahlil Gibran

I (Kenda) quit my church's youth group during my senior year of high school. The youth group of Grace United Methodist Church—a tiny Ohio farm church where the average age seemed to me to be about nine-hundred—operated as a close-knit band of church malcontents. We thought of ourselves as the "progressives" in our stodgy congregation, if you could call being "progressive" the fact that we sponsored dances and helped with Bible school and raised money for trips to Kings Island. In other words, we looked pretty much like our parents, except that we listened to Chicago and Amy Grant instead of Johnny Cash and the Gaithers. I don't remember playing a single icebreaker (we had known each other since primary choir) or breaking into small groups (on a good night, there were eight of us, scattered between sixth and twelfth grades). At the helm was a balding, sun-burned dairy farmer named "Trox," a good-natured soul who inexplicably heard God calling him to lead us—a role we considered more or less expendable.

By senior year, I was done.

I remember telling Trox it was because I was tired of babysitting younger, rowdier kids who were uninterested in heavy-duty "discussions" about God. That, of course, was only half true. What was also true was that my girlfriends at school had invited me to their "cool" youth group downtown.

"You would *love* Cindy and Nick," Ellen and Lisa cooed, referring to the hip husband-and-wife team who conducted a youth ministry four times larger than ours, thanks to an ecumenical arrangement between several downtown churches. They played games out of the *Ideas* series, Nick sang lead in a rock band, and last summer Cindy had taken some teenagers to Appalachia for something I had never heard of: a "mission trip." Their cool factor was off the charts.

"What do you do the rest of the time?" I asked them at school one Monday.

"Well," Ellen confided, edging a little closer to my locker, "last night we talked about orgasms. They asked us what we wanted to be doing when we died. And when it was Cindy's turn, she said she wanted to die during an orgasm."

I was hooked.

That was 1977. Youth ministry was an outpost of congregational life, vaguely approved by pastors and tended almost exclusively by generous volunteers. Adolescence seemed to fit neatly between the ages of twelve and eighteen; the first Gallup Youth Survey, piloted in 1977, focused exclusively on high school students. Mike Yaconelli and Wayne Rice's fledgling Youth Specialties company had moved out of Yaconelli's garage to join ranks with Zondervan three years earlier, but most youth leaders had never heard of them. Thom Schultz was still typing a little rag called *Group Magazine* on a typewriter in a spare   room.

In 1977, youth ministries in Catholic, Orthodox, and mainline churches were still regaining their footing from nearly a decade earlier, when the World Council of Churches had expressed concern over the "youth revolt" of a generation "disenchanted" with religion.[1] The National Catholic Youth Organization, consisting mostly of priests and nuns, had been reshaped into the National Federation of Catholic Youth Ministry, a professional organization made up of lay youth ministers. Mainline denominations' youth ministry offices were also experiencing a brief lull, unaware that many of them were on borrowed time. The World Council of Churches' recommendation that churches integrate young people into the mission of the church as a whole was beginning to be interpreted by American denominations as permission to slash denominational funds and personnel dedicated to youth ministry. The year 1977 was the calm before a storm of budget cuts just ahead, from which denominational youth organizations would not recover.

While I was attending our town's ecumenical youth group, one of youth ministry's true prophets, Charles Foster, was teaching Christian education and youth ministry at a seminary just five minutes up the road. Unfortunately, in 1977 youth ministry was a marginalized enterprise in seminaries as well. Seminaries tended to view youth ministry as the pesky stepchild of Christian education, a haven for immature theology students and largely irrelevant for everyone else. Years later, I learned about Foster's work through pastors I admired because they prioritized young people and approached youth ministry with uncharacteristic thoughtfulness—pastors who inevitably, I learned, had once had Foster for class.

Youth Ministry Comes of Age (Maybe)

More than three decades later, ministry with young people has exploded as a form of professional ministry, and consequently as a field of study in theological education, as churches struggle to respond to the shifts in culture and in adolescence that we have discussed in these pages. As we have noted, the postmodern age calls for serious reflection on ministry in general, which has created more demand for theologically prepared youth leaders. The early twenty-first century has seen youth ministry's first conscious attempts at self-reflection as an interdisciplinary field of study, profoundly shaping how we prepare leaders for children's, youth, young adult, and family ministries—all of which huddle under the "youth ministry" umbrella in explicit or implicit ways.

Youth ministry tends to serve as a galvanizing force, a place where theological factions and disenchanted churchgoers can come together out of a common and often urgent desire to "hand on the faith" to the young people we love—which most of us understand to mean inculcating a way of life that reflects our own religious values, for better and for worse. Since 1977 we have added enormously to the body of literature surrounding youth and young adult ministry. As the field has both expanded and consolidated, the signs of an emerging discipline are among us: a common language of specialization, a cadre of varied professionals, educational curricula and pedagogical self-awareness, and the beginnings of a research presence.[2]

> Youth ministry tends to serve as a galvanizing force, a place where theological factions and disenchanted churchgoers can come together out of a common and often urgent desire to "hand on the faith" to the young people we love.

If you are the kind of youth minister who loves kids but has no interest in the political terrain of youth ministry education, now is a good time to skip ahead. (We'll meet up again in the last paragraph of this section—or, if you're anxious to get started changing the church, jump to Appendix A and start developing "faith assets" in your congregation.) The research reported in the appendix would not have been possible apart from changes in the field of youth ministry itself, which this chapter summarizes. If you are in youth ministry for the long haul or if you prepare others for youth ministry leadership—or if you just worry about the oddball nature of our vocation in general—this chapter will help you map the ways in which youth ministry is "growing up."

Field or Discipline?

In the academy, "fields" are aptly named. They are the functional equivalent of the American frontier in 1862, when the Homestead Act gave 160 acres to anyone who would improve the land. A field's boundaries are largely in the eye of the beholder; fields are interdisciplinary to the point of cross-pollination. Belonging has less to do with your terminal degree than with whether you have earned your chops as a homesteader, noticeably improving the area. Fields create trouble for universities, which are used to dividing up the educational landscape into departments and majors. Fields have wild patches, unknown species, and lots of healthy outliers—unidentified sprouts around the edges that sometimes work their way into the middle. Students, faculty, and research in fields are hard to pin down, and nobody is quite sure what they're up to. Research may be wide rather than deep (after all, there's a lot to plough). ˉ

> A field's boundaries are largely in the eye of the beholder; fields are interdisciplinary to the point of cross-pollination.

"Disciplines," by contrast, are fields that have been tamed into gardens. They are much narrower than fields and controlled in what they grow. They are neatly bordered, carefully tended, have been fertilized by long traditions, and usually have gates with special keys (Ph.D.s or other official credentials). There are always a few people who jump the fence to get in, but most people behave respectably in a discipline (hence the word). Disciplines are nice to have around in higher education. Since students, faculty, and research cohere, they can be productive in ways that are recognized and understood by other disciplines. There are very few surprises from one season to the next; this year's discoveries lay the foundations for next year's crop.

We think of disciplines as being static, but in fact they evolve with a changing society; nursing, library science, information technology, biogenetic engineering, and film were all professional "fields" fifty years ago but now have disciplinary status and academic majors in major universities. Whenever a field moves toward becoming a discipline, there are gains to be had and risks to be incurred—especially in practical theology. All practical areas of inquiry struggle with boundaries, and theology adds slippery criteria like "faithfulness" that are hard to assess. On the one hand, if youth ministry adhered to the criteria of academic specialization, our future research would build on our current research, gaining new refinement and depth, and would be packaged in an empirical language that our colleagues could understand. Our thinking would be complex but not scattered and our students would be consistently trained and predictably capable. On the other hand, academic specialization could make our intellectual inquiry professionally self-centered and theologically shallow, simply because, as specialists, we no longer need the wisdom of other fields the way we once did. In social science, emerging disciplines readily submit themselves to the intellectual, behavioral, and social criteria of the academy. But in the interdisciplinary world of youth ministry, *spiritual maturity* is paramount— and notoriously hard to assess.

Most of us don't spend much time thinking about the evolution of youth ministry as a field or a discipline (and let me say at this point, you will live a long and happy life if you choose to ignore these debates altogether). At the same time, the effectiveness and longevity of youth ministry owes much to our academic maturity. Youth ministry's entrance into the academic world affects the research, literature, practices, and teaching available to churches. Yet to call youth ministry a "discipline" at all—a term that generally means we can locate it in a particular body of academic literature—suggests that pastoral effectiveness with young people (with all people) comes from mastering a discrete body of knowledge and from becoming adept at the skills related to it. It implies that we are "masters" of divinity—and that, as we pointed out in chapter 5, is an arrogant and impossible claim.

Specialists or Generalists?

"Specialization" is a hallmark of modernity.[3] With the printing press came an explosion of popular knowledge—too much to be mastered by any individual—and the culture of the "expert" was born. By the late twentieth century, professionalization meant becoming a specialist. Teachers prioritized one developmental level at a time—primary or secondary education? Colleges had majors—literature or business? Professional students chose specialty areas—pediatrics or gastroenterology? Tax law or litigation? Elementary or secondary school certification? We learned to privilege these specialists, believing that the depth of their knowledge means that they know "more" than generalists do.

In fact, this is true only at the technical level; what *is* true is that specialists know *differently* than generalists do. Being a specialist, like being a generalist, activates some intellectual capacities and disables others. What separates brilliant specialists from brilliant generalists is their epistemology (the nature of their knowledge); at issue is not how *much* they know, but the *way* they know, and the kinds of things they pay attention to. Specialists focus intensely on specific bodies of knowledge, mastering technical concepts, vocabularies, and nuances unavailable to most of us. Generalists, on the other hand, focus on *integrating* knowledge from *several* fields in a usable and coherent way.

Generalists do not, as a rule, become virtuosos on a single instrument; instead, they become innovators, improvisationalists, people energized by a measure of uncertainty and mess. True generalists are fluent in multiple discourses and cultural styles, and metaphorically "play several instruments" (perhaps not at concert quality). They pursue a disciplined eclecticism, borrowing widely but staying true to a single purpose. A generalist musician, for example—let's say an exceptional music teacher or a talented composer—cheerfully pilfers a huge repertoire of musical forms to memorably teach Bach's "Well-Tempered Clavier" or to compose a score that perfectly suits the *Twilight* series. We do not admire them for their faultless performances (Peter Schickele, a.k.a. "P.D.Q. Bach," purposefully builds mistakes into his concerts, and almost everything we hear from legendary composer John Williams is produced). We admire them for the genius ways their creations perfectly suit the occasions for which they are made.

Youth ministry—which, as we have noted, now contains a number of specialty areas of its own—came of age in this culture of specialization. Indeed, it is almost impossible for educated people today not to specialize in something. Generalists like Schikele and Williams are, after all, *musicians* (very accomplished ones), though their refusal to limit themselves to a single field or set of skills within their discipline accounts for much of their distinctiveness. Or take our family's general practitioner. His specialty is sports medicine (if you knew our household's total ineptitude for sports you would find this hilarious). But five minutes in "Dr. Lev's" office sees as many octogenarians as teenagers streaming in and out of his care. He attends conferences on cholesterol and cancer treatment, follows acupuncture and prescribes flaxseed. His effectiveness as a physician is based, not on his specialty, but on his medical *agility*. Over the years, Dr. Lev has developed a medical imagination, enabling him to move back and forth between many subjects and skills to treat *the particular patient before him*, the one dangling her legs over the edge of the examining table, awaiting a diagnosis and treatment plan that Dr. Lev has matched to the idiosyncrasies of being *her*.

The Risks of Intellectual Maturity

Despite calls to reclaim pastoral agility as a goal of theological education, most churches buy into the paradigm of expertise that dominates our culture.[4] When church leaders began to ask, "How can we improve the quality of ministry available to children, youth, emerging adults, and their families?" our first instinct was to develop "experts."

Today youth ministry majors and seminary specializations are increasingly common; producing "experts" is a booming business in youth ministry leadership formation. Graduate degrees in youth ministry frequently exempt students from other theological coursework to make room for classes that focus on the specialty skills of youth ministry. Continuing education events and publishers approach youth ministers as a niche market, assuming (correctly) that most church heads of staff will "opt out" if the brochure mentions youth ministry. Tapping into our culture's infatuation with experts—people who have contributed mightily to "raising the bar" for churches' ministries with young people—has improved youth ministry's professional status and solidified its reputation as a specialty ministry.

Such specialization, however, comes at a price. It makes it easier to separate youth ministry from ministry as a whole, creating the impression that adolescent discipleship formation is the province of "experts" rather than the responsibility of the entire faith community. A parallel narrowing occurs in scholarship too. Communication scholar Brenda Dervin warns that, when a field gains the status of another major subject and discipline, it also loses its healthy roots in basic disciplines (sociology, political science, linguistics, literature, and in our case, theology) while becoming more and more dependent on empirical and practical aspects of reality.[5] In short, we become more inward and insular, which undermines the vocation—indeed, the identity—of the church.

> Specialization makes it easier to separate youth ministry from ministry as a whole, creating the impression that adolescent discipleship formation is the province of "experts" rather than the responsibility of the entire faith community.

To become *less* integrated with general fields that inform the church's general ministry would be an ironic step backward for youth ministry, since much of what has motivated us to study youth ministry in the first place has been our dissatisfaction with young people's marginalization in the church, illustrated by the still-popular "the one-eared Mickey Mouse" model of ministry (see chapter 3). Much of the literature that now exists for children's, youth, young adult, and family ministries urges us to integrate young people more fully into the relationally rich practices of the congregation, even while offering teenagers important peer relationships as they grapple with faith.

There is little question that, thanks to the corporate structure of most North American congregations, youth ministry *is* a specialty profession—and the ability to specialize in a number of forms of youth ministry is one of the marks of its emerging maturity. The 2005 National Study of Youth and Religion found that 30 percent of (U.S.) teenagers studied came from congregations with a full-time youth minister (Figure 5.1); outside the U.S., full-time professional youth ministry leadership is extremely rare. In 2001, the "Transforming Youth Ministry" study reported a "mushrooming number of training organizations" in youth ministry, dedicated to supporting both volunteers and professionals through colleague networks and formal and informal youth ministry education.[6] In short, we are a far more sophisticated lot when it comes to ministry with young people than we were a generation ago, if we measure the maturity of youth ministry by academic standards.

Congregations with designated youth minister, full-time (U.S.) 30%
Conservative Protestants 44%
Mainline Protestants 37%
Black Protestants 41%
Roman Catholic 21%
Jewish 21%
Latter Day Saints 7%

Figure 5.1
Full-Time Youth Ministers (by denomination)[17]

But there is more to the story. Youth ministers are called to a pastoral vocation that exceeds a single specialty area. *How* we know matters as much as *what* we know. The hallmarks of pastoral identity are not only the depth of our knowledge but also the *shape of our lives and our imaginations,* our ability to envision how to serve Christ in situations that call for holy discernment, leadership, and action, and how to help young people do the same. If anything can prepare us for ministry with young people in the twenty-first century, it is more likely our ability to exercise a pastoral imagination than our ability to plan a sexuality retreat or Youth Sunday.

Pastoral Imagination:
Job #1 for Preparing Youth Ministers

To say that youth ministry is a pastoral vocation is to suggest that our work must be gauged according to pastoral criteria. Chief among the excellences of pastoral ministry is what Aristotle called *phronesis*, or the art of practical wisdom. Phronesis makes us agile practitioners who can tack back and forth between deep wells of knowledge, imagination, and courage to improvise faithfully in the moment calling for Christian action. A pastoral imagination, contends practical theologian Craig Dykstra, is

> the capacity to perceive the "more" in what is already before us. It is the capacity to see beneath the surface, to get beyond the obvious and the merely conventional, to note the many aspects of any particular thing or situation, to attend to the deep meanings of things.[8]

According to Dykstra, many pastors hear the call to develop a pastoral imagination as a daunting, discouraging, nigh-impossible task. Dykstra counters by citing British theologian David Ford for whom Christian faith is a matter of being overwhelmed. Ford describes Jesus Christ as the "embodiment of multiple overwhelmings": his immersion in the Jordan River, his temptation in the desert, his agony at Gethsemane, his betrayal, torture and crucifixion, dying as he cried, "My God, my God, why have you forsaken me?" Then came the resurrection, "the most disorienting and transformative overwhelming of all."[9] In baptism, observes Ford, we join Christ in a life of multiple overwhelmings. Christians are shaped by being overwhelmed.[10]

Such a view of Christian formation may ring true for people in youth ministry (who are overwhelmed most of the time), but it is not for the faint of heart. The good news, Dykstra reminds us, is that pastoral imagination is not an achievement but a gift; even our ability to receive this gift is by the power of divine grace:

> At the very heart of pastoral ministry lies the good news of a power that is not ours, a labor that ultimately is not our work, a grace that is not of our doing. The way is not so much one of earnest striving as it is "the 'active passivity' of letting ourselves be embraced, or letting ourselves be fed the food and drink that can energize us for" ministry.[11]

So how are we to assess our effectiveness in a "discipline" that is less the result of education than of being swept into the life of God, who calls us to become not simply experts, but vessels of suffering love. After all, we study youth ministry, not for the sake of advancing a discipline, but for the sake of advancing Christ. We are, by necessity, specialists who are evaluated by standards of academic excellence—standards that have given the church much needed rigor in our reflection on young people. But we are also pastors, in need of pastoral imagination and

114

interdisciplinary agility. Above all, we are Christians, committed to a counterintuitive community whose signature practices embody self-giving love and willing vulnerability before God and others, and whose integrity as a discipline is bound to virtues like collaboration and generosity, holy friendship and humility, as well as to as much depth in intellectual content as our eardrums can handle.

These standards directly challenge the highly specialized, individualistic, achievement-focused, competitive norms common to modern academia, which is one reason emerging disciplines like youth ministry education or adolescent discipleship formation do not "fit" into academic categories. Yet Christ calls us to attend to these pastoral variables, even as we become more proficient at mastering a recognized body of scholarly research. Is it possible to do both? Can youth ministry combine academic standards with the imitation of Christ? Can the practices and virtues of the Christian community that we covet for the young people in our care also characterize youth ministry as an emerging academic discipline?

Practical Theology: The Parent Discipline of Youth Ministry

Maybe. Much depends on whether we are willing to see ourselves as a practical theological discipline instead of as an "enriched" educational, psychological, or organizational one. Practical theology entails prayerful reflection on Christian life, and on those contexts where God's action intersects with the church's actions. Practical theology is concerned with how God reaches for human beings through concrete situations, and the concrete ways in which humans reach back.[12]

> Practical theology is concerned with how God reaches for human beings through concrete situations, and the concrete ways in which humans reach back.

1. Practical theology implies that youth ministry is theological.

To call youth ministry a form of practical theology sets it apart from most academic disciplines in at least four ways that distinguish all forms of practical theology. First, youth ministry is practical *theology*, so we can infer that the church's work with children, youth, emerging adults, and their families has *pastoral and theological significance*. It matters to the church. It matters to the kingdom of God. It influences the ways in which we imitate Christ—and because it is *prayerful* reflection on Christian action, doing youth ministry as practical theology *is* a way to imitate Christ. Youth ministry as practical theology simply cannot be reduced to either a social science or a liberal art.

2. Practical theology implies that youth ministry is interdisciplinary.

At the same time, to understand youth ministry as practical theology means that our work is *informed* by social science and the liberal arts. Practical theology is *interdisciplinary* (as well as cross-disciplinary, intradisciplinary, and so on). Youth ministry cannot be reduced to a single subject area. Practical theology honors the tension between specialists and generalists, but no one in ministry—least of all ministry with young people—can afford to build "silos" that separate youth, or youth leaders, from the rest of the church, or that separate the church from the rest of the world. While educational theory is essential to our work, assuming youth ministry is a "subarea" of educational ministry profoundly distorts the reality. The church's work with young people is a form of pastoral ministry, defined not by the task but by the *flock*—a flock that requires us to be thoughtful theologians-in-traffic, careful biblical exegetes, deft deliverers of pastoral care, skillful communicators who are keenly aware of community and interpersonal dynamics, and so on.

3. Practical theology implies that youth ministry reflects on God through Christian action.

In addition, youth ministry as practical theology offers a *way of knowing*—and a way of knowing *God*—that is distinctive. As I mentioned earlier, practical theology is concerned with those human situations in which God's action and human actions intersect. Technically, it is a "performative" theological discipline, which means we *do* things to know God, as well as think about them—and we assume that through these human actions, God does things as well. Practical theology's deepest truths are embodied truths, which is why Kierkegaard compared the Christian life to swimming: you can watch from on shore, admire the strokes, appreciate swimming's strength and grace. But eventually, if you want to understand swimming, you're going to have to get in the water.[13] In the same way, we can study prayer, admire prayers, appreciate people who pray—but we will never truly appreciate prayer until we *pray*. The practices of Christian life that identify us as Jesus' followers are practical theology's primary "texts." As practical theology, youth ministry focuses on practices that allow us to perceive God with and through young people.

This way of knowing is deeply embedded in Christian tradition. Christianity did not emerge as a collection of "great thoughts about Jesus." It emerged as a distinctive way of life that Jesus' followers eventually had to explain to newcomers. By retelling the stories and teachings of Jesus, and by reflecting on those stories' significance for the community, "doctrine" emerged. For example, today we tend to teach young people about the Eucharist *before* they participate in it. But if we lived in the first or second century, we would have saved this instruction until *after* newly baptized Christians took their first communion. Ancient church leaders believed that only by participating in the mysteries of Christ's presence in the bread and wine was it possible to truly recognize Christ's presence in them. In many ways, youth ministry intuitively continues this tradition, immersing young people in the "way" of Christian life, making connections between these practices and the stories and teachings of Jesus as we go.

4. Practical theology assumes youth ministry is particular.

A fourth way youth ministry as practical theology stands out from other theoretical disciplines is its emphasis on the *particular*. Practical theology listens intently to discoveries drawn from other disciplines but does not pretend to generate universal truths or one-size-fits-all practices of ministry. Like all practical wisdom, youth ministry starts on the ground, not with a theory, but with a teenager—let's call her Katt—who is seventeen and plays the piano and lives with her grandmother and her yellow cat. Unless we are too new to know better, we do not impose a "theory" of youth ministry on Katt, indebted as we are to theories of human development, sociology, education, and even other theological disciplines that help us understand Katt and her world. Katt pushes back, challenging these broad theories with her own human uniqueness. The theoretical literature is not irrelevant, but it is not universal either. Christian theology meets every adolescent's one-of-a-kind story with God's own one-of-a-kind story, the particularity of Jesus—a thirty-three-year-old Galilean who worked as a carpenter and whom we proclaim was God-made-flesh.

> Christian theology meets every adolescent's one-of-a-kind story with God's own one-of-a-kind story, the particularity of Jesus.

Discipling a Discipline

Locating youth ministry in the parent discipline of practical theology is fairly straightforward. Establishing it as a discipline in its own right is more difficult, especially if pastoral imagination serves as one of our norms. In some ways, of course, the term "discipline" exactly describes what we do. The word comes from the word "disciple"; throughout most of human history, education has been a discipline because it meant becoming a disciple of a master teacher. Humanist educators during the Enlightenment decoupled the "disciplines" from their religious roots, but the church's view that all knowledge comes from God, and that all learning should prepare us to serve Christ, suggests that for youth ministry to mature into a "discipline" is exactly right.

Yet so far we have no academic standard for assessing research and scholarship on the basis of discipleship, in youth ministry or any other field. This is partly because as an intellectual field, the study of youth ministry is too new for any one approach to dominate our scholarship. But it is also because it is unclear whether any one approach *should* dominate youth ministry scholarship. Like other so-called "emerging disciplines" (e.g., information technology, criminal justice, women's studies) youth ministry's interdisciplinary nature makes it difficult to evaluate. Whose standards should we use? Systematic theology deeply informs our work but misses youth ministry's performative dimensions. The arts provide models for assessing performance, but youth ministry is far less subjective; relating to a teenager is not a matter of taste, but a matter of fidelity to the gospel. Social and hard sciences offer methods for empirical research—but insert God into the equation, and science suddenly gets skittish. IBM vice president Gina Poole puts it succinctly:

> New fields of study, especially those requiring interdisciplinary involvement, are sometimes perceived as too "soft." But as we've seen with computer science and software engineering, acceptance is a matter of time. Higher education doesn't turn on a dime. It took nearly two decades from the time the first computer science course was offered before the first doctorate in computer science was granted in 1965.[14]

If youth ministry is a form of practical theological reflection, then we must evaluate our maturity as a field of study by posing questions that underscore our commitment to theology, and that acknowledge norms of interdisciplinarity, practice, and particularity. These questions tend to appeal to postmodern scholars, who are at home with a certain amount of ambiguity and who welcome eclecticism, community, embodiment, and context. Taken as a whole, these questions also have great integrity for ministry itself. However, they are not usually the criteria that modern institutions—especially universities—use to evaluate academic discourse. Clearly, we must incorporate the best of social scientific research and disciplined reflection at all levels of ministry with young people. Yet Christians maintain that spiritual, ecclesial, and theological maturity matter as well—and when forced to choose, these qualities matter *more*.

"New fields of study, especially those requiring interdisciplinary involvement, are sometimes perceived as too 'soft.'"—Gina Pool

---

Report Card for an Emerging Discipline

I have some reluctance about calling youth ministry a "discipline" (hence the quotation marks), despite its clear movement in that direction.[15] Since emerging disciplines never fit neatly into existing criteria for academic research (indeed, this is what makes them emerge), the question we must ask, as youth ministry moves from an interest area into an "emerging discipline," is whether youth ministry as practical theology can be researched and understood on its own terms. Can we evaluate our academic work according to the difference it makes—or fails to make—for a fifteen-year-old girl in Poughkeepsie? In the academy, disciplines tend to "emerge" (meaning, a field starts becoming tamed into a garden) when six markers can be discerned:[16]

1. *A common mission* that unites persons committed to addressing common needs and serving a common purpose;
2. *A common language* that gradually takes root among those in the field that allows them to identify common themes, causes, and objectives in their work;

3. *A cadre of professionals* who work in this field of interest at varied levels (for example, congregational middle high leaders, campus ministers, para-church staff members, Christian camp directors), and who are connected and served through professional networks (for example, professional guilds);

4. *Academic programs* that seek to prepare people for this mission through a specialized curriculum that fosters fluency in the field's specific language (coursework and degree programs in youth and young adult ministries), and that fosters professional participation in the larger "parent discipline" (practical theology);

5. *Academic research* emerging from this field of inquiry (the primary example of this in Western universities is the presence of doctoral dissertations);

6. *Distinctive pedagogies* that particularly suit the field of inquiry's identity and character (e.g., residencies for medical students, travel abroad for foreign language students, lab hours with fruit flies for budding geneticists). (See Figure 5.2.)

Missing from this list, of course, are those indicators that suggest a field's *spiritual* maturity, which we have discussed throughout this chapter. The following pages, therefore, evaluate our theological progress as well—but you may want to apply your own "grading criteria" as we proceed.

A common mission
A common language
A cadre of professionals
Academic programs
Academic research
Distinctive pedagogies

Figure 5.2
Markers of Emerging Disciplines

A Common Mission: Theological Education and Reform

Nature—and academics—abhor a vacuum. Like most new fields of study, the academic study of youth ministry emerged to address a series of "lacks": a lack of quality church leadership for children, teenagers, and young adults and their families; a lack of theological training for current leadership; a lack of research to assess whether anything we are doing makes any difference; a lack of systemic support from congregations or denominations—and a general lack of ecclesial interest on the part of young people themselves, which makes youth ministry a prime place to "test drive" alternative practices and ecclesial visions that may not win adherents from the congregation at large.

By the end of the twentieth century, colleges and seminaries (and, significantly, funders) had begun to identify youth ministry education as a gap they could fill. Armed with grants from the Lilly Endowment (or, rarely, independent funding), schools turned their attention to adolescent discipleship formation. Some of these efforts focused on seminarians and pastors; others focused on practitioners; many focused on teenage leaders themselves.

At the same time, academics and practitioners—concerned about the increasingly dire outlook for congregations generally—began to view youth ministry as a likely venue for initiating change in the church. History indicates that this is not a new role for youth ministry; youth ministry has often served as a kind of protest movement, calling into question practices that, to young people, seem transparently problematic.[17] Christian Endeavor modeled coeducational leadership a generation before women gained the right to vote in the U.S.; Young Life integrated clubs and leadership teams a generation before the civil rights movement. Historian Jon Pahl points out that Christian youth organizations like the Lutheran Walther League, the Catholic Young Christian Workers, Youth for Christ, and numerous African American youth ministries contributed to changing cultural attitudes toward gender, the middle class, media, and civil rights.[18]

> Youth ministry has often served as a kind of protest movement, calling into question practices that, to young people, seem transparently problematic.

To the degree that youth ministry's focus on education and reform is theologically driven (and is not just another defensive measure to shore up church membership), it clearly falls within the domain of practical theology. In fact, youth ministry stands to become even more significant as a context for shaping church leaders like Dietrich Bonhoeffer, Billy Graham, Pope John Paul II, and Bill Hybels of Willow Creek, whose visions of the church were provisionally tested in their days as youth ministers.

COMMON MISSION   Grade: B (needs to clarify theological thesis)

A Common Language: A Conundrum

Over time, emerging disciplines begin to share common terminologies—but youth ministry as a field of study is still in the "Goldilocks" stage, trying out terminology, searching for one that is "just right." What should we call this emerging discipline? We have already noticed that adolescence is a moving target, making the question of who youth ministry addresses very slippery. The phrase "youth ministry" is itself extremely problematic. It ignores youth ministry's relationship to other age groups (e.g., children and emerging adults), only vaguely describes the people it addresses, and in churches is often a code phrase for silliness that belies our current seriousness of purpose. "Youth *and*" designations underscore the interdisciplinary nature of the field but could go on endlessly: youth and young adults, youth and families, youth and mission, youth and discipleship, youth and children (and young adults, and families—and so on).

"Adolescent spiritual formation" sounds more academically respectable, and acknowledges the contributions of developmental theory and other social sciences. Yet each word in the phrase is problematic. Without a clear sense of when adolescence begins and ends, "adolescence" continues to mean one thing to social scientists and another to parents and congregations. "Spiritual" is one of those non-empirical words that bothers academics, and "formation" suggests youth ministry's debt to education, but not to God's transformation. Describing our work functionally might be a solution (e.g., "mission with young people," "discipleship formation with young people," etc.). This tactic clarifies youth ministry's purpose—although, as we have seen, there is not yet consensus on what our mission actually is. Furthermore, it invites another endless list of possibilities; is there any practice of the church that should *not* involve young people? As a matter of practical theology, a common language seems far away, and risks becoming a barrier that artificially narrows youth ministry's scope.

COMMON LANGUAGE   *GRADE: D (works hard, but not progressing)*

A Cadre of Professionals: A Significant Presence

One of the most obvious signs of youth ministry's maturation as a field of study is its increasing professionalization, which we have already discussed at length. Professional youth ministers are not new, though the model of a single professional youth minister leading hordes of young people—the "Pied Piper" image popularized in the 1940s and 1950s, when denominations had huge professional youth ministry staffs—is unrealistic today.[19] In 2005, the average salary of a full-time youth worker in the U.S. was just under $40,000—just under the national average of American workers everywhere. While salaries remain low in youth ministry, they have apparently become high enough that fewer full-time youth workers are moonlighting at second jobs. In 2003 about one in three full-time youth workers (29 percent) had another job outside the church; by 2005, that number dropped to about one in five (17 percent).[20]

Today resources, professional networks, and academic journals have swelled the support systems available to youth ministry specialists, including those called to teach and research youth ministry. Specialty areas have proliferated (e.g., campus ministry, young adult ministry, ministry with young families, senior high and middle high ministry, older elementary ministry, and so on). Doctoral students, housed in parent disciplines like practical theology, education, or sociology—and who increasingly participate in networks facilitated by guilds and peer associations—have begun to focus Ph.D. research on pertinent issues in youth ministry, and some prominent institutions explicitly encourage research in youth ministry in their doctoral programs.[21]

In some ways, professional guilds serve as Rorschach tests for a new field of study's growing pains. Commenting on the 2005 annual meeting of the International Association for the Study of Youth Ministry, beliefnet commentator Tony Jones—then a Ph.D. student in practical theology—observed:

The first generation of youth ministry professors were old and wise youth work-ers who were hired by colleges and seminaries to teach this new discipline of church-based youth work. The second generation, and the bulk of those cur-rently in most positions, hold terminal degrees in the social sciences (sociology, education, anthropology, cultural studies). And now there is an emerging genera-tion of scholars (among which I count myself) who are primarily theologians. Thus, there are social scientists with an interest in theology and theologians with an interest in social science. Both sides have the tendency to get arrogant, yet each side needs the other.[22]

While numerous organizations exist to support the secular study of adoles-cence, only a handful currently support youth ministry's theological interests and those who teach them, or publish academic journals to that end. Some, like the National Federation of Catholic Youth Ministry, focus on training profes-sional youth ministers but also function as networks for teachers, bishops, aca-demics, and researchers who collaborate to improve professional competency in Catholic educational and catechetical organizations. Others, like the Association of Youth Ministry Educators and the International Association for the Study of Youth Ministry, focus on professional development for professors in colleges and seminaries, and leave the training of professional youth minis-ters to entrepreneurial groups like *Group* and *Youth Specialties*, and to an ever-increasing number of continuing education events offered by colleges and seminaries.

CADRE OF PROFESSIONALS   *GRADE: B (has made great strides, enthusiastic contributor in youth ministry discussions, but research is uneven and the relationship between professionalization and faith matu-rity in adolescents remains muddled)*

Academic Programs: Proliferating

As churches began to recognize children's, youth, young adult, and family ministries as legitimate vocational options for pastors and educators, aca-demic programs in youth ministry began to proliferate. "Proliferation" is a relative term; most are small programs located in evangelical undergraduate colleges, with mainline liberal arts institutions and Catholic universities and seminaries are slowly but steadily adding to their number.[23]

Yet the curricular maturation of youth ministry is far from complete. Several problems dog youth ministry education at the curricular level, both in terms of what we teach and who teaches it. Academic programs fill a crit-ical need but fail to address the vast majority of youth workers who are volunteers; what legitimizes these programs is the fact that students who enroll in academic youth ministry programs tend to wield more influence in churches than volunteers, and often train volunteers in various capacities. For this reason, the content of youth ministry curriculum has far-reaching impact. Jack and McRay's research on undergraduate youth ministry education programs (2005) found that students in these programs generally receive a background in biblical and theological studies, augmented by large servings of psychology, sociology, and educational theory, with various ministry courses sprinkled throughout. Yet Jack and McRay's study also revealed a dearth of educational offerings that fostered critical thinking, theological reflection and integration, empirical sophistication, attention to globalization or cultural "others," or pastoral (as opposed to therapeutic) identities among youth ministry graduates.[24]

Despite expanding curricular opportunities, coursework related to youth ministry (like children's ministry and emerging adult ministry) still tends to be "outsourced" to wise professionals instead of taught by regular faculty. This strategy brings great practical wisdom to students but reinforces youth ministry's peripheral status, and many practitioners struggle to strike a balance between praxis and theological reflection. Equally worrisome is the amount of so-called soft money supporting youth ministry in colleges and seminaries. Typically, grant-supported programs (in theological settings as in secular ones) are considered experimental or auxiliary to institutions' core values—nice, but not necessary. Grant money allows for unparalleled creativity—but at the cost of permanency. Soft money tends to create temporary faculty positions and temporary programs, which makes research difficult and faculty influence brief. Most leaders of such programs (typically youth ministers whose entrepreneurial skills have been honed by years of "making do") demonstrate remarkable resourcefulness within such institutional constraints. Yet outsourced and grant-supported youth ministry programs are a double-edged sword. On the one hand, grants have garnered unprecedented academic attention for youth ministry in the early twenty-first century. On the other hand, the temporary nature of grant funding contributes to youth ministry's marginalization in academic settings.

ACADEMIC PROGRAMS　　*GRADE: C+ (Shows vast improvement but has difficulty fully participating in academic discussion)*

Academic Research: A Hopeful Sign

For most of the twentieth century, youth ministers relied on anecdotal evidence to determine the effectiveness of their work with young people. By the 1990s, however, churches began to scrutinize their practices of youth ministry, revealing a paucity of research that could guide them. Youth ministry's first foray into academic research was as a consumer: we borrowed research from secular fields and adapted them for our needs in ministry. Marketing research, psychology, sociology, cultural anthropology, and educational theory all provided invaluable data that helped us understand our work with adolescents. Youth ministers learned to be deft interdisciplinary synthesizers, adept at cross-disciplinary conversations that still allow us to draw, unabashedly, from research in disparate fields for the sake of living out the gospel with teenagers.

> Youth ministry's first foray into academic research was as a consumer: we borrowed research from secular fields and adapted them for our needs in ministry.

While these interdisciplinary skills deepened youth ministry's intellectual work appreciably, we overlooked a significant point: that theology contributes to the interdisciplinary discussion as well, and that youth ministry has its own contributions to make to theology and social science. Thanks to the high percentage of youth ministry professors who are sociologists, psychologists, and educators, nontheological empirical research still dominates youth ministry research. Yet by the 1990s, we had begun—somewhat intuitively—to leverage decades of experience with young people to theologically reflect on adolescent development, leadership, and mission. What we learned was that much of what is true for ministry with adolescents is also true for the entire church. Inevitably, questions of importance to the whole church fall first to the young, starting with questions of identity: Who are we, the church, called to be in a cyber-connected universe? What is the role of the pastor for the Facebook generation? In a world where adolescence seems to be expanding and contracting simultaneously, what is the purpose of youth ministry? Questions that will undoubtedly shape the twenty-first century church, but that Christian young people are already grappling with, include:

Future Research Directions for Youth Ministry

Hermeneutics and youth ministry	• What does an adolescent perspective on biblical texts contribute to the tradition of the church • What do cultural perspectives on youth ministry contribute to Christian tradition? • How do theological perspectives on youth ministry condition the way we appropriate the Bible for youth ministry?
Youth ministry and the lifecycle paradigm	• What are the limits of the lifecycle paradigm as a basis for understanding adolescent growth and maturity? • How might we think about adolescence if we considered maturity a spiritual, rather than a psychosocial, phenomenon?

Leadership formation and youth ministry	• How do we teach young people "how to fish" instead of giving them fish? • How does leadership formation differ (e.g., poor congregations vs. wealthy ones, Latino vs. Anglo communities, Protestant vs. Catholic vs. Orthodox, American youth ministry vs. sub-Saharan African youth work, etc.)?
Congregational cultures and youth ministry	• What does blurring the line between adolescence and adulthood do to the way intergenerational dynamics play out in youth ministry? • How does youth ministry navigate full participation in congregational culture without tempting burnout?
Youth ministry and missiology	• What are we to make of the increasing convergence between youth ministry and missional theology? • Why do missional churches tend to grow out of youth ministries?
Introducing new voices to youth ministry	• What can be learned about ministry with emerging generations from churches "at the edges" of current youth ministry literature? • What can ethnic minority congregations or immigrant congregations teach us about identity formation? • What can small or rural congregations teach us about kinship models of community? • How can Catholic and Protestant youth ministries learn from one another? • What can "alternative paradigm" churches teach us about emerging adults' relationship with culture and tradition? • What can youth ministers learn from other church leaders? (heads of staff, custodians, musicians, etc.)

Not only does youth ministry model interdisciplinary thinking, it helps advance Christian theories of leadership and adolescence, and invites us to rethink ecclesiology in culturally specific ways. Instinctively, youth ministers tend to employ practical theological methods in their work. As a result, youth ministry provides a lively laboratory for learning how Christian communities can contribute to interdisciplinary scholarly dialogue.

ACADEMIC RESEARCH   *GRADE: C+ (Shows vast improvement, particularly in terms of practical theological reflection; consistency and quality of work remains erratic)*

Distinctive Pedagogies: Still Evolving

Most professional fields develop pedagogies that immerse students in conditions, real or simulated, that enact situations and evoke practices indigenous to their field of study. Aspiring doctors have residencies, new teachers do student teaching, budding counselors log clinical hours. Even future academics immerse themselves in scholarly reflection and class presentations, on the assumption that the disciplined habits of mind required by scholarly inquiry should be practiced in doctoral seminars. Ministry with young people makes certain generalizations about adolescent learning styles (namely, that young people are more likely to actively, rather than passively, engage material—an assumption that has been both complicated and intensified by participatory media culture). However, youth ministry as a field of study for *adults* is still awaiting a distinctive pedagogy.

In fact, youth ministry pedagogy has much to offer theological education generally, since the issues confronting youth ministry as an emerging discipline tend to confront theological education as a whole. Youth ministry education gravitates toward coaching, mentoring, and apprenticeship pedagogies because they tap into youth pastors' relational instincts. As we have seen, situated learning stresses participation and education-in-context, and helps explain the power of retreats, campus mission trips, and other "immersion experiences" in the Christian life. Transformative learning—intended for adults—offers a method for evoking paradigm shifts that youth ministers employ instinctively, almost without exception. Even without reading the theory, what youth leader has not presented a "disorienting dilemma" to teenagers, in order to decenter them long enough to entertain a new idea or practice?[25]

And yet, when it comes to teaching adults *about* youth ministry, most of us teach the way we were taught—which is to say, we teach youth ministry the way we teach everything else. Furthermore, while the educational methods we use with teenagers may offer our best hope for modeling and developing pastoral imagination (for all areas of theological education, not youth ministry alone), the links between discipleship formation and educational methods remain implicit and underutilized.

DISTINCTIVE PEDAGOGIES   *GRADE: B (Enormous natural talent here, but not living up to potential. Need to apply ourselves)*

Growing Pains in a Growing Field

On a 12-point scale, we get a C+ overall as an emerging discipline, slightly above average and tipping toward "not bad." We're not failing, and in fact we have made noticeable and impressive strides, but there is plenty of room for improvement. To move "up" to full disciplinary status in the academy requires straight A's. As the scope of youth ministry broadens to include academic preparation, the theological purpose of the field inevitably challenges many of the norms of modern professional life. Unless we redefine what we mean by "academic discipline," youth ministry faces two problems in its journey toward disciplinary status. First, it is likely to have difficulty meeting the criteria for academic longevity, in part because longevity is still difficult for youth ministry leaders, and also because the norms of youth ministry challenge the competitive, individualistic, achievement-oriented habits of academic culture. Second, in the absence of clearly articulated (and widely shared) goals related to faith formation and practical theology, youth ministry is likely to capitulate to the standards of social sciences, overlooking the very standards that Christians deem crucial to forming and living as disciples of Jesus Christ.

> Is academic respectability a pipe dream for youth ministry, and must we sell our souls to get it? Or do we sell our souls without it?

In the meantime, the most important question facing us is one of integrity. Daily, those of us who teach others in ministry must ask ourselves and each other, "How do we live the life we teach about?" How do we practice the kind of soul-full ministry we covet for young people themselves, when the culture-at-large seems anything but redemptive? How do we become means of grace in our communities, even academic ones? Is academic respectability a pipe dream for youth ministry, and must we sell our souls to get it? Or do we sell our souls without it? Is youth ministry a harbinger of things to come in the church and in theological education generally, an example of an emerging discipline for a postmodern church, a model for integrating the imagination, experience, and courage that finds its truest expression, not in academic criteria, but in young people themselves?

Much will depend on your ministry, and the intentionality with which you pursue these questions. The end of this book has yet to be written, for the conversations we have started on these pages are ongoing, and are being shaped by ministries like yours. These pages represent our stick in the sand, a marker of how far we can see the tide coming in from where we sit. But where scholars place the marker next depends largely on where God takes your ministry, and on where God takes you. We are watching with gratitude and anticipation. Carry on.

Further Reading on Themes in This Chapter

Dykstra, Craig. "Pastoral and Ecclesial Imagination," in Dorothy Bass, ed., *For Life Abundant*. Grand Rapids: Eerdmans, 2008, 41–61.

Foster, Charles, et al. *Educating Clergy: Teaching Practices and Pastoral Formation*. San Francisco: Jossey-Bass, 2005.

Jacks, Andrew S., and Barrett W. McRae. "Tassel-Flipping: A Portrait of the Well-Educated Youth Ministry Graduate," *Journal of Youth Ministry* 4 (Fall 2005), 53-73.

Lave, Jean, and Etienne Wenger. *Situated Learning: Legitimate Peripheral Participation.* Cambridge, England: University of Cambridge, 1991.

Mezirow, Jack. *Transformational Dimensions of Adult Learning.* San Francisco: Jossey Bass, 1991.

Osmer, Richard R. *Practical Theology: An Introduction.* Grand Rapids: Eerdmans, 2008.

Pahl, Jon. *Youth Ministry in Modern America, 1930–present.* Peabody, MA: Hendrickson, 2000.

Paulsell, Stephanie. "Pastoral Agility and Intellectual Work," lecture, Yale Divinity School (April 2003), *Harvard Divinity Bulletin,* http://www.hds.harvard.edu/news/bulletin/articles/paulsell.html

Schön, Donald. *Educating the Reflective Practitioner.* San Francisco: Jossey-Bass, 1987.

THE STUDY OF EXEMPLARY CONGREGATIONS IN YOUTH MINISTRY: ASSETS FOR DEVELOPING SPIRITUALLY MATURE YOUTH

(www.exemplarym.org)

The 2004 Exemplary Youth Ministry study used mixed methods to do quantitative studies at 118 congregations whose young people consistently demonstrate spiritual maturity (see Appendix B) in seven denominations (Assemblies of God, Evangelical Covenant, Evangelical Lutheran [ELCA], Presbyterian Church [USA], Roman Catholic, Southern Baptist, and United Methodist), and returned to 21 of these congregations (representing rural, suburban, and urban contexts and small, medium, and large congregations, as well as the seven denominations) for qualitative research, including site visits and interviews with leadership, parents, and teenagers.

CONGREGATIONAL ASSETS

1. Faith maturity

God's living presence—Congregation members possess a collective sense of God's living presence in community, at worship, through study, and in service.
Centrality of faith—Congregation members recognize and take part in God's sustaining/ transforming life and work.
Emphasis on prayer—Congregation members practice the presence of God as individuals and as a community through prayer and worship.
Focus on discipleship—Congregation members are committed to knowing and following Jesus Christ.
Emphasis on Scripture—Congregation members value the authority of Scripture for their life and mission.
Centrality of mission—Congregation members witness, seek justice, serve, and promote moral responsibility.

2. Pastoral leadership strength

Exercises spiritual influence—Pastor(s) know and model the transforming presence of God in life and ministry.

Demonstrates interpersonal competence—Pastor(s) build a sense of community and relate well to adults and youth.

Supports youth ministry—Pastor(s) understand, guide, and advocate for youth ministry.

Supports leaders—Pastor(s) affirm and mentor youth and adults leading youth ministry.

3. Congregational qualities

Supports youth ministry—Congregation makes ministry with young people a high priority.

Demonstrates hospitality—Congregation values and welcomes all people, especially youth.

Strives for excellence—Congregation sets high standards, evaluates, and engages in continuous improvement.

Encourages thinking—Congregation welcomes questions and reflection on faith and life.

Creates community—Congregation reflects high quality personal and group relationships.

Encourages support groups—Congregation engages members in study, prayer, and conversation about daily faith.

Promotes worship—Congregation expands and renews spirit-filled, uplifting worship in the congregation's life.

Fosters ethical responsibility—Congregation encourages individual and social moral responsibility.

Promotes service—Congregation sponsors outreach, service projects, and cultural immersions both locally and globally.

Demonstrates effective practices—Congregation engages in a wide variety of ministry practices and activities.

4. Youth involvement

Participates in the congregation—Youth are engaged in a wide spectrum of congregational relationships/practices.

Assumes ministry leadership—Youth are invited, equipped, and affirmed for leadership in congregational activities.

YOUTH MINISTRY ASSETS

1. Youth minister strength

Provides competent leadership—Youth minister reflects superior theological, theoretical, and practical skill and knowledge in leadership.

Models faith—Youth minister is a role model for youth and adults, reflecting a living faith.

Mentors faith life—Youth minister assists adult leaders and youth in their faith life, both one-on-one and in groups.

Develops teams—Youth minister reflects clear vision and attracts gifted youth and adults into leadership.

Knows youth—Youth minister knows youth and is sensitive to changes in youth culture, using these understandings in ministry.

Establishes effective relationships—Youth minister enjoys effective relationships with youth, parents, volunteers, and staff.

2. Youth and adult leadership

Peer ministry—Youth practice friendship, caregiving, and outreach, supported by training and caring adults.

Adult-youth mentoring—Adults engage youth in faith and life, supported by informed leadership.

Training—Youth and adult leaders evaluate and equip youth and adults for ministry in an atmosphere of high expectations.

Vibrant faith—Youth and adult leaders possess and practice a vital and informed faith.

Competent volunteers—Youth and adult volunteers foster authentic relationships and effective practices with youth within a clear vision strengthened by training and support.

3. Youth ministry effectiveness

A caring environment—Youth ministry provides multiple nurturing relationships and activities, resulting in a welcoming atmosphere of respect, growth, and belonging.

Quality relationships—Youth ministry develops authentic relationships among youth and adults, establishing an environment of presence and life engagement.

Focus on Jesus Christ—The life and ministry of Jesus inspires the ministry's mission, practices, and relationships.

Consideration of life issues—Youth ministry values and addresses the full range of young people's lives.

Use of many approaches—Youth ministry intentionally and creatively employs multiple activities appropriate to its mission and context.

4. Parental involvement

Possess strong parental faith—Parent(s) possess and practice a vital and informed faith.

Promote family faith practices—Parent(s) engage youth and family in conversations, prayer, Bible reading, and service that nurture faith and life.

Reflect family harmony—Families express respect and love and create an atmosphere promoting faith.

Foster parent-youth relationships—The congregation offers parent/youth activities that strengthen parent/youth relationships.

THE STUDY OF EXEMPLARY CONGREGATIONS IN YOUTH MINISTRY: CHARACTERISTICS OF SPIRITUALLY MATURE YOUTH

(www.exemplarym.org)

According to the Exemplary Youth Ministry Study (2004), the fruit of "faith assets" in a congregation are spiritually mature youth (for a description of the study, see Appendix A). In this study, a spiritually mature young person exhibits the following characteristics:

Demonstrates a Personal Spirituality

- Seeks spiritual growth, both alone and with others
- Is heard referring to having prayer, devotions, and meditation times
- Asks sincere and searching questions about the nature of a life of faith in God
- Prefers and attends gatherings where he or she can learn more about the Christian faith
- Accepts opportunities for learning how to speak naturally and intelligently about his or her faith
- Is involved in Bible study and/or prayer groups
- Joins Christian groups to build friendships and learn how to be a friend

Believes God Is Present in the World

- Speaks openly about seeking or experiencing God's guidance
- Is heard asking peers what God has recently done in their lives or the lives of others
- In times of trouble, reassures others that God is active to make things work out all right in the long run
- Occasionally speaks of having been keenly aware of the presence of God

Acts Out of a Commitment of Faith

- Speaks publicly about his or her relationship with Jesus Christ

- When providing a rationale for his or her actions will sometimes cite specifics of Christian faith
- In conversation with family and friends brings up topics of faith or Christian living
- Prays for people especially needing God's help

Is Active with God's People

- Regularly attends worship services
- Has willingly participated in two or more of the following:
  ○ taught Sunday school, Bible class, or Vacation Bible School
  ○ served with a group to improve conditions at school or neighborhood
  ○ made a presentation before a faith group or in worship
  ○ helped raise money for a Christian project or mission trip
  ○ served on a congregational or denominational committee or task force
- Regularly contributes money to a congregation or faith project

Possesses a Positive, Hopeful Spirit

- Enjoys being with other spiritually mature Christian teenagers, as evidenced by his or her laughing, singing, and conversation
- Shows a gracious, loving attitude to people not easy to like (e.g., the difficult, rude, shunned, loser)
- Has friends of widely diverse socioeconomic, ethnic, and religious background or persuasion
- Has been heard describing the Christian faith as a necessary force in society, helping people develop attitudes of understanding, sympathy, and cooperation
- Is known for his or her general optimism, trust, and positive expectation of other people, being convinced that one person can do much to make the world a better place
- Is eager, responsive, and cooperative rather than unresponsive, disinterested, and apathetic

Lives Out a Life of Service

- Gives portions of time and money for helping people
- Attends conferences or workshops that present the challenges of service professions such as the ordained ministry
- Speaks out publicly against specific social injustices
- Offers comfort or support to friends or neighbors, either by talking or by action (personal presence, help with routine tasks, transportation, visit in hospital, etc.) as they face death or tragedy
- Defends a friend or acquaintance who is being talked about when he or she isn't there

- Organizes and participates in study or action groups to address injustice or immorality
- Is involved in activities of service related to church, community, or world
- Is assuming responsibility for some aspect of his or her youth ministry

Lives a Christian Moral Life

- Is heard referring to seeking help from Scripture in deciding what is right and wrong
- Actively seeks to discourage friends from cheating at school
- Has a reputation for not participating in activities such as lying, stealing, substance abuse, etc. and has a reputation for honesty, integrity, hospitality, and acts of kindness

NOTES

Oh My God: An Introduction

1. Kate Zernike, "Generation OMG," *New York Times* (March 7, 2009), http://www.nytimes.com/2009/03/08/weekinreview/08zernike.html, accessed April 2, 2009.

2. The "Youth and Theology" series is a partnership between the Princeton Theological Seminary Institute for Youth Ministry and Abingdon Press.

3. Gregory of Nazianzus, *Orations of Gregory of Nazianzus*, "In Defense of His Flight to Pontus," Oration II, Section 22, trans. Charles E. Brown and James E. Swallow, *The Nicene and Post-Nicene Fathers Series* (1893), http://www.ccel.org/ccel/schaff/npnf207.iii.iv.html, accessed September 27, 2007. The original uses gender-specific God-language.

1. Haunting Questions

1. Names have been changed.

2. C.f. Victoria Flood, "Results: Youth Ministry Resources Questionnaire, Mailed October 2002," unpublished report (Evangelical Lutheran Church in America, Department for Research and Evaluation, August 2004), archive.elca.org/research/reports/dcm/YMResources.pdf (accessed April 3, 2009).

3. Christian Smith with Melinda Lundquist Denton, *Soul Searching: The Religious and Spiritual Lives of American Teenagers* (New York: Oxford University Press, 2005), 265.

4. For examples of relevant research from those mentioned, see Dean Hoge, *Commitment on Campus: Changes in Religion and Values over Five Decades* (Philadelphia: Westminster Press, 1974) and *Vanishing Boundaries: The Religion of Mainline Protestant Baby Boomers* (Louisville, KY: Westminster John Knox Press, 1994); Sara Little, *Youth, World and Church* (Richmond, VA: John Knox Press, 1968); Michael Warren, *Youth and the Future of the Church* (New York: Seabury Press, 1982) and *Youth, Gospel, Liberation* (San Francisco: Harper & Row, 1987); Merton Strommen, *Five Cries of Youth* (New York: Harper & Row, 1974); The Barna Group, www.barna.org; The Higher Education Research Institute (www.heri.ucla.edu, especially the work of Alexander and Helen Astin et al., "The Spirituality of Higher Education Project" [Los Angeles: UCLA, 2007]); The Search Institute (www.search-institute.org); Herschel and Ellen Thornburg, *The Journal for Early Adolescence and the Journal of Adolescent Research*; Jeffrey Arnett, *Emerging Adulthood* (New York: Oxford University Press, 2004); Sharon Daloz Parks, *The Critical Years* (San Francisco: Harper & Row, 1986); Christian Smith with Melinda Lundquist Denton, *Soul Searching* (New York: Oxford University Press, 2005); Robert Wuthnow, *After the Baby Boomers* (Princeton, NJ: Princeton University Press, 2007). These represent the tip of

the iceberg; recently, fields like media studies, social psychology, cognitive neuroscience, and of course practical theology have added significantly to the range of research influencing the church's ministry with adolescents.

5. Peter Hastings and Dean Hoge, "Changes in Religion Among College Students, 1948–1974," *Journal for the Scientific Study of Religion* 15:3 (September 1976), 221–35.

6. Michael Warren, *Youth and the Future of the Church* (New York: The Seabury Press, 1982), 8–9.

7. D. Michael Lindsay, "Youth on the Edge," *The Christian Century* (October 4, 2003), 26–29.

8. Cf. Wuthnow, *After the Baby Boomers*, 17–18; also see http://www.usa today.com/news/religion/2007-08-06-church-dropouts N.htm (accessed July 11, 2009).

9. Smith, 52. The research team suggests that contributing factors could include low levels of parental involvement in ongoing religious formation, less emphasis on youth formation from dioceses and parishes compared to other churches, and lower enrollments in Catholic high schools and formation programs for youth.

10. Cf. Smith and Denton, 126.

11. Hal Marcovitz and Gail Snyder, *Gallup Youth Survey: Major Issues and Trends* (Broomall, PA: Mason Crest Publishers, 2004); Smith, 31.

12. The National Study of Youth and Religion found that American teenagers, even those who say religion matters to them, possess little understanding of historically orthodox church teachings, few religious practices, and virtually no religious language to either critique or construct a worldview informed by (much less infused with) Christian faith. Cf. Christian Smith and Melinda Denton, *Soul Searching: The Religious and Spiritual Lives of American Teenagers* (New York: Oxford University Press, 2005), 49, 266. For a longitudinal look at these teenagers during the college years, see Christian Smith, *Souls in Transition* (New York: Oxford University Press, 2009). Christian Smith and Patricia Snell, on the other hand, find an overall pattern of continuity between the religious lives of teenagers nd those of emerging adults (see *Souls in Transition: The Religious and Spiritual Lives of Emerging Adults* [New York: Oxford, 2009], 208).

13. Roland Martinson, "The Challenge," FaithFactors, unpublished research conducted 1992–1996 at Luther Theological Seminary, St. Paul, MN; personal conversation (July 13, 2009).

14. Cf. Tim Clydesdale, *The First Year Out: Understanding American Teens after High School* (Chicago: University of Chicago Press), 2007.

15. The Barna Group, "Teens Evaluate the Church-Based Ministry They Received as Children," Barna Update, http://www.barna.org/barna-update/article/5-barna-update/124-teens-evaluate-the-church-based-ministry-they-received-as-children (accessed April 4, 2009).

16. Smith, 129.

17. Arnett, *Emerging Adulthood*, 166.

18. Arnett expresses surprise at how little relationship seemed to exist between the religious identities of emerging adults and their religious upbringings. See Jeffrey Arnett, *Emerging Adulthood: The Winding Road from the Late Teens through the Twenties* (New York: Oxford University Press), 174. For research that emphasizes the continuity between childhood religious training and religious identity, see "Adolescent Religious Development and Commitment: A Structural Equation Model of the Role of Family, Peer Group, and Educational Influences," *Journal for the Scientific Study of Religion*, 31:2 (1992), 131–152; R. L. Dudley and R. L. Wisbey, "The Relationship of Parenting Styles to Commitment to the Church among Young Adults," *Religious Education* 95 (2000), 39–50; Mark Finley and Steven R. Mosely, *What My Parents Did Right* (Nampa, ID: Pacific Press, 2001); Carol E. Lytch, "The Role of Parents in Anchoring Teens in Christian Faith," *Family Ministry* 13 (1999), 33–38.

19. See Christian Smith with Patricia Snell, *Souls in Transition* (Oxford: Oxford University Press), 2009.

20. The Barna Group, "Most Twentysomethings Put Christianity on the Shelf Following Spiritually Active Teen Years," Barna Update, http://www.barna.org/barna-update/article/16-teensnext-gen/147-most-twentysomethings-put-christianity-on-the-shelf-following-spiritually-active-teen-years (accessed April 4, 2009).

21. Andrew Root, *Revisiting Relational Youth Ministry* (Downers Grove, IL: InterVarsity Press, 2007), 78.

22. Ibid., 79.

23. It is fair to wonder whether teenagers would give a straight answer to researchers asking them directly about their faith. While NSYR researchers took the standard precautions customary in empirical social scientific research on human subjects, and talked to the teenagers (and their parents) prior to face-to-face interviews (sometimes multiple times), it is difficult to know how forthright teenagers were. The two dozen researchers conducting the interviews, however, agreed that they did not sense duplicity in the young people interviewed; teenagers did not seem to be reaching for words to describe religion as though it were something so meaningful that words eluded them. On the contrary, most teenagers were remarkably articulate about other complex subjects. Researchers' clear sense was that the problem in the religious portion of the interview was unfamiliarity, and discomfort, with religious language itself, and a paucity of practice using it. Many teenagers said "no one had ever asked them" to talk about their religious views before. For a more detailed discussion, see Kenda Creasy Dean, *Almost Christian: What the Faith of American Teenagers Is Telling the American Church* (New York: Oxford University Press, 2010), especially chapter 7.

24. Smith, 118–71.

25. Ibid., 162–3.

26. Ibid., 118–71.

27. For example, subsequent research in the United Kingdom since Smith

and Denton's study yielded similar conclusions. See Sara Savage, Sylvia Collins-Mayo, Bob Mayo with Graham Cray, *Making Sense of Generation Y: The World View of 15-25-year-olds* (London: Church House Publishing, 2006).

28. Warren, *Youth, Gospel, Liberation,* 43.

29. Ibid.

30. Ibid., 42.

31. Warren proposes a "new vision" for youth ministry that foreshadows the discussion of practices, which has become dominant twenty years later. For Warren, this wholistic approach to youth ministry includes: (1) *the ministry of the word,* encompassing all activities by which the church maintains and proclaims the meanings that bind it together, including evangelization, catechesis, theology (systematic reflection on the experience of Christian living and tradition), and worship; (2) *the ministry of worship,* by which a community embodies its understandings and its group life ritually; (3) *the ministry of guidance and counsel,* including education and those activities by which a community comforts the troubled and shares its wisdom about the human condition; and (4) *the ministry of healing,* by which a community follows Jesus' mandate to free the captives, feed the hungry, bind up the wounded, and be a force for justice. (Warren, *Youth and the Future of the Church,* 11.)

32. We assume that youth ministry includes those entering as well as completing adolescence, which now includes the mid-elementary school ages through emerging adulthood, as well as ministry with these young people's families. This broad scope is not always self-evident. The expansion of adolescence in the West throughout the twentieth century is now a widely accepted phenomenon, as puberty begins earlier and social and economic conditions push adulthood further into the twenties and even early thirties. The unifying task of the adolescent and emerging adult life stage(s) is the task of identity formation—a task that is completed in emerging adulthood, and therefore has unique dimensions as young people negotiate decisions about intimacy, vocation, and ideology to complete identity formation.

33. Merton Strommen, Karen Jones, and Dave Rahn, *Youth Ministry That Transforms* (Grand Rapids: Youth Specialties Books/Zondervan, 2001), 20–21.

34. Ibid., 9–10.

35. Rick Lawrence, "3 Dirty, Rotten Youth Ministry Lies," *Group Magazine* (September–October 2006), 77, cited in DeVries, 93. For research about the time it takes to become an expert in a field, cf. Mikhail Csikszentmihalyi, *Creativity: Flow and the Psychology of Discovery and Invention* (New York: HarperCollins), 1996; Jane Piirto, *Understanding Creativity* (Scottsdale, AZ: Great Potential Press), 2004; Malcolm Gladwell, *Outliers* (New York: Little, Brown and Company, 2008), 37ff.

36. D. Andrew Zirschky, "Beyond Fakes and Phonies: Toward a Theological Understanding of Authenticity in Youth Ministry Leadership," paper presented at the annual meeting of the Association of Youth Ministry Educators, Atlanta, GA (October 18, 2008).

37. Cf. Sarah Arthur, *The God-Hungry Imagination* (Nashville: Upper

Room Books, 2007); Kenda Creasy Dean and Ron Foster, *The Godbearing Life: The Art of Soul-Tending for Youth Ministry* (Nashville: Upper Room Books, 1998); Duffy Robbins, *The Ministry of Nurture* (Grand Rapids: Zondervan, 1990); Katherine Turpin, *Branded* (Cleveland, OH: Pilgrim Press, 2006); David White, *Practicing Discernment with Youth* (Cleveland, OH: Pilgrim Press, 2005); Mark Yaconelli, *Contemplative Youth Ministry* (Grand Rapids: Zondervan, 2006).

38. DeVries, 39.

39. Ibid.

40. Karen Jones, "Refining the Image: A Vocational Perspective on Youth Ministry," *Christian Education Journal* 2 (Fall 1999), 9–16.

41. Tracy Schier, "Christian Smith on the National Study of Youth and Religion," *Resources for American Christianity*, http://www.resourcingchristianity.org/ (accessed February 21, 2009).

2. Daunting Challenges

1. Graham Cray et al., *Mission-shaped Church: Church Planting and Fresh Expressions of Church in a Changing Context* (London: Church House, 2004). The report actually described the gap between the church and culture generally but acknowledged that young people experienced the greatest distance between their own cultural experience and the Anglican Church. The report launched the Anglican/Methodist "Fresh Expressions" movement, encouraging Anglicans to establish churches based on perceived mission, and to allow the church to take whatever form best addresses the mission at hand.

2. Sara Savage, Sylvia Collins-Mayo, Bob Mayo with Graham Cray, *Making Sense of Generation Y: The World View of 15-25-year-olds* (London: Church House Publishing, 2006), 157. Savage is senior research associate for the Psychology and Christianity Project at the University of Cambridge.

3. Ibid.

4. For a breathtaking example, see the senior adult choir's hip hop entry on YouTube, http://www.youtube.com/watch?v=K1kjkUAA9VM (accessed February 27, 2009).

5. On the "branding" of children, see Susan Linn, *Consuming Kids: The Hostile Takeover of Childhood* (New York: The New Press), 2004; Susan Gregory Thomas, *Buy, Buy Baby: How Consumer Culture Manipulates Parents and Harms Young Minds* (New York: Houghton Mifflin), 2007; and Eric Schlosser, *Fast Food Nation* (New York: Houghton Mifflin), 2002.

6. Talcott Parsons, *The Social System* (Glencoe, IL: Free Press, 1951), 208. Sociologist Talcott Parsons referred to each new generation of youth as a "barbarian invasion"—the dominant culture must either conquer them, or be conquered by them.

7. Dr. Seuss (Theodor Seuss Geisel), *Horton Hears a Who!* (New York: Random House, 1954).

8. Smith, 76.

9. Ibid., 79.

10. The real problem, says feminist Letty Russell, is that Christians are usually of the world but not in it. Cited by Cindy Rigby, "Umble Pie," *Austin Presbyterian Theological Seminary Windows* (Summer, 2008), 16, www.austinseminary.edu/page.cfm?p=417 (accessed April 10, 2009).

11. Joseph Kett, *Rites of Passage: Adolescence in America, 1790-present* (New York: Basic Books, 1978), 73–74.

12. Anthony M. Platt, *The Child Savers: The Invention of Delinquency* (Chicago: University of Chicago, 1969), 99.

13. G. Stanley Hall, *Adolescence: Its Psychology, and Its Relation to Physiology, Anthropology, Sociology, Sex, Crime and Religion* (New York: D. Appleton), 1904.

14. For a helpful summary of Hall's work in religious psychology, see Hendrika Vande Kemp, "G. Stanley Hall and the Clark School of Religious Psychology," *American Psychologist* 47 (1992), 290-98.

15. Hall's view of adolescence as a period of "storm and stress" view of adolescence remains persistent, even though he had no empirical evidence to back it.

16. James Stuart Olson, *Historical Dictionary of the 1950s* (Westwood, CT: Greenwood Press, 2000), 283. By 1999, the American teenager had $94/week to spend *on average* (David Plotz, "The American Teenager: Why Generation Y?" *Slate.com* (September 17, 1999), http://www.slate.com/id/34963/ (accessed April 4, 2009).

17. Erik H. Erikson, *Identity, Youth and Crisis* (New York: W.W. Norton, 1968), 128ff.

18. See the literature review on the subject by Sandra Steingraber, *The Falling Age of Puberty in US Girls: What We Know, What We Need to Know* (Breast Cancer Fund, 2007), available online at http://www.breastcancerfund.org/site/pp.asp?c=kwKXLdPaE&b=3291891 (accessed April 14, 2009).

19. Sandra Steingraber, *The Falling Age of Puberty in U.S. Girls: What We Know, What We Need to Know* (Breast Cancer Fund, 2007), 10. The Steingraber report is the first comprehensive review of the literature on the declining age of puberty in the U.S. http://www.breastcancerfund.org/site/c.kwKXLdPaE/b.3266509/k.27C1/Falling_Age_of_Puberty_Main_Page.htm (accessed November 15, 2009).

20. Cf. Richard A. Settersten, Jr., "Becoming Adult: Meanings and Markers for Young Americans," working paper for the Network on Transitions to Adulthood (March 2006), MacArthur Foundation. Also see Richard A. Settersten, Jr., Frank F. Furstenberg, Jr., and Rubén G. Rumbaut, eds., *On the Frontier of Adulthood: Theory, Research, and Public Policy* (Chicago: University of Chicago Press, 2005).

21. Jeffrey Arnett, *Emerging Adulthood: The Winding Road from the Late Teens through the Twenties* (Oxford and New York: Oxford University Press), 2006. Sharon Daloz Parks foreshadowed Arnett's argument two decades earlier in *The Critical Years: The Young Adult Search for a Faith to Live By* (San Francisco: Harper & Row, 1986).

22. Ibid., 165.

23. Philip Graham, *The End of Adolescence* (London: Oxford University Press, 2004), 1.

24. Robert Epstein, *The Case against Adolescence: Rediscovering the Adult in Every Teen* (Sanger, CA: Quill Driver Books/Word Dancer Press, 2007), 355.

25. Epstein goes so far as to call religious groups "enemies of the teen" because they perpetuate myths of teen helplessness and incompetence, "[having lost] sight of the important roles that young people played in the Bible," 358.

26. David F. White, in Brian Mahan, Michael Warren, and David F. White, *Awakening Youth Discipleship* (Eugene, OR: Wipf and Stock, 2007), 4.

27. Cf. Kate Zernike, "Generation OMG," *The New York Times* Week In Review (March 7, 2009), http://www.nytimes.com/2009/03/08/weekin review/08zernike.html?pagewanted=1&_r=4&ref=weekinreview; Lizzie Ratner, "The New Victorians," *The New York Observer* (July 10, 2007), http://www.observer.com/2007/new-victorians (accessed March 11, 2009).

28. We avoid the term *student* because not all young persons are students, and because it reduces the young person's identity to a role she or he plays in society.

29. Paul Tillich, *The Protestant Era* (Chicago: University of Chicago Press, 1948), http://www.religion-online.org/showchapter.asp?title=380&C=101 (accessed February 26, 2009).

30. A version of Grace and the foot clinic appears in chapter 6 of Don Richter, *Mission Trips That Matter* (Nashville: Upper Room Books, 2008).

31. Cf. Zygmunt Bauman, *Liquid Modernity* (Cambridge, UK: Polity Press, 2000); and Pete Ward, *Liquid Church* (Carlisle, Cumbria, UK: Paternoster Press, 2002).

32. The Nicene Creed commends belief in "one holy catholic and apostolic church." The Apostles' Creed speaks of belief in "the holy catholic church."

33. For our purposes, "place is a specific convergence of people, story, and earth." Place is located, but not every location is a place. "Space" can be measured in cubic feet or square miles—but "place" is thick and embodied, inhabited and known. A place is known most fully from within. Dorothy C. Bass, "Placing Christian Formation," unpublished Robert Jones Lecture delivered at Austin Presbyterian Theological Seminary (February 2008).

34. See Andrew Walls, *The Missionary Movement in Christian History: Studies in the Transmission of Faith* (New York: Orbis, 1996), 5ff.

35. Jon Bonne, "Are We Done with the 40-Hour Work Week?" MSNBC.com (August 25, 2003), http://www.msnbc.msn.com/id/3072426/ (accessed March 9, 2009); "'I Can't Sleep'—It's a Huge and Growing Class of Americans: The Worn-Out, Stressed-Out Denizens of a Sleepless Netherworld. More Than 82 Million Suffer from Insomnia—Nearly 40% of All Teens and Adults." *Business Week–New York 3867 (2004): 66–74. In The Twenty-Four-Hour Society*, Martin Moore-Ede attributes the Three Mile Island, Bhopal, Chernobyl, Exxon

Valdez, and Challenger disasters at least in part to human fatigue (Reading, MA: Addison-Wesley, 1993), 5–7.

36. See "Lack of Sleep Americans' Top Health Problem, Doctors Say," CNN report, http://www.worldsleepfoundation.com/news.asp (accessed March 9, 2009). The Challenger disaster, the Chernobyl nuclear reactor meltdown, and the Exxon Valdez oil spill were partly linked to people suffering from a severe lack of sleep.

37. Fred P. Edie, *Book, Bath, Table, and Time* (Cleveland, OH: Pilgrim Press, 2007), 168.

38. Dorothy C. Bass, Receiving the Day (San Francisco: Jossey-Bass, 2000), 87.

39. Sabbath-keeping involves acts of resistance. Families who covenant not to shop on this day, who refrain from commercial television, homework, and committee meetings, resist the urge to become enslaved to a 24/7 calendar. I know of one community in which Sunday morning softball practices were rescheduled when enough Christian players and parents cried foul. Singing prayers of praise and remembrance, telling stories of hope, visiting the lonely, enjoying nature, sharing our lives with others, reading, playing, and most importantly, feasting are all time-honored practices of Sabbath. The center-piece of the Jewish Shabbat is the family feast, but many Christians struggle to have family meals together. Feasting one day out of seven, with family and friends, frees youth and adults from fast-food monotony and information-byte exchanges, while teaching that life is for *being* as well as for doing, and offering a foretaste of God's heavenly banquet table.

40. In *Family-Based Youth Ministry* (Downers Grove, IL: InterVarsity Press, 1994), Mark DeVries underscores the importance of viewing youth within the context of their families. Youth activities that threaten family ties must be critiqued and modified, claims DeVries. Instead, DeVries suggests models that allow young people to maintain their family identities as a necessary dimension of their faith formation.

41. Gordon W. Lathrop, *The Pastor: A Spirituality* (Minneapolis: Fortress, 2006), 59–75.

42. "Associating in one's mind with certain brands gives a sense of identity: one identifies one's self with certain images and values that are associated with the brand." William T. Cavanaugh, *Being Consumed: Economics and Christian Desire* (Grand Rapids: William B. Eerdmans, 2008), 46.

43. William T. Cavanaugh, *Theopolitical Imagination* (London: T & T Clark, 2002), 111.

44. Cited by Katherine Paterson, "I Love to Tell the Story," *Proclaiming the Gospel in a Wired World: Princeton Lectures on Youth, Church and Culture* (Princeton, NJ: Princeton Theological Seminary, 2001), 113. Available online at http://www2.ptsem.edu/iym/content.aspx?id=3892 (accessed April 14, 2009).

45. Flannery O'Connor, *Mystery and Manners: Occasional Prose*, ed. Sally and Robert Fitzgerald (New York: Farrar, Straus & Giroux, 1970), 192.

46. Sarah Arthur, *The God-Hungry Imagination* (Nashville: Upper Room, 2007), 77.

47. As historian Diana Butler Bass points out, American culture has shifted from being a univocal religious society (with a relatively unified set of external authorities) to being a multivocal one ("of many voices"), "in which the individual is the final arbiter of truth." *The Practicing Congregation: Imagining a New Old Church* (Washington, DC: The Alban Institute, 2004), 25.

48. Mary Belenky, et al., *Women's Ways of Knowing* (New York: Basic Books, 1997), 168–69. The "third disestablishment" of the church shifts religious authority in North America to the authority of individual subjectivity. Cf. Philip Hammond, *Religion and Personal Autonomy: The Third Disestablishment in America* (Columbia, SC: University of Columbia), 1992; Loren Mead, *More than Numbers: The Way Churches Grow* (Washington, DC: The Alban Institute), 1993.

49. Writing about the de facto Christendom that characterizes the U.S. and Canada, Douglass John Hall points out, "Whereas the old, European forms of Christian establishment were legal ones…ours have been cultural, ideational, and social," which are much harder to spot. "One suspects," Hall concludes, "that our very refusal of *formal* patterns of Christian establishment has blinded us to the power of our *informal* culture-religion pattern" (*The End of Christendom and the Future of Christianity* [Eugene, OR: Wipf and Stock, 1997], 29).

50. Catholics were the first to successfully resist this cultural hegemony, establishing parochial schools in the 1600s to counter latent Protestantism (and sometimes overt anti-Catholicism) in colonial education. See "A Brief Overview of Catholic Schools in America," National Catholic Education Association, http://www.ncea.org/about/HistoricalOverviewofCatholicSchools InAmerica.asp (accessed March 31, 2009).

51. Stanley Hauerwas, *After Christendom? How the Church Is to Behave If Freedom, Justice, and a Christian Nation Are Bad Ideas* (Nashville: Abingdon, 1991), 18–19.

52. Fifteen percent of Americans identified themselves as "nones" (having no religious affiliation), the fastest growing group in the 2008 American Religious Identification Survey. See Cathy Lynn Grossman, "Nones Now 15% of Population," *USAToday* (March 9, 2009), http://www.usatoday.com/news/religion/2009-03-09-aris-survey-nones N.htm (accessed March 31, 2009).

53. For one recent example, see Lovett H. Weems and Ann A. Michel, *The Crisis of Younger Clergy* (Nashville: Abingdon, 2008). On the decline of religious affiliation in the U.S., see Grossman, http://www.usatoday.com/news/religion/2009-03-09-american-religion-ARIS N.htm (accessed April 14, 2009).

54. This distorted religious creed was "Moralistic Therapeutic Deism," introduced in chapter 1. Christian Smith with Melinda Denton, *Soul-Searching: The Religious and Spiritual Lives of American Teenagers* (Oxford: Oxford University Press, 2005).

55. Douglas John Hall, "Finding Our Way into the Future," *For Such a Time*

as This: Princeton Lectures on Youth, Church and Culture (Princeton, NJ: Princeton Theological Seminary, 2006), 28. Available online at http://ww2.ptsem.edu/iym/content.aspx?id=3892 (accessed April 14, 2009).

56. Hall, *The End of Christendom*, 52.

57. Ibid., 47–48. Italics original.

58. Amy L. Sales and Gary A. Tobin, *Church and Synagogue Affiliation: Theory, Research, and Practice*, Contributions to the study of religion, no. 42, (Westport, CT: Greenwood Press, 1995), 38.

59. Hall, T*he End of Christendom*, 35–39, 57.

60. Kenda Creasy Dean, *Almost Christian: What the Faith of American Teenagers Is Telling the American Church* (New York: Oxford University Press, 2010), forthcoming.

3. Enduring Themes

1. With gratitude for the insights of Nathan Stucky especially, and the "Mennonites with Milkshakes," whose contributions were invaluable in constructing this chapter.

2. The male language of "master" and disciple in this case implies experience, not domination. The master-apprentice relationship has historically involved some abusive power dynamics, but master-apprentice relationships can also imply mutuality and care. See Jean Lave and Etienne Wenger, *Situated Learning: Legitimate Peripheral Participation* (Cambridge: Cambridge University Press), 1991.

3. Anna Carter Florence, "A Prodigal Preaching Story and Bored-to-Death Youth," *Theology Today* 64 (July 2007), 235.

4. Ibid., 236.

5. Ibid., 238.

6. Stuart Cummings-Bond, "The One-Eared Mickey Mouse," *Youthworker* (Fall 1989), 76.

7. Florence, 239.

8. On the "preferential option for the young" in the biblical narrative, see Kenda Creasy Dean, "Youth," *New Interpreters Bible Dictionary* (Nashville: Abingdon, 2009), in press.

9. Florence, 240.

10. The Greek word *epepsen* is rare in the New Testament, but Florence points out that it appears in both Acts 20 and in the prodigal son story (240–41). Both scenes imply resurrection; in Luke 15:24, the father of the wayward son proclaims: "This son of mine was dead and is alive again!"

11. Ibid., 242–43.

12. See Dale Blythe and Eugene Roehlkepartain, *Healthy Communities, Healthy Youth: How Communities Contribute to Positive Youth Development* (Minneapolis: Search Institute), 1993.

13. Shauna Hannan, untitled sermon, Miller Chapel, Princeton Theological Seminary (April 24, 2008).

14. Ibid.

15. Mark DeVries, unpublished address, Center for Youth Ministry Training (February 10, 2007).

16. Andrew Root, *Revisiting Relational Youth Ministry: From a Strategy of Influence to a Theology of Incarnation* (Downers Grove, IL: InterVarsity Press, 2007), 17.

17. Rolf Jacobson, ed., *Crazy Talk: A Not-So-Stuffy Dictionary of Theological Terms* (Minneapolis: Augsburg, 2008), 113.

18. Sometimes interpreted as "common" or "preventing" grace, this grace comes to us solely through God's initiative, prompting good, preventing evil, nudging us toward the recognition that Christ is right under our noses (cf. John Calvin, *Institutes of the Christian Religion* (Philadelphia: Westminster Press, 1960), II:2. John Wesley, "On Working Out Our Own Salvation" (Sermon #85, 1872), http://new.gbgmumc.org/umhistory/wesley/sermons/85/). A case can be made that divine grace is especially palpable in the liminal, developmental space of adolescence that has not yet been claimed by other social roles or institutional commitments.

19. Protestants limit sacraments to two commanded by Jesus—baptism and the Lord's Supper—while Catholics add confirmation, penance, anointing of the sick, holy orders, and marriage.

20. Eastern Orthodoxy, like Catholicism, recognizes seven Holy Mysteries: baptism, chrismation, the Eucharist, confession, holy unction, marriage, and ordination. These rites are considered occasions of divine-human encounter that enable union with God.

21. Martin Luther, *On the Freedom of Being a Christian*, ed. Mark Tranvik (Minneapolis: Fortress Press, 2008), 83.

22. Fred Edie, *Book, Bath, Table and Time: Christian Worship as Source and Resource for Youth Ministry* (Cleveland, OH: Pilgrim Press, 2007), 71.

23. See Paul Ricouer, *Interpretation Theory: Discourse and the Surplus of Meaning* (Fort Worth, TX: Texas Christian University Press, 1976), especially chapter 3.

24. F. C. Happold, cited by Nadia Delicata, unpublished dissertation, "Staged Present: Attending to the Mystical on the Stage of Working Memory," Department of Psychology, Faculty of Education, University of Malta, Tal-Qroqq, Msida MSD06, Malta (April 1999), 2.2; http://nadia.delicata.net/ (accessed March 29, 2009).

25. "Art's ability to move human beings makes it a primary channel for God's self-revelation precisely because of its capacity to speak to the human heart.... Art is a medium uniquely capable of participating in God's own revelatory means of self-communication." Edie, 82–84.

26. Garrett Green, *Imagining God: Theology and the Religious Imagination* (San Francisco: Harper & Row, 1989), 109.

27. Sarah Arthur, *The God-Hungry Imagination* (Nashville: Upper Room, 2007), 23; Smith and Denton, 131.

28. Richard Florida, *The Rise of the Creative Class: And How It Is*

Transforming Work, Leisure, Community and Everyday Life (New York: Basic Books, 2002). Florida believes 38 million Americans (30 percent of employed people) belong to this social class, which he understands to "share a common creative ethos that values creativity, individuality, difference, and merit." Because they are paid to create, they have more autonomy and flexibility than other socioeconomic classes (8). On the relationship between youth and creativity, see David W. Galenson, *Old Masters and Young Geniuses: The Life Cycles of Creativity* (Princeton, NJ: Princeton University Press), 2006) and Henry Jenkins, "Confronting the Challenges of Participatory Culture," white paper (Chicago: MacArthur Foundation), 2006. Available online at: digitallearning.macfound.org/atf/cf/%7B7E45C7E0-A3E0-4B89-AC9C-E807E1B0AE4E%7D/JENKINS_WHITE_PAPER.PDF (accessed April 15, 2009).

29. Arthur, 27. Italics original.

30. Ibid., 30.

31. Cited in ibid., 21.

32. Kenda Creasy Dean, *Practicing Passion: Youth and the Quest for a Passionate Church* (Grand Rapids: Eerdmans, 2004), 11.

33. Ibid.

34. Erwin Fahlbusch and Geoffrey William Bromiley, *The Encyclopedia of Christianity* (Grand Rapids: Eerdmans, 1999), 743.

35. Wynton Marsalis, with Geoffrey C. Ward, *Moving to Higher Ground: How Jazz Can Change Your Life* (New York: Random House, 2009), 12.

36. Ibid., 13.

37. Ibid., 12.

38. Ibid., 17.

39. Ibid., 7.

4. Promising Possibilities

1. Bruce Main, "Reflections: By Bruce Main," UrbanPromise USA Blog, posted January 21, 2008, http://www.urbanpromiseusa.blogspot.com/ (accessed April 14, 2009).

2. It is generally accepted among textual scholars that vv. 9-20 are not part of the original text of Mark. See notes in *The New Oxford Annotated Bible, New Revised Standard Version* (New York: Oxford University Press, 1991), 91NT.

3. Eugene Peterson notes that church leaders need to "be attentive to the divine action already in process so that the previously unheard word of God is heard, the previously unattended act of God is noticed.... What has God been doing here? What traces of grace can I discern in this life? What history of love can I read in this group? What has God set in motion that I can get in on?" in Eugene Peterson, *The Contemplative Pastor: Returning to the Art of Spiritual Direction* (Grand Rapids: Eerdmans, 1989), 61.

4. Biblical scholars note that the Gospel of Mark alerts the reader that God is at work in our realm, calling us to act: "Jesus is out of the tomb, on the

loose!... Jesus has promised an end. That end is not yet, but the story gives good reasons to remain hopeful even in the face of disappointment" (Donald Juel, *A Master of Surprise: Mark Interpreted* [Minneapolis: Augsburg Fortress, 1994], 113, 120). Also see Brian Blount, "Is the Joke on Us? Mark's Irony, Mark's God, and Mark's Ending," in *The Ending of Mark and the Ends of God: Essays in Memory of Donald Harrisville Juel*, ed. Beverly R. Gaventa and Patrick D. Miller (Louisville, KY: Westminster John Knox Press, 2005).

5. See Andrew Root, "Youth Ministry as an Integrative Theological Task: Toward a Representative Method of Interdisciplinarity," *The Journal of Youth Ministry* 5 (Spring 2007), 33–50.

6. *Renewing the Vision: A Framework for Catholic Youth Ministry* (Washington, DC: National Conference of Catholic Bishops, 1995), 10. Italics original.

7. Ibid. In his 1995 message to the World Day of Prayer for Vocations, Pope John Paul II stated: "This is what is needed: a Church for young people, which will know how to speak their heart and enkindle, comfort, and inspire enthusiasm in it with the joy of the Gospel and the strength of the Eucharist; a Church which will know how to invite and welcome the person who seeks a person for which to commit his whole existence; a Church which is not afraid to require much, after having given much; which does not fear asking from young people the effort of a noble and authentic adventure, such as that of following the Gospel." Cited in *Renewing the Vision*, 10.

8. Some of the material in this section appears, in expanded form, in Kenda Creasy Dean, *Almost Christian: What the Faith of Our Teenagers Is Telling the American Church* (Oxford and London: Oxford University Press, 2009).

9. Cited by Merton Strommen, et al., *Youth Ministry That Transforms* (Grand Rapids: Zondervan, 2001), 150.

10. John Westerhoff argues that "an ecology of institutions" that once shared the task of religious socialization in the U.S. has disintegrated. For Westerhoff, the demise of faith formation in public setting, families, public schools, the church (as the center of civic life), and religious periodicals has left church school to do what six institutions once did together—and church school "is failing." Westerhoff omits institutions of formation like parochial schools and Christian colleges, which arguably have more impact on religious identity than "religious periodicals." See *Will Our Children Have Faith?* (Harrisburg, PA: Morehouse Publishing; Toronto: Anglican Book Centre, 2000), 10–12.

11. Dean R. Hoge, et al., "Desired Outcomes of Religious Education and Youth Ministry in Six Denominations," *Review of Religious Research* 23 (March 1982), 230–54.

12. See K. C. Dean, "A Review of the Literature on Protestant, Catholic, and Jewish Religious Youth Organizations in the U.S.," working paper (Washington, DC: Carnegie Council on Adolescent Development), 1991.

13. As identified by Strommen, et al., in *Youth Ministry That Transforms*, 155.

14. The studies are not commensurate; Hoge studies only six denominations

(and did not seek a nationally representative sample, so regional differences are not reflected); the Carnegie study interviewed only leaders of denominational youth offices rather than youth ministers themselves; and Strommen's research surveyed more than 2,000 youth ministers—the largest study of its kind—but the sampling technique was not random. Still, these studies are the best indicators we have of the church's perceptions of the aims of youth ministry over the past five decades. This chart is indicative, not conclusive.

15. Stanley Hauerwas, "Why Did Jesus Have to Die?", unpublished lecture (Princeton, NJ: Princeton Theological Seminary Institute for Youth Ministry Youth Forum, 3 May 2007).

16. I heard this phrase originally from Darrell Guder (though it is widely quoted by others).

17. Darrell L. Guder, *The Continuing Conversion of the Church* (Grand Rapids: Eerdmans, 2000), 147.

18. Ibid., 150.

19. The term *missional church* was coined in 1998 by Darrell Guder, et al., in their book *Missional Church: A Vision for the Sending of the Church in North America* (Grand Rapids: Eerdmans, 1998).

20. "Decree on the Church's Missionary Activity," *Ad Gentes Divinitus*, 7 December 1965, in *Vatican Council II: The Conciliar and Post-Conciliar Documents*, ed. Austin Flannery (Northport, NY: Costello Publishing Company, 1975), 814.

21. For a detailed discussion of the missional church's significance for youth ministry, see K. C. Dean, *Outing the Emperor*, especially chapter 5.

22. Cathy Lynn Grossman, "Most Religious Groups in USA Have Lost Ground, Survey Says," *USAToday* (March 17, 2009), http://usatoday.com/news/religin/2009-03-09-american-religion-ARIS N.htm (accessed March 31, 2009).

23. Ibid.

24. David White, "Pedagogy for the Unimpressed," in *Awakening Youth Discipleship: Christian Resistance in a Consumer Culture*, ed. Brian J. Mahan, Michael Warren, and David F. White (Eugene, OR: Cascade Books, 2008), 37.

25. Karl Barth, *Church Dogmatics IV.3.2*, trans. G. W. Bromiley (Edinburgh: T.&T. Clark, 1962), 575.

26. Thanks to Dr. Rhonda Van Dyke Colby, Director of the Institute for Church Professions at Shenandoah University, for sharing this comment from a youth pastor at an Episcopal church in Winchester, Virginia.

27. "Emerging Church," Wikipedia, http://en.wikipedia.org/wiki/Emerging_church (accessed July 17, 2008).

28. See Don Richter, *Mission Trips That Matter* (Nashville: Upper Room), 2008.

29. For a discussion of how difficult it is for the church to be countercultural in a culture that loves, co-opts, and commodifies attempts at counterculture, see Ted A. Smith, "Christ and Counter Culture" unpublished lecture (Princeton, NJ: Princeton Theological Seminary Institute for Youth Ministry

Youth Forum, January 7, 2008), available at www.ptsem.edu/iym.

30. For an engaging discussion of the relative merits of age-segregated congregations, see Bruce Reyes-Chow, "Location, Location, Location: Ministry and Living in the 21st Century," in Neil Presa, ed., *Insights from the Underside* (Elizabeth, NJ: Broadmind Press, 2008), www.opcusa.org/vision.htm.

31. http://sarcasticlutheran.typepad.com/sarcastic lutheran/2009/03/so-what-is-the-emerging-church.html

32. Commission on Children and Risk, "Hardwired to Connect: the New Scientific Case for Authoritative Communities," Institute for American Values, 9 Sept 2003, http://www.americanvalues.org/html/hardwired_press_release.html (accessed April 15, 2009).

33. See Jeffrey Arnett, *Emerging Adulthood: The Winding Road from the Late Teens through the Twenties* (New York: Oxford University Press, 2004).

34. Jason Brian Santos, *A Community Called Taize* (Downers Grove, IL: InterVarsity Press, 2008), 129.

35. Several characteristics of Web 2.0 technology foster adolescent belonging: (1) Teenagers belong where they are known and seen; (2) they belong where they are able to be vulnerable, to be themselves, and to be with people who behave the same way; (3) they belong where they participate; (4) they belong to complex group and individual identities, and therefore to multiple communities at once; (5) they see belonging as unhinged from place and time; they belong 24/7 and they do not associate belonging with a "place" (Andrew Zirschky, "Belonging 2.0: Youth and Technology," unpublished lecture [Princeton, NJ: Princeton Theological Seminary Continuing Education Series], November 1, 2007). As Zirschky suggests, there is no inherent reason these elements of belonging cannot characterize congregations as well.

36. For a detailed discussion of the influence of globalization on the faith of American teenagers, see chapter 3, "God Versus Glitz," in Richard R. Osmer and K. C. Dean, eds., *Youth, Religion, and Globalization: New Research in Practical Theology* (Münster, Germany: Global, 2007).

37. Zirschky, "Belonging 2.0: Youth and Technology."

38. The study, *A Generation Unplugged* (presented by Harris Interactive at the CTIA Wireless, IT and Entertainment Conference, September 2008), surveyed more than 2,000 teens ages 13-19 from across the U.S. Cited in "Keep Up If You Can: Teens Are Taking Cellular Use to New Levels," *Harris Interactive Trends and Tudes* 8 (January 2009), 1, 3.

39. Danah Boyd, "Why Youth (Heart) Social Network Sites: The Role of Networked Publics in Teenage Social Lives," in *MacArthur Foundation Series on Digital Learning—Youth, Identity, and Digital Media Volume*, ed. David Buckingham (Cambridge, MA: MIT Press, 2008), 119–42. As adults increase their internet usage (55 percent of internet users are between the ages of 33–55; millenials make up 30 percent of the internet-using population), young people still lead in social uses of the internet. Sydney Jones and Susannah Fox, "Generations Online in 2009" (January 28, 2009), www.pewinternet.org/Reports/2009/Generations-Online-in-2009.aspx (accessed April 3, 2009).

40. Cf. Cornell University and University of Maryland researchers, Joseph Price, et al., "The Time Use of Teenagers" (2006), paa2007.princeton.edu/down load.aspx?submissionld=71143 (accessed April 3, 2009).

41. Danah Boyd cites three reasons the passion for social networking may be fading among teens: (1) "too much drama" (especially on MySpace); (2) "it's not my space anymore" (adults have infiltrated sites like Facebook, preventing it from being private teen space); and (3) a desire to "keep it real" (maintain face-to-face relationships). Cited by Anastasia Goodstein, "The P's on Facebook and Youth Social Networking Fatigue," YPulse (April 2, 2009), http://www.ypulse.com/the-ps-on-facebook-youth-social-networking-fatigue (accessed April 2, 2009).

42. Zirschky, "Belonging 2.0: Youth and Technology."

43. A resurgence of interest in practical theology in the late twentieth century has fueled interest in contemporary faith practices. Craig Dykstra and Dorothy Bass were instrumental in engineering the faith practices discussion for youth ministry (cf. Dorothy C. Bass, et al., *Practicing Our Faith* (San Francisco, CA: Jossey-Bass, 1997). A constellation of diverse authors in youth ministry have drawn on the work of Bass and Dykstra, Alistair MacIntyre, Pierre Bourdieu, and/or Michel de Certeau for youth ministry, including Fernando Arzola, Dori Baker, Kenda Creasy Dean, Fred Edie, Tony Jones, Joyce Ann Mercer, Don Richter, Andrew Root, Jason Santos, Tim van Meter, Michael Warren, David White, and Mark Yaconelli, to name a few.

44. Kenda Creasy Dean and Ron Foster, *The Godbearing Life: The Art of Soul-Tending for Youth Ministry* (Nashville: Upper Room, 1998), 107. The Valparaiso Project on the Education and Formation of People in Faith describes Christian practices as "things Christian people do together over time to address fundamental needs and conditions of humanity and all creation in the light of and in response to God's active presence for the life of the world in Jesus Christ." Craig Dykstra and Dorothy C. Bass, "Times of Yearning, Practices of Faith," in *Practicing Our Faith*, 5.

45. Craig Dykstra, *Growing in the Life of Faith: Education and Christian Practices* (Louisville, KY: Westminster John Knox Press, 2006), 66.

46. Describing this life, Brother Lawrence wrote: "There is not in the world a kind of life more sweet and delightful than that of a continual conversation with God. Those only can comprehend it who practice and experience it." For free downloads of Brother Lawrence's classic *Practicing the Presence of God*, go to http://www.practicegodspresence.com/brotherlawrence/.

47. Tom Beaudoin, *Virtual Faith: The Irreverent Spiritual Quest of Generation X* (San Francisco, CA: Jossey-Bass, 1998), 74. This definition differs slightly from the one offered by Vatican II, which emphasized the role of the priest in offering the blessing associated with sacramentals.

48. While sacramentals often involve tangible objects, they are not objects; it is the act of blessing associated with the object and the experience of surrendering these objects to God that matters. Only at our invitation does the Holy Spirit transform these objects into vehicles that pave the way for Christian transformation. "Sacramentals," *New Advent Catholic Encyclopedia*,

http://www.newadvent.org/cathen/13292d.htm (accessed March 18, 2009). See Beaudoin, 74.

49. Beaudoin, 74.

50. For the Wesleys, "seeking justice" especially meant opposing slavery. John Wesley was careful to distinguish outward means of grace from the action of the Holy Spirit, reminding his followers that God is free to bestow grace without any outward means of grace being present at all. See Sermon 16, "The Means of Grace" (1872 edition, Thomas Jackson, ed.), http://new.gbgm umc.org/umhistory/wesley/sermons/16/.

51. Barbara Brown Taylor, *The Preaching Life* (Cambridge, MA: Cowley Publications, 1993), 104–5.

52. For the complete list of suggestions, see Smith and Denton, 265–71.

53. Christian Smith and Patricia Snelling, *Souls in Transition: The Religious and Spiritual Lives of Emerging Adults* (Oxford: Oxford University Press, 2009), 180ff.

54. See the Exemplary Youth Ministry Study at www.exemplarym.com. The study concluded that mature Christian young people: (1) *seek spiritual growth, both alone and with others*; they pursue questions, guidance and commitment through conversation, study, Bible reading, prayer, small groups, retreats, etc; (2) *are keenly aware of God,* and view God as active and present in their own life, in the lives of others, and in the life of the world; (3) *act out of a commitment to faith in Jesus Christ,* privately and publicly, through regular worship, participation in ministry, and leadership in a congregation; (4) *make Christian faith a way of life* by recognizing God's "call" and integrating their beliefs into conversation, decisions, and actions in daily life; (5) *live lives of service* by being involved in caring for others and addressing injustice and immorality; (6) *reach out to others* who are different or in need through prayer, hospitality, conversation, and support; (7) *exercise moral responsibility* by living with integrity and utilizing faith in making considered moral decisions; (8) *speak publicly about faith* by speaking openly about Jesus Christ and God's participation in their own lives and in the world; (9) *possess a positive, hopeful spirit* toward others and toward life. The congregational assets leading to these qualities in adolescents are listed in Appendix A.

55. Victoria Flood, "Results: Youth Ministry Resources Questionnaire, Mailed October 2002," unpublished report (Evangelical Lutheran Church of America, Department for Research and Evaluation), August 2004, archive elca.org/research/reports/dcm/YMResources.pdf (accessed April 3, 2009).

56. These are the emphases that undergird the pedagogical philosophy of Harvard's Derek Bok Center for Teaching and Learning, according to Jim Wilkinson, Director of the Bok Center. Personal interview (Cambridge, MA), April 30, 2009.

57. Mark DeVries, *Sustainable Youth Ministry* (Downer's Grove, IL: InterVarsity Press, 2008), 53.

58. Jerome Bruner, *The Process of Education* (Cambridge, MA: Harvard University Press, 1977), 33.

59. See Jean Lave and Etienne Wenger, *Situated Learning: Legitimate Peripheral Participation* (Cambridge: Cambridge University Press), 1991.

60. Cf. Sarah Arthur, *The God-Hungry Imagination: The Art of Storytelling for Postmodern Youth Ministry* (Nashville: Upper Room Books, 2007), 147; Robin Maas, "Christ and the Adolescent: Piper or Prophet?" (Princeton, NJ: Princeton Lectures on Youth, Church, and Culture, 1996), www.ptsem.edu/iym); Kenda Creasy Dean and Ron Foster, *The Godbearing Life: The Art of Soul-Tending in Youth Ministry* (Nashville: Upper Room), 1998; Andrew Root, *Revisiting Relational Youth Ministry: From a Strategy of Influence to a Theology of Incarnation* (Downer's Grove, IL: InterVarsity Press), 2007; Mark Yaconelli, "Becoming a Spiritual Guide: Formation in Contempletive Youth Ministry," in *Growing Souls: Experiments in Contemplative Youth Ministry*, ed. Mark Yaconelli (Grand Rapids: Zondervan), 2007.

5. Emerging Competencies

1. In his book, *The Teaching Ministry of Congregations* (Louisville, KY: Westminster/John Knox Press, 2005), Richard Osmer provides a helpful, more expansive understanding of exhortation. He draws upon Paul Ricoeur's work to further understand exhortation as more than simply admonishing or encouraging one another. Osmer argues for an understanding of exhortation as an identity-shaping moral ethos of a community (such as a congregation) that applies practical moral reasoning and moral practices that shape the community's own vision but also make claims not only upon the community but also more broadly as the community lives and interacts with the whole world.

2. See Parker Palmer, *A Hidden Wholeness* (San Francisco: Jossey-Bass, 2004).

3. Ralph Waldo Emerson, *Natural History of Intellect and Other Papers* (London: Routledge, 1903), 103.

4. Regin Prenter, *Spiritus Creator*, trans. J. M. Jensen (Philadelphia: Muhlenberg Press, 1953), 102.

5. See Larry Shelton, "John Wesley's Approach to Scripture in Historical Perspective," Wesley Center for Applied Theology/Wesley Center Online, wesley.nnu.edu/wesleyan_theology/theojrnl/16-20/16-02.htm (accessed April 4, 2009).

6. Barbara Brown Taylor, *The Preaching Life* (Cambridge and Boston: Cowley Publications, 1993), 47.

7. See John M. Bracke and Karen B. Tye, *Teaching the Bible in the Church* (St. Louis, MO: Chalice, 2003).

8. See Stanley Hauerwas, *Unleashing Scripture* (Nashville: Abingdon, 1993).

9. See Parker Palmer, *The Courage to Teach* (San Francisco: Jossey-Bass, 1998).

10. Stephen Rosen, "Professional Conduct" (lecture), Derek Bok Center for Teaching in Learning, Harvard University. See also the Bok Center online at

http://bokcenter.harvard.edu/icb/icb.do. Rosen does not include "love" in his outline, nor does he include "know and love God." In the Bible, however, knowing is a relational construct; knowing God, and to be known by God, implies loving God and being loved by God. Love, therefore, is an appropriate translation of knowledge for Christian teaching.

11. Mark Yaconelli, *Contemplative Spirituality* (Grand Rapids: Zondervan, 2006), 21–22.

12. Ibid., 22.

13. Ibid., 19.

14. Mike King, *Presence-Centered Youth Ministry: Guiding Students into Spiritual Formation* (Downers Grove, IL: InterVarsity Press, 2006), 181.

15. David Elkind, *All Grown Up and No Place to Go* (Cambridge, MA: Perseus Books, 1998), 21. Elkind argues that adolescents with a *patchwork self* are more vulnerable to the influence of others because they have no inner "gyroscope." Consequently, these adolescents experience more stress because they must always look to others for approval and coping strategies. I argue, unlike Elkind, that the development of a theological center predicated on the immanence of transcendence of God combats this patchwork self.

16. St. John of the Cross, a sixteenth-century Catholic reformist, Spanish mystic, and Carmelite monk and priest wrote a poem titled *Dark Night of the Soul* in 1585. This phrase is attributed to him. The poem narrates the journey of the soul from its bodily home to union with God. It happens during the night, which represents the hardships and difficulties the soul meets in detachment from the world and reaching the light of the union with the Creator. There are several steps in this night, which are related in successive stanzas. The main idea of the poem can be seen as the painful experience that people endure as they seek to grow in spiritual maturity and union with God.

17. Robert Dykstra, *Counseling Troubled Youth* (Louisville, KY: Westminster/John Knox Press, 1997), 5.

18. Seward Hiltner, *Preface to Pastoral Theology* (New York: Abingdon Press, 1958), 43.

19. Dykstra, 5.

20. Thomas G. Long, *Beyond the Worship Wars: Building Vital and Faithful Worship* (Bethesda, MD: Alban Institute, 2001), 18.

21. Ibid.

22. See Leonard Sweet, *Postmodern Pilgrims* (Nashville: Broadman and Holman, 2000), 60. The rise of the participatory culture is an ongoing theme for Sweet in a number of his books. This one provides a nice, succinct summary on the rise of the participatory culture.

23. Terri Apter, *The Myth of Maturity* (New York: Norton, 2001), 108.

24. Christian Smith with Melinda Denton, *Soul Searching: The Religious and Spiritual Lives of American Teenagers* (Oxford and New York: Oxford University Press, 2006), 56.

25. Frederick Buechner, *Wishful Thinking: A Theological ABC* (San Francisco: Harper One, 1993), 95.

26. Brian Mahan, *Forgetting Ourselves on Purpose: Vocation and the Ethics of Ambition* (San Francisco: Jossey-Bass, 2002).

27. Cf. Pope St. Gregory I and Terrence Kardong, *The Life of St. Benedict* (Collegeville, MN: The Order of St. Benedict, 2009).

28. See St. Benedict's Rule 59, found in St. Benedict, *The Rule of St. Benedict in English*, ed. Timothy Fry (Collegeville, MN: The Liturgical Press, 1982), 81. Some later orders prohibited oblates until puberty; today the term refers to lay affiliates of religious orders, who adapt the rule for life outside the monastery.

29. Gregory and Kardong, 116.

30. Rule 3.3, found in *The Rule of St. Benedict*, 25.

31. Rule 2, found in *The Rule of St. Benedict*, 21–25.

6. A Maturing Discipline

1. Paul Goodman, "The New Reformation," *The New York Times Magazine* (September 14, 1969), SM32.

2. These categories are adapted from a presentation by MIT professor Paul Penfield, Jr., "What Is a Discipline?" ABET Board of Directors (Baltimore, MD, March 16, 2002), http://www-mtl.mit.edu/~penfield/pubs/abet-02.html (accessed April 5, 2009), and corroborated by looking at articles from countless "emerging disciplines" (ranging from nanotechnology to cinema studies to nursing) that are asking the same questions we are.

3. For further elaboration on this thesis, see Peter Berger, *The Homeless Mind: Modernization and Consciousness* (New York: Random House, 1973).

4. Stephanie Paulsell, "Pastoral Agility and Intellectual Work," lecture (New Haven, CT: Yale Divinity School, April 2003), *Harvard Divinity Bulletin*, http://www.hds.harvard.edu/news/bulletin/articles/paulsellhtml (accessed April 16, 2009).

5. Brenda Dervin, cited by Kaarle Nordenstreng, "Discipline or Field? Soul-Searching in Communication Research," *Nordicom Review*, Jubilee Issue (2007), 212–13.

6. Merton Strommen, Karen Jones, and Dave Rahn, *Youth Ministry That Transforms* (Grand Rapids: Youth Specialties/Zondervan, 2001), 303.

7. Christian Smith, with Melinda Denton, *Soul Searching: The Religious and Spiritual Lives of American Teenagers* (New York: Oxford University Press, 2005), 51.

8. Craig Dykstra, "Keys to Excellence: Pastoral Imagination and Holy Friendship," Sustaining Pastoral Excellence Forum (January 22, 2004), http://www.divinity.duke.edu/programs/spe/articles/200506/dykstra-pl.html.

9. David Ford, *The Shape of Living* (Grand Rapids: Baker Books, 1998), 46. Ford's thesis offers a theological corollary to the developmental theory of Robert Kegan, who argues that human development proceeds by successive experiences of finding ourselves "in over our heads" (Robert Kegan, *In Over Our Heads* [Cambridge, MA: Harvard University Press, 1994]).

10. Ford, 49.

11. Dykstra, summarizing Ford, 89.

12. Andrew Root explains the significance of locating youth ministry in the context of practical theological reflection: "Practical theology is essentially a theology of action and practice. And it is here that youth ministry scholarship should see itself. Youth ministry is a practical theological discipline that seeks to construct a theology of action/practice for younger generations of people. Therefore, the common identity of those in youth ministry scholarship (as well as with those in the broader fields of the ministry arts) is *not* in application [of theology], but in the fact that we are theologians of action/practice. We are those in the theological faculty that attend to reflection on God's action in concrete locations where young people are present, seeking to construct theories born from practice that lead individuals and communities into faithful performative action in the world" (Andrew Root, "Practical Theology: What Is It and How Does It Work?" *Journal of Youth Ministry* 7 [Spring 2009], 71).

13. Sören Kierkegaard, *Fear and Trembling*, C. Stephen Evans and Sylvia Walsh, eds. (Cambridge, UK: Cambridge University Press, 2006), 31.

14. Gina Poole, "A New Academic Discipline Needed for the 21st Century," *Triangle Business Journal* (April 6, 2007), http://www.bizjournals.com/triangle/stories/2007/04/09/focus4.html (accessed May 31, 2008).

15. What is at stake in this conversation is ultimately academic credibility, and the consequent widespread inclusion of youth ministry as a discipline in academic institutions. Take, for instance, the debate over whether education is a "discipline" or a "field" in Chinese universities: "The dispute on attributes of education, as a discipline, has been going on for a long time. However, there is still no clear answer to it (Tang, 2002). Many scholars try to avoid answering this question, because it is not easy to do, and it has potentially negative impacts on the status of education. It is very easy to bring education into a dilemma: if education is declared as a nondiscipline, it will then be excluded naturally from curriculums of many educational institutions, which will disgrace the dignity of education." Wang Hongcai, *Journal of Xiamen University* 1 (Arts and Social Sciences), 2006, 72. http:/www.springerlink.com/content/p7u427091107273w/ (accessed April 5, 2009). The parallels between this discussion and the one youth ministry and other emerging disciplines are undergoing in the United States are striking.

16. These markers are drawn from a consensus reading of literature on emerging disciplines in the social sciences.

17. The relationship between young people and reform is long-standing: Francis of Assisi renounced his father's consumerism and pledged to build Christ's church at twenty-three; George Whitefield ignited the First Great Awakening with his preaching tour of America at twenty-four; Martin Luther King, Jr. led the Montgomery Bus Boycott at twenty-six.

18. Jon Pahl, *Youth Ministry in Modern America, 1930–Present* (Peabody, MA: Hendrickson, 2000).

19. Strommen, 27.

20. Rick Lawrence, "2005 Youth Ministry Salary Survey," *Group*

(November/December 2005), http://findarticles.com/p/articles/mi qa3835/is _200511/ai n15742856/ (accessed April 5, 2009).

21. An incomplete list includes Candler School of Theology, Fuller Theological Seminary, Luther Theological Seminary, Princeton Theological Seminary, Trinity International University [Chicago], Kings College at the University of London, Trinity Theological College in Singapore, and the University of Pretoria in South Africa.

22. Tony Jones, "Reflections on IASYM," *Theoblogy*, http://theoblogy.blog spot.com/2005/01/reflections-on-iasym.html (accessed April 5, 2009).

23. History and theology both play a part in the strong presence of youth ministry in conservative schools. Youth ministry has long been part of fundamentalist and evangelical Protestantism, thanks in part to the communitarian (and sometimes sectarian) ways many churches in these traditions understand the church, to the theological urgency these traditions assign to "saving" young people, and to the high priority placed on evangelism in general. By the 1990s, however, devastating losses of youthful members forced mainline Protestant schools to look seriously at the quality of adolescent discipleship formation in mainline churches, and—largely with the support of Lilly Endowment funds—both colleges and seminaries in these traditions began experimenting with curricular offerings in youth and young adult ministry. Some of these experiments developed models of theological education for high school students themselves, while others focused on practitioner, undergraduate, or graduate teaching. A number of significant research projects were launched that focused on young people, churches, and faith development. Project lists are available at www.lillyendowment.org/religion.html.

24. Andrew S. Jack and Barrett W. McRay, "Tassel-Flipping: A Portrait of the Well-Educated Youth Ministry Graduate," *Journal of Youth Ministry* 4 (Fall 2005), 53–73.

25. Cf. Donald A. Schön, *The Reflective Practitioner* (New York: Basic Books, 1983); Jean Lave and Etienne Wenger, *Situated Learning Theory* (New York: Cambridge University Press, 1991); Jack Mezirow, *Learning as Transformation* (San Francisco: Jossey-Bass, 2000).

INDEX OF AUTHORS CITED

INDEX OF SELECTED TOPICS